GALATIANS

BELIEF

*A Theological Commentary
on the Bible*

GENERAL EDITORS

*Amy Plantinga Pauw
William C. Placher*[†]

GALATIANS

NANCY ELIZABETH BEDFORD

WJK WESTMINSTER
JOHN KNOX PRESS
LOUISVILLE · KENTUCKY

© 2016 Nancy Elizabeth Bedford

First edition
Published by Westminster John Knox Press
Louisville, Kentucky

16 17 18 19 20 21 22 23 24 25—10 9 8 7 6 5 4 3 2 1

Book design by Drew Stevens
Cover design by Lisa Buckley
Cover illustration: © David Chapman/Design Pics/Corbis

Library of Congress Cataloging-in-Publication Data
Names: Bedford, Nancy Elizabeth, author.
Title: Galatians / Nancy Elizabeth Bedford.
Description: First edition. | Louisville, Kentucky : Westminster John Knox
Press, 2016. | Series: Belief: a theological commentary on the Bible |
Includes index.
Identifiers: LCCN 2015051050| ISBN 9780664232719 (hbk : alk. paper) | ISBN
9780664262068 (pbk : alk. paper)
Subjects: LCSH: Bible. Galatians--Commentaries.
Classification: LCC BS2685.53 .B43 2016 | DDC 227/.407--dc23 LC record available at http://lccn
.loc.gov/2015051050

Contents

Publisher's Note

William C. Placher worked with Amy Plantinga Pauw as a general editor for this series until his untimely death in November 2008. Bill brought great energy and vision to the series, and was instrumental in defining and articulating its distinctive approach and in securing theologians to write for it. Bill's own commentary for the series was the last thing he wrote, and Westminster John Knox Press dedicates the entire series to his memory with affection and gratitude.

William C. Placher, LaFollette Distinguished Professor in Humanities at Wabash College, spent thirty-four years as one of Wabash College's most popular teachers. A summa cum laude graduate of Wabash in 1970, he earned his master's degree in philosophy in 1974 and his PhD in 1975, both from Yale University. In 2002 the American Academy of Religion honored him with the Excellence in Teaching Award. Placher was also the author of thirteen books, including *A History of Christian Theology, The Triune God, The Domestication of Transcendence, Jesus the Savior, Narratives of a Vulnerable God,* and *Unapologetic Theology.* He also edited the volume *Essentials of Christian Theology,* which was named as one of 2004's most outstanding books by both *The Christian Century* and *Christianity Today* magazines.

Series Introduction

Belief: A Theological Commentary on the Bible is a series from West-minster John Knox Press featuring biblical commentaries written by theologians. The writers of this series share Karl Barth's concern that, insofar as their usefulness to pastors goes, most modern commentaries are "no commentary at all, but merely the first step toward a commentary." Historical-critical approaches to Scripture rule out some readings and commend others, but such methods only begin to help theological reflection and the preaching of the Word. By themselves, they do not convey the powerful sense of God's merciful presence that calls Christians to repentance and praise; they do not bring the church fully forward in the life of discipleship. It is to such tasks that theologians are called.

For several generations, however, professional theologians in North America and Europe have not been writing commentaries on the Christian Scriptures. The specialization of professional disciplines and the expectations of theological academies about the kind of writing that theologians should do, as well as many of the directions in which contemporary theology itself has gone, have contributed to this dearth of theological commentaries. This is a relatively new phenomenon; until the last century or two, the church's great theologians also routinely saw themselves as biblical interpreters. The gap between the fields is a loss for both the church and the discipline of theology itself. By inviting forty contemporary theologians to wrestle deeply with particular texts of Scripture, the editors of this series hope not only to provide new theological resources for the church but also to encourage all theologians to pay more attention to Scripture and the life of the church in their writings.

We are grateful to the Louisville Institute, which provided funding for a consultation in June 2007. We invited theologians, pastors, and biblical scholars to join us in a conversation about what this series could contribute to the life of the church. The time was provocative and the results were rich. Much of the series' shape owes to the insights of these skilled and faithful interpreters, who sought to describe a way to write a commentary that served the theological needs of the church and its pastors with relevance, historical accuracy, and theological depth. The passion of these participants guided us in creating this series and lives on in the volumes.

As theologians, the authors will be interested much less in the matters of form, authorship, historical setting, social context, and philology—the very issues that are often of primary concern to critical biblical scholars. Instead, this series' authors will seek to explain the theological importance of the texts for the church today, using biblical scholarship as needed for such explication but without any attempt to cover all of the topics of the usual modern biblical commentary. This thirty-six-volume series will provide passage-by-passage commentary on all the books of the Protestant biblical canon, with more extensive attention given to passages of particular theological significance.

The authors' chief dialogue will be with the church's creeds, practices, and hymns; with the history of faithful interpretation and use of the Scriptures; with the categories and concepts of theology; and with contemporary culture in both "high" and popular forms. Each volume will begin with a discussion of *why* the church needs this book and why we need it *now*, in order to ground all of the commentary in contemporary relevance. Throughout each volume, text boxes will highlight the voices of ancient and modern interpreters from the global communities of faith, and occasional essays will allow deeper reflection on the key theological concepts of these biblical books.

The authors of this commentary series are theologians of the church who embrace a variety of confessional and theological perspectives. The group of authors assembled for this series represents more diversity of race, ethnicity, and gender than any other commentary series. They approach the larger Christian tradition with a critical respect, seeking to reclaim its riches and at the same time to acknowledge its shortcomings. The authors also aim to make available to readers a wide range of contemporary theological voices from many parts of the world. While it does recover an older genre of writing, this series is not an attempt to retrieve some idealized past. These commentaries have learned from tradition, but they are most importantly commentaries for today. The authors share the conviction that their work will be more contemporary, more faithful, and more radical, to the extent that it is more biblical, honestly wrestling with the texts of the Scriptures.

William C. Placher
Amy Plantinga Pauw

Acknowledgments

In some ways, the arc of this book begins and ends with my students at Garrett-Evangelical Theological Seminary. Several years ago I taught a seminar on Galatians as a way of thinking through what it would mean for us to read Scripture "as theologians." I want to thank Daniel Cho, Ryan Hansen, Char Heeg, Carol Hill, Annie Lockhart-Gilroy, and Anita Munden for many enlivening conversations in the course of that semester. As I was working on the rough draft of this book, I conducted an independent study on Galatians with Laura Harris-Adams and Michael Jarboe. All through a busy fall semester we met to read and discuss the Galatian commentaries by Augustine, Jerome, Luther, and Calvin and to bat around some of the ideas in this book. I also discussed the Galatian commentaries by Luther and Calvin more recently in an independent study with doctoral candidates Christopher Hunt and Deborah Pagels. I want especially to thank Jason Okrzynski, who helped me search for the bibliography in the early stages of the book, and Kate Hanch, who read the rough draft and made many useful suggestions. Many students have asked me when I would write more books in English: here is one that I hope will be helpful to you in your ministries.

My colleagues Cheryl Anderson and Barry Bryant in particular were generous with their insights as I tried to think through some thorny implications of Paul's theology. Thanks also to David Balch for his thoughtful suggestions. Insights from the doctoral seminar in hermeneutics that I periodically teach with Lallene Rector also found their way indirectly into this text, as did conversations about hermeneutics with my former colleagues from Instituto

Universitario ISEDET in Buenos Aires, Mercedes García Bach-
mann and Diana Rocco. I continue to be amazed at the collective
wisdom of my colleagues both at Garrett and at ISEDET, and I am
profoundly grateful for their influence on my life and my theology.
Thanks also to Amy Plantinga Pauw for thinking of me as she began
to edit this series: I would not have come up with the idea of a theological commentary on my own, but I think I've been itching to try
my hand at one since the long-ago days before doctoral studies when
I couldn't quite decide whether to become a biblical scholar or a systematic theologian.

Garrett-Evangelical kindly made possible a sabbatical leave in the
fall of 2011, which allowed me to immerse myself in Galatians. Reba
Place Church, the Mennonite congregation in Evanston to which
I belong, offered me the opportunity to preach a number of times
from Galatians, for which I am grateful, especially to our lead pastor
Charlotte Lehman as well as to all the folks at church who at various
points asked me, "Still working on that book?" Thanks always to Lisa
Knaggs for her constant support and friendship through the years
and for great conversations about Paul and Pauline theology. Many
lively exchanges around the dinner table with my husband, Daniel
Stutz, and our three daughters, Valeria, Sofía, and Carolina, were
food for thought and made their way into my own conversations
with Paul and his interpreters. One of my main hermeneutical concerns as a theologian is how to interpret Scripture and tradition in a
way that will be life-giving to my daughters, and this book was written with that question always in the back of my mind. My parents,
Benjamin and La Nell Bedford, were the first to teach me to "read
the Bible as a theologian." To them this book is gratefully dedicated.

Introduction
Why Galatians? Why Now?

Some years after the death and resurrection of Jesus, possibly between 53 and 57, but maybe as early as the late 40s, Paul wrote a letter to a group of Galatian congregations in Anatolia (or Asia Minor), located in present-day Turkey. There are actually two candidates for the designation "Galatia" in the ancient world. Either of them would intersect with what we know of Paul's ministry. Galatia may mean a Roman province of that name located in southern Galatia, established by Augustus in 25 BCE. Alternatively, it may refer to the traditional region of a group of Celtic tribes often called "Galatians," living around Ancyra, Pessinus, and Tavium, who had migrated there in the third century BCE.[1] The latter group is identified with what is often called the "North Galatian" hypothesis.

Several Christian congregations in the Roman province of southern Galatia are mentioned in Acts 16:1–2 (Iconium, Lystra, and Derbe), but it is unclear whether they can be identified with the "Galatians" of our letter. The debate about how to identify the "Galatia" of the epistle has continued for centuries, at many different levels, not all of them geographical. Jerome, for example, derives "Galatians" from the Hebrew *galath,* meaning removed or carried away. This allows him to relate their designation to the "removal" (*translatio*) of the Galatians from the true gospel of Jesus.[2] Luther quotes Jerome and then adds, "Some people think that we Germans

1. Brigitte Kahl, *Galatians Re-Imagined: Reading with the Eyes of the Vanquished* (Minneapolis: Fortress, 2010), 34.
2. See Jerome, *Commentary on Galatians,* in *The Fathers of the Church: A New Translation,* vol. 121, trans. Andrew Cain (Washington, DC: The Catholic University of America Press, 2010), 73.

2 INTRODUCTION

are descended from the Galatians, and there may be some truth in this." He thinks that, like the Galatians of Paul's epistle, his own German people are ardent in the beginning but soon lose their enthusiasm, and he wishes that they were "steadier and surer."[3]

It is not entirely clear from Galatians itself who exactly the recipients of the letter may have been. This may explain why the sociocultural context of the addressees has sometimes been overlooked in the interpretation of the epistle. Nevertheless, in recent years a number of scholars have underlined the fact that the Galatians were a colonized people living in an imperial context and that this is important to take into account in understanding the epistle. Aliou Cissé Niang, for example, holds that the addressees of Paul's letter, whom he calls Celts/Gauls/Galatians, were "living under imperial/colonial Rome" and were viewed as the "barbaric" others of classic civilization. In this reckoning, the "Galatians" probably were the descendants of ancient Celtic tribes who settled in Anatolia.[4] As such, they would have been touched by the older Phrygian culture in the region (which included worship of Adgistis, the "Mother of the Gods")[5] as well as by wider Hellenistic influences. They would quite possibly also have encountered diasporic Judaism, which was present in Asia Minor, as evidenced in the settlement of several hundred Jewish families in the region, following orders by Antiochus.[6] For that matter, Sardis in Lydia was the site of one of the largest ancient synagogues ever discovered.[7] In time, these "Galatians" would have been colonized and at least partially "Romanized." This may have been the cultural context in which Paul, as an "Apostle to the Uncircumcision," proclaimed that the good news of Jesus Christ was "about breaking down social boundaries, dismantling taboos,

3. Martin Luther, *Luther's Works*, vol. 26, *Lectures on Galatians, 1535 Chapters 1–4*, ed. Jaroslav Pelikan (Saint Louis: Concordia Publishing House, 1963), 47.
4. Cf. Aliou Cissé Niang, *Faith and Freedom in Galatia and Senegal: The Apostle Paul, Colonists and Sending Gods* (Leiden: Brill, 2009), 47–50.
5. Adgistis was her Phrygian name, but she was worshiped under many other names, many of them identified with particular mountains. Cf. Susan M. Elliott, "Choose your Mother, Choose your Master: Galatians 4:21–5:1 in the Shadow of the Anatolian Mother of the Gods," *Journal of Biblical Literature* 118 (1999): 661–83.
6. Cf. Flavius Josephus, *The Jewish Antiquities, Books 1–19*, trans. Henry St. J. Thackeray et al., LCL (Cambridge: Harvard University Press, 1930–1965), 12.148–53.
7. A. Thomas Kraabel, Review of Paul R. Trebilco, *Jewish Communities in Asia Minor*, *Catholic Biblical Quarterly*, 55 (1993): 186–87.

and overthrowing and challenging human institutions that dehumanize people."[8]

Davina Lopez reminds us that the Galatians (whom she likewise identifies with the Celts/Gauls, or in Greek, *Keltoi/Galatai*) would have been perceived as the "quintessential barbarians" from the perspective of imperial power. The Celts/Gauls appear in ancient Roman inscriptions, texts, and images as "stereotypical representatives of those who must be conquered," placed symbolically on the negative side of such binaries as civilized/uncivilized, male/female or Romans/nations.[9] This means, as Brigitte Kahl makes clear, that the "Galatians/Gauls/Celts," regardless of their physical location, need to be understood in ways that transcend a single ethnic or geographical identity. She reminds us that "Galatians" is "a term soaked with memories, fears, and aggression that are completely absent from our New Testament dictionaries." The Galatians function as a symbol of the "barbarians par excellence," of the vanquished enemies of Rome, and of "the history of the conquest of lawlessness by law." In sum, for the dominant culture of the time, the "Galatians" would have been the "others" of an imperial order that painted itself as the essence of civilization and legality.[10] The reality of empire traverses the theological themes of the letter and is a presence always latent in Paul's awareness of power relations within the community and in his championship of grace and freedom.

Paul mentions in the letter that he found gracious hospitality among the believers in Christ of the Galatian churches just when he needed it: at a time when he was suffering from an ailment possibly having to do with his eyes. In Galatians 4:13 he says, "You know that it was because of a physical infirmity that I first announced the gospel to you," and in verse 15 he adds, "had it been possible, you would have torn out your eyes and given them to me." For a missionary, preacher, and apostle such as Paul, it would have made for a strong bond to have been welcomed generously by the Galatians at a vulnerable time in his life. For the community to have taken his

---

8. Niang, *Faith and Freedom*, 8.
9. Davina Lopez, *Apostle to the Conquered: Reimagining Paul's Mission* (Minneapolis: Fortress, 2008), 103.
10. Kahl, *Galatians Re-Imagined*, 51.

preaching to heart would have been doubly satisfying. It would also likely have seemed akin to a personal betrayal if those same communities seemed on the brink of abandoning his interpretation of the gospel for one quite contrary to it.

The Galatian churches were most likely made up primarily of followers of Jesus who were not Jewish by birth.[11] It is possible that some of the Galatians were Gentile proselytes within Judaism who had come to confess faith in Jesus while most others were pagan converts to the way of Jesus without exposure to Judaism outside of the preaching of the gospel. Here we find potential seeds of conflict. There were many Gentiles interested in Judaism and sympathetic to it, both as God-fearers and proselytes, but for Gentiles to become part of the Jesus movement without simultaneously adhering to Judaism would have been surprising or even scandalous. It seems to have caused quite a stir in the young church in Jerusalem and beyond for Paul to present himself as an apostle to the Gentiles, espousing the hitherto unheard-of conviction that non-Jewish believers did not need also to become observant Jews in order to follow Jesus.

The community around the Jerusalem church, which was the mother church of the other nascent ecclesial communities and had among its leadership people like John, Peter, and James the brother of Jesus, was forced (in part by Paul) to make a decision about this matter of non-Jewish followers of Jesus. To speak of "Christians" and "Christianity" at this early juncture is admittedly anachronistic, but difficult to avoid in practice. At any rate, the massive incorporation into the Jesus movement of Gentiles who increasingly became "Christians" without also becoming observant Jews (a development synonymous with Paul's mission) is one of the reasons that the faith community later known as "Christianity" became identifiable as something other than a sectarian movement within Judaism. The apostles in Jerusalem concluded that while Jewish followers of

---

11. J. Louis Martyn states unequivocally that "Just as there were no Jewish communities in the Galatian cities, and no former Jews in the Galatian churches, so no Jews are addressed in the Galatian letter, and no Jews are being spoken about in the letter." J. Louis Martyn, *Galatians: A New Translation with Introduction and Commentary,* Anchor Bible (New York: Doubleday, 1997), 40. I agree that the letter is by no means an anti-Jewish polemic and that the community was primarily made up of Gentiles, but the presence of Paul himself puts an observant Jew into the mix.

Jesus would continue to be Jewish, Gentile believers in Christ did not necessarily have to convert to Judaism fully in order to follow Jesus, though they were to avoid certain actions that would be offensive to Jewish disciples of Jesus. Luke tells this story in Acts 15, and Paul gives his version in Galatians 2. The two accounts are slightly different, but they agree on the principle that contextual versions of Christianity are legitimate ways to receive the good news of the gospel in new places.

Not all scholars believe that the conflicts that appear in Galatians were between Jewish and Gentile followers of Jesus, or what we might call (for lack of a better term) "Jewish Christians" and "Gentile Christians." Mark Nanos, for example, holds that the basic conflict reflected in the epistle is properly described as "intra-Jewish," not "intra-Christian." He detects differences between "Jewish subgroups and non-Christ-believing Jewish authorities" who disagree on how to incorporate non-Jews into the community. Some (non-Christ-believing Jews) would have considered proselyte conversion the only appropriate way for full inclusion of Gentiles in the community, whereas others (Christ-believing Jews) would have not. They would all have appealed to the Torah but come to different conclusions on the basis of the relevance they claimed for Jesus and their ideas about the place of non-Jews in the age to come.

My own reading leads me to see the tensions in the epistle as arising primarily between Jewish and Gentile followers of Jesus (i.e., so-called "intra-Christian" rather than "intra-Jewish" tensions). However, Nanos's point that the question of the place of Gentiles in God's economy significantly predates institutional Christian identity or factionalism between Christian groups is well taken.[12] Any intra-Christian debate at that time was embedded in a larger Jewish context, which had among its riches a long tradition of how to deal with Hellenistic cultures and the "righteous ones" among the pagans. That is one reason that some of the "fiercest debates within first-generation Christianity," which had precisely to do with the question of "whether or to what extent" the boundaries marking off

---

12. Mark Nanos, *The Irony of Galatians: Paul's Letter in First-Century Context* (Minneapolis: Fortress, 2002), 6–9 et passim.

"Christian" Jews from "Christian" Gentiles should be maintained,
can said to have been formulated "entirely in Jewish terms."[13]

The larger Jewish community of the time in all its variety, including emerging groups of Jewish followers of Jesus, is without question the "mother" of Pauline theology, even as the Jewish Paul is—at
least in his own estimation—the apostle and "mother" of non-
Jewish Christians in Galatia. There is in this sense no tension
between "Pauline" and "Jewish" Christianity, since Paul's interpretation of how Gentiles could come to be heirs of God's promise to Abraham emerged from a Jewish worldview that was by no
means exclusively his own. As a Jewish interpreter of Paul, Nanos
warns Christian readers to be wary of anti-Jewish themes and attitudes to be found even in those non-Jewish Christian interpreters
of Galatians who emphatically try to avoid anti-Jewish attitudes
and rhetoric. He points out that latent anti-Jewish themes remain in
such interpretations, especially whenever the Pauline version of the
gospel is painted as if it were something absolutely new and in discontinuity with the God of the Old Testament or as if God's revelation were exclusively linked to the Christian faith. Connected to this
problem is the persistently negative valuation of Jewish Christians
in Galatians (the so-called Judaizers) by many Christian commentators, an attitude easily spread to non-Christian Jews as well.[14]

It is therefore important to keep in mind that Paul is addressing
a specific group when he writes the epistle to the Galatians: namely,
"Gentiles who have already believed in Christ and received the Spirit
of God as a testimony to their new status as righteous ones among
the people of God."[15] Put succinctly, Paul's letter advocates the inclusion of Gentiles as Gentiles into the community of the people of God.
Paul does not think that Gentiles should first have to become proselytes in order to belong to God's people. His critique of the practice
of circumcision and of the need to abide by dietary guidelines or
other aspects of the law is not meant as a rejection of Judaism or of

13. John Dunn, "Echoes of Intra-Jewish Polemic in Paul's Letter to the Galatians," *Journal of Biblical Literature* 112 (1993): 459–77.
14. Cf. Mark D. Nanos, "How Inter-Christian Approaches to Paul's Rhetoric Can Perpetuate Negative Valuations of Jewishness—Although Proposing to Avoid That Outcome," *Biblical Interpretation* 13 (2005): 255–69.
15. Nanos, *The Irony of Galatians*, 15.

a Christian Jewish alternative. What he rejects is the need to require such practices of Gentile followers of Jesus who were not previously proselytes. Paul adamantly holds that it is not necessary for Gentiles to become full-fledged Jews in order to follow Jesus, in part because the apostle does not advocate "sameness" or homogeneity but rather the way of Jesus from within particularity.[16] As Paul will argue in the heart of the epistle, in Christ there is ample room for difference and heterogeneity. For that reason, equality in Christ (as advocated in Gal. 3:28) does not lead to the erasure of differences but rather aims at breaking down hierarchical relationships among many different people and groups.

A further point at stake here is that wherever the gospel is received, the people who accept it have to figure out the balance between what is good and worth keeping from the community's ancestral legacy and what needs to be given up or transformed in light of the gospel as it can best be interpreted in a given time and place. Accordingly, it is not necessary for non-Jews to become Jews in order to be Christians, though Christians accept the Hebrew Bible as Scripture and respect the faith of Jesus; it is also not necessary for Jews to cease being Jews if they do follow Jesus any more than Paul gave up his Jewish faith and identity. Even if he had wanted to, Paul could not have discarded his cultural, educational, and religious identity of origin. Clearly, he had no desire to do so; he knew that his heritage was precious.

However, given the work of the Holy Spirit not only in Judaism but also in renewing the face of the whole earth, it is not only Paul's heritage that is valuable. By an extension of the principles applied by the early church, people from the global South, for instance, should not have to adhere to the canons of Western Christendom in order to become Christians. Christianity has been present in Europe for a long time, but it is not a European or a Western religion; it does not belong to any particular geographical region or cultural sphere. As C. S. Song argues, the gospel does not have to make a detour through Paris or London on its way from Jerusalem to Beijing. The norms, theological concepts, and cultural idiosyncrasies developed

16. Cf. Pamela Eisenbaum, "Is Paul the Father of Misogyny and Antisemitism?," *Cross Currents* 50 (Winter 2000–2001): 517–18.

by Western churches are not essential for the expression of the gospel in Asia.[17] Those of us who profess the Christian faith are all one and we are all equal in Christ, certainly, but we are not all identical. Whatever our background and heritage, if we are to follow Jesus, we will have to sift through our traditions and try to rediscover both their ambiguities and their liberating potential in light of the good news of Jesus Christ.

This exciting principle is not always easy to uphold. George Tinker, writing from an American Indian perspective, points out that temporal categories, such as historicity, have been primary to Eurocentric biblical interpretations of the reign or commonweal of God to the detriment of spatiality. Spatial categories, in particular the categories of place and of land, are extraordinarily important to Amerindian spirituality, which leads Tinker to underline the importance of creation as a whole in Christian thinking about the *basileia* rather than to focus only on an anthropocentric historicity. From this perspective, the way of Jesus Christ has to be an actual path, in a real place, never an abstraction, and the reign of God is about the hegemony of a Creator who calls us "to assume our rightful place in the world as humble two-leggeds in the circle of creation with all the other created."[18] According to Paul's understanding in Galatians, then, it would not be necessary for a member of an Indian nation of the Americas first to become a "Western Christian" in order to follow Jesus; in fact, such a requirement would constitute a distortion of the good news.

That does not mean that Amerindian Christians would be expected to cut themselves off from the wider Christian traditions or that they are immune to cultural shifts and hybridity but rather that the exact contours of faithfulness to the path of Jesus should be allowed to emerge in freedom through the guidance of the Spirit, not according to a colonial template. The freedom to develop faithful communities in a particular context actually can allow people to find meaningful connections to wider traditions, both those belonging to

---

17. Choan-Seng Song, "From Israel to Asia: A Theological Leap," *Ecumenical Review* 28 (July 1, 1976): 252–65.
18. George E. Tinker, *Spirit and Resistance: Political Theologian and American Indian Liberation* (Minneapolis: Fortress, 2004), 113, cf. 93–99.

the Christian faith and those of the community's ancestors or neighbors who were not Christian. In them, the community can learn to discern the healing, transformative work of the Spirit.

The great thing about the decision made by the early church, at least as it was interpreted by Paul in Galatians, was that it opened the door for much creativity and locally based solutions about how to follow Jesus in a given place and time. Any given culture will have both liberating and oppressive aspects that need to be deepened or transformed, as the case may be. As part of the task of discernment it is particularly helpful to look at a given context from the perspective of gender to see how cultural practices are manifested in the concrete bodies of men and women. Paul does this in Galatians as he ponders the significance of male circumcision in emerging Gentile Christian communities. Musimbi Kanyoro makes a similar point as she constructs an African feminist hermeneutic in a Kenyan context. On the one hand, she affirms African culture as "the thread which strings our beliefs and social set-up together." On the other, she warns that any particular culture is a two-edged sword, because some aspects of it "are embraced without considering their oppressive nature." As the "gospel comes face to face with African traditions," she along with other African women theologians are "asking the church in Africa to be a witness of God's liberation."[19] It is in this kind of tension between the celebration of culture and its critique that a critical ecclesiology—or more widely, a critical theology—is born.

Particularity does not imply a lack of unity or relationship. The larger Christian community is united across time and space by having a common Scripture. Even more importantly, it is held together by the Holy Spirit, who sheds light on those Scriptures. From the perspective of Christian history, however, it becomes clear that one unintended outcome of the decision of the early church that gave such freedom to contextual responses to the gospel was that as Jewish Christians became a minority in the wider Christian church, anti-Jewish sentiments and practices reared their heads. Some

19. Musimbi R. A. Kanyoro, "The Challenge of Feminist Theologies," in *In Search of a Round Table: Gender, Theology and Church Leadership*, ed. Musimbi Kanyoro (Geneva: WCC Publications, 1997), 179–80.

people even used Paul's writings to justify anti-Semitism. Jewish children living in majority Christian societies continue to be familiar with the ugly story of being accused of having "killed Jesus." One pertinent question that arises, then, is whether the principle of contextuality, as fleshed out by Paul in Galatians and inherited by the Christian movement, is inherently anti-Jewish and therefore flawed or whether it can be retrieved and given new life in a context of interfaith respect. Even if we are convinced that it is the latter, and that it is a principle of great value, it will be a conviction continually put to the test by Christianity's own checkered history.

The theme of the relationship between Jewish and Gentile followers of Jesus and the need for a contextual Gentile form of the Christian faith should not obscure the wider imperial context in which both Galatian Jews and Galatian Gentiles were the "Others" of a Rome that was convinced it was the embodiment of law, order, civilization, and excellence. "Jews and Gentiles of all stripes in Galatia," as vanquished peoples, "had to come to terms with each other and with the omnipresent realities of Roman colonialism."[20] When Paul develops his ideas about faith and about the law, it is not only the Torah that sets the terms of the discussion but also the Roman *nomos*.

In the time of Paul the Roman imperial presence was simply "the most basic reality of life." In other words, as Brigitte Kahl shows, it would have been impossible to have any debate about the terms of "Jewishness" apart from the "Romanness" of Galatia (wherever its exact geographical location) or indeed of Judea, Samaria, Galilee, or anywhere else in the empire where Jewish and Gentile followers of Jesus were to be found. In Kahl's words, "whatever the subject of contention between Paul and his 'stupid Galatians' regarding *Jewish* law and *Jewish* affiliation, it was *Roman* law that ultimately defined and enforced what was licit or illicit."[21] Then as now, imperial power is known and experienced by people of many different religious convictions. It is presupposed, often naturalized, and therefore can be almost invisible in their discussions, yet it is present and often sets the terms of the debate.

20. Kahl, *Galatians Re-Imagined*, 7.
21. Ibid., 6–7.

Paul's struggle to find a liberating expression of the gospel of Jesus in the Galatian context as a Jewish follower of Christ living in the shadow of empire and called to share the gospel with the "barbarians" is a theme that can be illuminating to us today. On the one hand, despite the distortions of some later interpretations of Pauline theology, Paul himself is unwilling to fall into the disagreeable Christian habit of anti-Jewish rhetoric and behavior. On the other hand, unlike later Christendom models with their equally unhealthy habit of accommodating faith to empire or other forms of hegemony in "this evil age," Paul is looking for concrete ways to subvert the dominant system by "running well" (Gal. 5:7) according to God's Spirit of transformation and liberation—something we also are called to do in our own time, space, and place.

Freedom is a central theme of Galatians. It is not the freedom to consume or to dominate but the freedom to love and to be transformed ever more in God's image and likeness. Because dominant ideas in society often interpret freedom as the capacity to do whatever we like and especially to amass power, money, and possessions, the theme of freedom—as Paul understands it—is a difficult one to make our own. We tend to take detours that lead us to false dichotomies such as "law versus gospel" or "flesh versus spirit" that seem at first sight to be taken from Paul's letter but miss the heart of his message.

As a case in point, the valuable Reformation insight about the centrality of justification by faith, based in large part on Galatians, has too often led to making the law into a simple foil for faith or into a caricature of what torah means both for the Old and the New Testament. What in Paul functions as a dialectical relationship in which the law is valued and respected becomes an excuse for bashing those who are thought to observe the law in an "outmoded" way: namely, Jews or any other group of opponents such as (in Luther's case) Anabaptists or the Roman Catholic hierarchy. While "justification by faith" was a liberating insight in the context of a church that had become legalistic and stifling, the theology of Galatians cannot be reduced to this one theme. Pauline "justification" cannot be helpful theologically without being related to the wider liberating work of the Holy Spirit in society.

Clearly, just as in the "search for the historical Jesus" one learns at least as much about the person searching for Jesus as one does about Jesus, a given interpretation of Galatians will reflect the interests and concerns of its interpreters. Augustine wrote his commentary on Galatians in the short period when he was a priest, before becoming bishop. His intention was primarily pastoral; he wanted to see how Paul built Christian community and how the epistle could serve as a model of how to give and receive correction.[22] Jerome, who was primarily a Hebrew Bible scholar and mostly wrote commentaries on Old Testament books, dictated his commentary (along with commentaries on Philemon, Ephesians, and Titus) in response to a request from his mentor and friend Paula and her daughter Eustochium. He also mentions that he writes for the benefit of another patron and student of the Scriptures, Marcella, as a kind of consolatory exegesis on the loss of her mother.[23] This was at a time when he was struggling to find the proper balance between classical influences and his reading of Christian interpreters such as Origen, and so writing about Galatians functioned as a contextual hermeneutical exercise for him as well. In his commentaries Luther found parallels between his own situation, surrounded by many adversaries, and that of Paul. Each of these perspectives sheds light on our interpretation of the text, yet none of them are the "definitive" interpretation of Galatians. The reservoir of meaning of the text is deep enough to keep giving of itself in new ways to those who are willing to engage it.

Nevertheless, beyond our various standpoints as contemporary readers, it is worth remembering that Paul can be difficult to understand simply because he dictated his text in the heat of the moment and at times sacrificed precision to passion. As Luther (himself at times a tempestuous writer) remarks, Paul "speaks with great fervor, and anyone who is fervent when he speaks cannot be very precise about following the rules of grammar and the principles of rhetoric."[24] Along those same lines, I have to admit that in writing a

22. See Eric Plumer, "Preface and Acknowledgments" in *Augustine's Commentary on Galatians: Introduction, Text, Translation, and Notes,* Oxford Early Christian Studies (Oxford: Oxford University Press, 2003), ix–x.
23. See Andrew Cain, "Introduction," in Jerome, *Commentary on Galatians,* 17.
24. Luther, *Luther's Works,* vol. 26, *Lectures on Galatians, 1535 Chapters 1–4,* 92.

book such as this one it is difficult to be consistent grammatically and, for instance, to maintain the third person plural when writing about the addressees of the epistle. It is true that Paul is dictating a letter to the Galatians (to "them"), but as one who identifies as a Christian, I also experience the text as written to "me" and to "us." The very pneumatology of Paul's text pushes me in that direction, inasmuch as I accept his premise from Galatians 4:6 that the Spirit of the Son sent into "our" (though some manuscripts read "your") hearts is still at work in "us." Even so, as a contemporary reader of the epistle, I find that not all passages in the letter speak to me equally, so that some sections seem addressed more specifically to "them" and only indirectly to "us," while others seem immediately relevant both to "them" and to "us." Finding the fruitful interstices between "them" and "us," and between "then" and "now," denying neither of them, never collapsing them into one, yet finding a place to stand (and read) as we are caught between worlds, is one of the main challenges of reading the Bible as a theologian.

My use of "we" also makes transparent my point of departure, in that I am admittedly reading and writing as part of a hermeneutical community made up primarily of people who identify in some measure with following Jesus in faith. I am a teaching and writing theologian in an academic setting and therefore part of a vital community of teachers and learners. Equally important, though, is that I am part of a (Mennonite) community of faith. Both in my work as a seminary professor and in my life as a church member, I try to be a theologian for the church and for the world. The latter means that I take on as part of my responsibility the task of helping remind the church (including myself) that the gospel of Jesus Christ should be good news for all people, whether or not they belong to a church. Last, the use of "we" reflects the *nosotros* and *nosotras* of my Latin American roots and my commitment to what Latino and Latina theologians in the United States have called a *teología en conjunto*. This is a theology constructed collectively even if a given person sometimes articulates it.[25] Everything that I write and think is directly or indirectly

25. A paradigmatic example is José David Rodríguez and Loida I. Martell-Otero (eds.), *Teología en Conjunto: A Collaborative Hispanic Protestant Theology* (Louisville, KY: Westminster John Knox Press, 1997).

indebted to my "life together" with others in many intersecting communities both in the Southern and the Northern hemispheres and
thus is a reflection of it. To say "we" in thinking of the meaning of
Galatians "for me and for us" is therefore a reflection of the embedded, diverse, and collaborative quality of life in community that to
me seems central to the Christian faith; it does not mean that I think
I have the authority to "speak for" or "instead of" other people.

As Friedrich Schleiermacher puts it in explaining the heart of
hermeneutics, to interpret a text means to enter into a conversation
with it, question it directly, and allow oneself to be questioned by
it.[26] At the very least, reading Galatians should allow us to enter into
a fruitful dialogue with Paul, whether or not we can agree with him
on every (or any) point he is making.

In the interpretive attempt represented by this book, I am particularly concerned about themes such as gender equality, antira-
cism, the problem of Christian supersessionism, God's option for
the poor, the ambiguous legacy of Pauline theology, and the possibility of a liberating, de-colonial and counter-hegemonic hermeneutic of Scripture. Paul's Christology of the "wonderful exchange"
(understood as a Trinitarian dynamic that is much more encom-
passing than substitutionary atonement), the strong pneumatological undercurrents of the epistle, and the principle of freedom for
contextual expressions of a discipleship of equals seem to proffer
hopeful possibilities for reading Galatians—and the gospel of Jesus
generally—as good news in many different geographical, cultural,
and historical contexts. It seems to me that the epistle has much to
offer. I see it as a window that can be used by the Spirit of Life to let
in some fresh air and healing light to sometimes dark ecclesial cor-
ners and to instill in those who follow Jesus renewed hope for living,
loving, and steadfastly resisting injustice in troubled times.

26. Cf. Friedrich Schleiermacher, *Hermeneutics and Criticism*, trans. Andrew Bowie
(Minneapolis: Fortress, 2004), 90–157.

A. 1:1-5

Introduction/Salutation

Paul's very first statement in the letter is meant to establish that he is an apostle, a messenger or agent who is sent out as the bearer of a commission. According to Paul, this commission was given to him by God when—through the action of the Holy Spirit—he became a witness of the resurrected Christ. Such an apostleship, Paul claims, is not merely the result of human decisions or ambitions. It is not instantiated by human beings (*ouk ap'anthrōpōn*) or from or through a human being (*di'anthrōpou*) but rather through (*dia*) Jesus Christ and the First Person, confessed as "Father," who resurrected Christ from the dead. Wrapped up in Paul's statement about the nature of his apostleship, and inseparable from it, is therefore the confession of Jesus Christ as one who rose from the dead and was shown to be on a par with God.

This is the only explicit mention of the resurrection in Galatians, and yet the fact that Paul opens the epistle with a proclamation of God's commitment to the victory of life over death is an indication of its importance to Paul and to the theology of the letter. By beginning with a reference to the life-giving work of the God of the resurrection, Paul makes clear that the God who has called and commissioned him is committed to overcoming slavery, alienation, and the powers of "the present evil age" (v. 4), bringing the way of liberation and transformation even into spaces—such as the crucifixion of Jesus Christ by Roman imperial power—where it would seem there is no way forward.

In his influential commentary on the epistle, Jerome (ca. 347–420) supposes that one reason Paul appealed to divine authority to establish his apostleship was to confute those who might have pointed out that he was not an apostle in the same sense as Peter or the other members of the core group of disciples who accompanied Jesus during his lifetime. His affirmation may therefore have been meant as a "preemptive response" to his opponents.[1] Possibly building on the taxonomy of apostleship first developed by Origen (ca. 185–254), Jerome states that there are four kinds of apostles.[2] First, there are those who are apostles not by or through human effort but through God, such as Isaiah and the other true prophets as well as Paul himself. Second, there are those who are apostles by God's doing but who are called through humans, such as Joshua son of Nun. Third, there are those who are not sent by God but by humans as a result only of human effort, such as persons who are ordained bishops because of human favor and partisanship. And, finally, there are those who are sent neither by God nor by other people but by themselves: namely, false prophets and false apostles.[3]

In his 1519 commentary on the same text, Martin Luther (1483–1546) quotes Jerome approvingly and places in the third category all the "gluttonous and glory-hungry creatures" who offer themselves for places of power in the church, whereas in the fourth category are the "thieves and robbers" of John 10:8, the most dangerous of all. For Luther what is central is not even whether such people speak the truth occasionally, since even demons can do so, but rather the work of the Holy Spirit, who inspires those who are called legitimately.[4]

Whether or not Paul is a true apostle, sent by God and empowered by the Holy Spirit to bring transformative good news that is congruent with the way of Jesus Christ, is something that the Galatians—and present-day readers of the epistle—are challenged to discern. Indeed, whether or not Paul (or any other spokesperson for the gospel) is a genuine harbinger of good news is a subtext that flows through the entire epistle and on through the history of its

---

1. Jerome, *Commentary on Galatians*, in *The Fathers of the Church: A New Translation*, vol. 121, trans. Andrew Cain (Washington, DC: The Catholic University of America Press, 2010), 60–61.
2. See translator's footnote 31 in Jerome, *Galatians*, 62. Only a few fragments of Origen's commentary on Galatians are extant.
3. Jerome, *Galatians*, 62–63.
4. Martin Luther, *Luther's Works*, vol. 27, *Lectures on Galatians, 1535 Chapters 5–6, 1519 Chapters 1–6*, ed. Jaroslav Pelikan (Saint Louis: Concordia Publishing House, 1964), 163–66.

interpretation. What gives force to the introduction, and to the letter as a whole, is not, however, the nature of Paul's apostleship but
rather the dynamic action of the triune God, in whose work and
grace we as human beings are invited to share. That dynamism is the
force that keeps the epistle in motion, spinning continuously like
a top that has been wound up by God's involvement in the world.
All through Galatians, the theme will be how, through the work and
gifts of God's Spirit, we are given the kind of agency characteristic of
Christ: namely, the capacity to live freely in the world as a "new creation" (6:15) without any restrictions other than truly to love one
another.

Already in the first verse, we see the powerful dynamic between
the "Father" and the "Son" at work, and it is no surprise that the
Trinitarian implications of the passage were of great interest to early
commentators. In his version of the Greek text, no doubt keenly
aware that the opening words of the epistle reflect the kind of divine
economy he wants to excise from the scriptural witness, Marcion
(second century CE) omits the agency of God the Father altogether.[5] Chrysostom (ca. 347–407), on the other hand, points out that
Paul mentions the Son and the Father (v. 1) and then the Father followed by the Son (v. 3), and argues on that basis that it cannot be
said that either is inferior to the other.[6]

Theodoret of Cyrus (ca. 393–ca. 460) for his part argues that
the use of the preposition "through" (*dia*) with respect to both the
Father and the Son (v. 1) indicates that there is no difference in
their nature. Furthermore, the affirmation that the Father has raised
the Son from the dead shows how the two Divine Persons share in
the harmony of the mystery of the incarnation: both the Son and the
Father are providers of the New Covenant, and the "Father in his
own person is a sharer in this providential arrangement."[7]

Paul mentions the "Father" three times in these first five verses of
the letter. The "Father" is described as having raised Jesus from the
dead, as our source of grace and peace (along with Jesus), as desiring

5. Cf. Jerome, *Commentary on Galatians*, 65.
6. John Chrysostom, *Commentary on the Epistle to the Galatians and Homilies on the Epistle to the Ephesians* (Oxford: John Henry Parker, 1840), 5
7. "The Letter to the Galatians," in Theodoret of Cyrus, *Commentary on the Letters of St. Paul*, vol. 2, trans. Robert Charles Hill (Brookline, MA: Holy Cross Orthodox Press, 2001), 2.

our liberation, and as worthy of eternal glory. A distinct marker of the identity of the "Father," whom the Christian tradition calls the "First Person" of the Trinity, is given at once: Paul is speaking of the God who raised Jesus from the dead and who is not to be thought of or worshiped in isolation but whose very mention is intertwined with the life, death, resurrection, and liberating work of Jesus Christ. Likewise, Paul blesses the churches of Galatia by granting them grace and peace from "God our Father and the Lord Jesus Christ" (v. 3).

What we find in this short passage is doubly significant from a theological perspective. First, the "Father" and the "Lord Jesus Christ" are linked inextricably, so much so that it would be impossible to unravel the threads that hold their narrative together. "LORD" or *Kyrios* is the name used in Greek translations of the Old Testament to denote YHWH. Paul's use of "Lord Jesus Christ," and the way he associates "God our Father" with "the Lord Jesus Christ" as a joint source of grace and peace are suggestive of a "high" Christology, though not a docetic one that denies the true humanity of Christ, as we shall see when Paul comes to discuss the contours of the Christian life. Second, "God the Father" as depicted by Paul, is One whose character has to do with a deep commitment to our liberation and flourishing. That is why it is God's "will" that we might be set free (v. 4). Though the metaphor "Father" is indisputably masculine, we are not confronted here with a one-dimensional male divinity that desires to tyrannize us but rather with the kind of God whose compassion and love overflow all gender categories and deconstruct rigid boundaries of all kinds.

The implications of Paul's convictions about God's character and intentions for creation are radical and lead him to envision fruitful and equitable possibilities of relationship among human beings, as can be seen in Galatians 3:28 and 6:2. At the same time he seems to be hesitant about the consequences of what his own theology can unleash when it is worked out materially, for instance, in the roles of men and women in specific congregations. This can be seen paradigmatically in his instructions to the congregation in Corinth, where on the one hand he assumes that women pray and prophesy publicly and even gives advice as to how they should dress when they do so (1 Cor. 11:5) and on the other recommends that they should not speak out in public (1 Cor. 14:34). In Galatians the question of gender is addressed more indirectly and yet is constantly present throughout the letter. It is a theme that needs to be made explicit in order to see whether Paul's gospel gives women as well as men traction for flourishing in this life.

For Paul, the Father is the author of the resurrection and the Son gave himself to set us free from this present evil age (v. 4). This self-giving or self-bestowing took place according to the "will of our God and Father," certainly, yet Paul's focus here is not on sacrifice or sub-stitutionary atonement but on God's work of liberation in and with us. According to these verses, the Son of God is not a passive, sacrifi-cial lamb who is slain: the Son of God gave or offered himself (*dontos eauton*). In other words, the Son chose to walk a path of solidarity with our condition, entering into this messy and unjust human sys-tem in order to set us free. As Chrysostom puts it, the ministry that "he undertook was free and uncompelled."[8] We need to be careful when we talk about sacrifice, especially when we demand sacrifices from other people. This "present evil age," the system under which we live, demands human sacrifices for the good of the market, for the good of Dow Jones, for the good of multinational corporations, for the good of the military-industrial complex, and for the good of the few who concentrate most of the wealth in the world. Jesus came to put an end to a sacrificial system that requires victims. He becomes one of us that we might become as God is, able to live abundantly.

The reference to the "present evil age" does not mean that the world itself is evil or that God's beautiful creation is not good. It refers, rather, to the fact that the way that we have organized our life on this earth distorts God's good creation. As Augustine (354–430) puts it in his commentary on the passage, with an eye to refuting dual-istically minded Christians who believe that all material existence is fundamentally bad and only disembodied spirituality is good, a house is not malignant or evil in itself; we call it evil if evil deeds are done in it.[9] Jesus comes to make that house—our world—the kind of place where life can flourish. He liberates us from conformity to the

8. Chrysostom, *Commentary on the Epistle to the Galatians,* 8.
9. Eric Plumer, *Augustine's Commentary on Galatians: Introduction, Text, Translation, and Notes,* Oxford Early Christian Studies (Oxford: Oxford University Press, 2003), 129.

present system, which tries to entice us.[10] Elsa Tamez makes explicit the political connotations of the phrase in verse 4 and understands the "perverse world" as the situation of Roman imperial domination "with all of its enslaving religious beliefs," including the principalities and powers both of society and of the cosmos.[11]

From a gender perspective, the letter serves up several challenges, already evident in these initial verses. Paul, a male writer, invokes God using male-centered metaphors such as "Father." He does use generic language about humans (*anthrōpos*) to make clear that his commission as an apostle is not "from human authorities" (v. 1) but then returns to male language to establish that he is not alone but is writing the Galatians with the support of others (v. 2). The NRSV translates this as "all the members of God's family who are with me," adding in a footnote that literal translation of the Greek is "all the brothers" (*adelphoi*). Who are the *adelphoi* who are with Paul in the writing of the letter? In Pauline literature the expression often indicates an entire community (Eph. 6:23) and the relations of the members of a Christian community amongst themselves (Rom. 8:29; 1 Cor. 5:11). In the face of the predominantly masculine language of the New Testament, it is a good idea here consciously to assume the presence of women and not their absence rather than the all-male mental images possibly evoked by the literal translation "brothers," because we know from Christian and non-Christian historical sources that from the beginning the Christian movement was attractive to women and to the oppressed of any gender.[12]

In reading Galatians, then, we can imagine with the NRSV that the *adelphoi*, the siblings in Christ in the company of whom Paul composes his letter, are not exclusively—or even primarily—male. In the same way, the *adelphoi* who are the recipients of Galatians (3:15; 5:11,13; 6:1,18) are not exclusively male, either. But it might be a good idea to press the idea further. Can we hope that for Paul,

10. Cf. Bruno the Carthusian, "Complete Galatians," in *The Bible in Medieval Tradition: The Letter to the Galatians*, ed. and trans. Ian Christopher Levy (Grand Rapids, : Eerdmans, 2011), 134.
11. Elsa Tamez, *Contra toda condena: La justificación por la fe desde los excluidos*, 2nd. ed. (Costa Rica: DEI, 1993), 91.
12. As can be seen, for instance, in Pliny the Younger's letter to Trajan; see Pliny, *Epistulae* X.97, http://www.bartleby.com/9/4/2097.html, where he writes of his torture of two female slaves who were said to officiate in Christian assemblies.

apostleship is not about the establishment of male authority and that his invocation of "God the Father" is not about the celebration of a male deity? Will Paul in this letter give us reason to believe that God is "no respecter" of gender, race, ethnicity, class, and religion? Will the agency of the Son who entered into our reality lead in turn to greater agency and empowerment for both women and men, both slave and free, both Greek and Jew? It is a hypothesis worth testing out and one that might make a difference in discerning whether Paul is truly an apostle sent by God and not by human—or by male—commission.

FURTHER REFLECTIONS
The Chiastic Structure of Galatians

The outline that I am proposing for Galatians emerges from a theological reading of the themes in the epistle as a "chiasm": that is, as a structure shaped roughly as an *x* (the Greek letter *chi*), where the top and bottom halves are somewhat symmetrical and parallel to each other, so that they can be represented as A-B-C-X-C'-B'-A'. I am not arguing that Paul had a detailed, precise chiastic outline in mind before he dictated his letter but rather that his thought probably flowed in ways consonant with such a structure, such as happens to many of us today when we preach a sermon or write a speech and develop it in three points. Admittedly, a chiastic structure is not the only way to organize the material, and there are probably as many outlines as there are commentators on the letter. However, some of them have indeed concluded that the literary figure of the chiasmus is influential in the structure of the letter and more importantly, for my argument, have located the beginning of chapter 4 as its center.[13] There is something esthetically and theologically satisfying in finding that both from a literary and from a structural standpoint God (and not Paul himself or Paul's struggles with his opponents) is at the center of Paul's letter.

13. The work of John Bligh provides a classic example of this. In his book *Galatians: A Discussion of Paul's Epistle* (London: St. Paul Publications, 1969), iii and 37–42, he argues that the central chiasm of the epistle is 4:1–10.

In my proposed outline, the "Introduction and Salutation" (1:1–5) are mirrored by the "Final Blessing and Conclusion" (6:18), and so they are labeled A and A' respectively. The same happens with B (1:6–2:21) and B' (6:1–17), both titled "The Gospel Is Truly Good News" and with C (3:1–3:27) and C' (4:8–5:26), both titled "Walking by Faith in Freedom." The very center of the *chi* (3:28–4:7) marks the theological heart of the letter and deals with the Trinitarian dynamic at the heart of God's relationship with creation. The section has an implicitly Trinitarian structure, built around the Son (3:28, "Equality in Christ"), the Father (3:29–4:5, "Adoption as God's Children"), and the Holy Spirit (4:6–7, "The Spirit of the Son"). The theological structure of the epistle shows that though themes such as justification by faith and the place of the law in the life of Christian communities do have their place, it is the character of the liberating and loving God manifested as Son, Father, and Spirit, as well as the empowering, life-giving relationship of human beings to God, that enliven Paul's letter with its themes of goodness, freedom, and justice.

B. 1:6–2:21
The Gospel Is Truly Good News

1:6–10
Do Not Mistake the Nature of the Gospel

Paul turns abruptly to the matter that is heavy on his heart. He skips the expression of thanksgiving for his addressees often found in his letters (see Rom. 1:8; 1 Cor. 1:4; Phil. 1:3). Instead, immediately after the initial salutation he moves quickly, with little fanfare, to a fundamental question: How is it possible that the Galatians have turned away so quickly to "another gospel" (*heteron euangelion*)? Paul speaks forcefully, in the first person singular: "I am astonished" (v. 6). Perhaps his use of the present tense indicates that he is continuing to marvel at what he considers the extraordinary obtuseness of the Galatians but also that his surprise is open-ended and subject to change rather than fixed, as it would be over a matter that was over and done with. He may be able to persuade them to change course if their embrace of "another gospel" turns out to be a nine days' wonder rather than a firm commitment on their part.

Paul says that he is dumbfounded to see that the Galatians are so quickly abandoning the One who called them: that is, God.[1] The apostle likes to use the idea of being "called" in the sense of an invitation by God to participate in the company of those being transformed by the gospel (see Rom. 8:30; 9:24; 1 Cor. 1:9). That this call is one that involves the work of Christ and of the Holy Spirit is

---

1. Luther thinks that in this passage it is Christ who is doing the calling; cf. Martin Luther, *Luther's Works*, vol. 26, *Lectures on Galatians, 1535 Chapters 1–4*, ed. Jaroslav Pelikan (Saint Louis: Concordia Publishing House, 1963), 47.

implicit in verse 6 in that it is a call in or by grace (*en chariti*). Some
manuscripts specify that the call is in "the grace of Christ;" others
say simply "grace," while yet another set of witnesses, including Origen and Theodoret, transmit the reading "by the grace of God."[2] At
any rate, the One who has called the Galatians (none other than
God as manifested by grace in Christ) is now—as Paul sees it—
rapidly being abandoned by the Galatians. They are changing over
or transferring their loyalties to another gospel. The accusation is
indeed a grave one, as it amounts to
idolatry, for they are putting their
confidence in another gospel that is
in reality no gospel at all, not least
because it does not amount to good
news.

> It is the Father himself, he is
> saying, the giver of the Law,
> who called you to this Gospel.
>
> "The Letter to the Galatians," in
> Theodoret of Cyrus, *Commentary on the
> Letters of St. Paul*, vol. 2, trans. Robert
> Charles Hill (Brookline, MA: Holy
> Cross Orthodox Press, 2001), 3.

What is ostensibly so horrifying
to Paul has been shown throughout
Christian history to be quite a common pattern: the Christian church
has been rather prone to quick distraction and to drifting away from
the good news for the poor, for instance, in the direction of "other"
gospels. Such non-gospels lack substance, for, as Paul puts it, they
are not really gospels at all. Still, there will always be those willing to
promote alternative gospels, including messengers of great beauty
and attraction (v. 8). Put succinctly, not everything that passes for
the gospel is in fact the good news of Christ. The gospel can be
misrepresented.

The question of the falsification or "perversion" of the gospel is
made more complicated by the history of the Christian faith, especially as it has been exercised within the logic of Christendom.
Christianity has too often been made uneasy by those who seem
"different" or "abnormal" from the perspective of the dominant.
This can lead to developing a theology in which those persons or
movements that make the powerful or the privileged uncomfortable
are pushed aside, depicted as immoral, or portrayed as somehow

---

2. Bruce Metzger, *A Textual Commentary on the Greek New Testament* (Stuttgart: United Bible
   Societies, 1975), 589.

ontologically deficient. Whenever the "least of these" are considered "perverted," then it is the good news of the gospel that is distorted.

In view of such theological accommodations to power, Marcella Althaus-Reid turns perversion on its head and proposes an "indecent theology" able to make the reality of those pushed aside, along with their "theological perversions," central to the good news. She pays particular attention to poor women and to "sexual dissidents," that is, to those who do not conform to commonly accepted norms that regulate sexuality in a given time and place. She reminds us that even well-intentioned theologies, such as Latin American feminist and liberation theologies, have often functioned in ways that exclude human beings from the expression of life abundant, for example, by repressing queer sexuality.[3] Her subversion of "perversion" indirectly picks up a Pauline theme that is sometimes obscured, since Paul can also be quoted to shore up "normalcy." Paul's awareness of the ambiguity of religion and how easily it can lend itself to perverseness puts him in continuity both with the prophetic critique of religion in the Old Testament and with a necessary contemporary hermeneutic of suspicion that does not confuse wariness in the face of religion with the rejection of faith in God.

The verb translated "to pervert" by the NRSV (*metastrepsai*) in verse 7 can evoke the idea of sleight of hand as well as of any change of a thing into its opposite. (It is the same verb used in James 4:9: "let your laughter be turned into mourning and your joy into dejection.") As Jerome points out, in Galatians the expression refers to undermining the gospel of Christ by "causing what is in front to appear behind, and vice versa."[4] In other words, Paul holds that some people who want to confuse or disturb the Galatians desire to change the gospel into something harmful. It is sobering to realize how easily religious faith can be distorted and become alienating, but it is also bracing to find that Paul, despite his zeal for the faith, begins his message to the Galatians with the conviction that not everything that glitters in the nascent Christian faith movement is necessarily good news. It is not

---

3. Cf. Marcella Althaus-Reid, *Indecent Theology: Theological Perversions in Sex, Gender, and Politics* (New York: Routledge, 2000), 52.
4. Jerome, *Commentary on Galatians*, in *The Fathers of the Church: A New Translation*, vol. 121, trans. Andrew Cain (Washington, DC: The Catholic University of America Press, 2010), 73.

the attractiveness of the messenger that Paul considers central but rather the character of the message. He is teaching us to discern and ask: Is this truly the good news of Jesus Christ?

The "gospel of Christ" (v. 7) can mean either a gospel that comes from Christ as its author or a gospel that purely exhibits Christ.[5] The first is the "subjective genitive" and the second the "objective genitive." It would probably be a mistake to pit either of these dimensions against the other. Christ brings a message, and at the same time Christ inhabits the message. The further christological point here is that the concrete and particular (even at times uncongenial) person of Jesus is inextricably bound up in this good news. There is no escape into abstraction or generalities: the gospel cannot be detached from the incarnation.

In verses 8–9 Paul then enunciates a principle that is helpful for biblical interpretation and for spiritual discernment generally: no matter how persuasive and attractive the purveyors of a given message may be, their function as messengers (whether earthly or heavenly) is not in itself a criterion of the authenticity of the message. As Paul expresses it, if he and his close collaborators or, indeed, even if an "angel from heaven" were to preach another gospel rather than the good news of Jesus Christ, it would merit rejection. In other words, we are invited by Paul himself to interpret —whenever it becomes necessary— "with Paul against Paul," in a hermeneutical move we might call *Paulus contra Paulum*. Said otherwise, should Pauline theology become distorted or should Paul's own words be used in toxic ways, Paul himself authorizes us to disregard them.

Paul's rhetorical strategy is one of excess: he clearly thinks that it is no more likely that he himself would distort the gospel than that a heavenly messenger would do so, and yet apostles do sometimes get confused, and nonangelic figures can pose as heavenly ones, so caution is at all times required. Discernment is never optional in listening to discourse about God. Paul's approach presupposes that nobody is infallible and that the community of faith has an important role in the process of discernment, even communities of Christians such as the Galatians, who seem to frustrate Paul greatly because of

5. John Calvin, *Calvin's Bible Commentaries: Galatians and Ephesians*, trans. John King (Forgotten Books: 2007), 21. Calvin believes it is the latter.

their inconstancy. In that hermeneutical task, church members as part of an interpretive community have two important helps: the work of the Holy Spirit in guiding them (pneumatological dimension) and the nature of the gospel that they have already received (christological dimension).

Paul underscores the seriousness of the matter (v. 9) by declaring twice that to be fooled by false messengers and by distorted gospels is to be accursed (*anathema*). In the Septuagint, the Greek *anathema*, a translation of the Hebrew *cherem*, was used in various senses, sometimes positively, to describe something set apart for God (as in the case of certain offerings; see Lev. 27:28). It could also mean something set apart for destruction (such as Jericho in Josh. 6:17) or something accursed (Zech. 14:11). In the New Testament it takes on a purely negative sense. Paul seems to apply the idea especially to the christological realm: to confuse the good news of the gospel with a false gospel is to be cut off from the liberation brought by Jesus. He uses the expression in Romans 9:3 to speak of what it would mean for him personally to be separated from Christ. In 1 Corinthians 12:3 he makes the point that a person who is led and inspired by the Spirit will not make the mistake of calling Jesus "anathema." Finally, in 1 Corinthians 16:22, he declares "anathema" those who do not love Jesus Christ, presumably because they have cut themselves off from the good news of the gospel.

The "other gospel" which is not really a gospel at all, is "anathema," as are those who proclaim false gospels, because they cut people off from the good news. Luther compares this to a tree that is torn out of its place and soon withers and becomes barren.[6] In the Middle Ages Paul's "anathema" in Galatians was commonly assumed to be the same thing as excommunication from the church.[7] Paul's meaning is deeper than that: it has to do with the willing rejection of a way of life that pushes aside the glorious freedom in Christ promised to the children of God. As Luther says, Paul would prefer to be "ostracized, accursed, execrated, cut off and disgraced rather than that the

6. Martin Luther, *Luther's Works,* vol. 27, *Lectures on Galatians, 1535 Chapters 5–6, 1519 Chapters 1–6,* ed. Jaroslav Pelikan (Saint Louis: Concordia Publishing House, 1964), 175.

7. Haimo of Auxterre (d. 855), for instance, interprets "anathema" to mean separation from the church; see his *Galatians,* in *The Bible in Medieval Tradition: The Letter to the Galatians,* ed. and trans. Ian Christopher Levy (Grand Rapids: Eerdmans, 2011), 83.

truth of the Gospel be endangered," and that goes for himself, for the
other apostles, and for the very angels of heaven.[8]

Paul is not hurling curses around in a facile manner. He realizes that to make such vigorous avowals will not endear him to his listeners (v. 10). However, he apparently feels compelled to speak so forcefully because he wants to establish the gravity of what he thinks is happening among the Galatians. In the end, he has to try to be faithful to what he understands as the gospel, while rejecting any distortions that might

> The pope, Luther, Augustine, Paul, an angel from heaven—these should not be masters, judges, or arbiters but only witnesses, disciples and confessors of Scripture.
>
> Martin Luther, *Luther's Works*, vol. 26, *Lectures on Galatians, 1535 Chapters 1–4*, 58.

turn that good news into bad news. The tension between pleasing people and seeking God's approval is one known to anybody who tries to live out the Christian faith, but it is not easy to figure out in practice, as Paul discovers multiple times during his ministry, since he always seems to be clashing with various opponents.

Though he ends the section with rhetorical questions contrasting God's approval with human approval, Paul does care about the opinions and welfare of the people to whom he ministers, or he would not bother to try to persuade the Galatians. It would not be possible to minister at all, if one were fully indifferent to one's human interlocutors, and it would be self-defeating to "labor for the express purpose of displeasing" people.[9] On the other hand, conflict is inevitable in ministry as in all sustained human interactions. The important thing—as Augustine points out—is to please human beings in a way that also pleases God and serves truth, not acting in order to achieve some sort of personal glory.[10] In other words, "making friends and influencing people" is for Paul not an end in itself or a means to achieve personal gain but has meaning only inasmuch as it serves to glorify God. At the same time, God's glory and God's

8. In his 1519 Commentary; see *Luther's Works*, vol. 27, *Lectures on Galatians, 1535 Chapters 5–6, 1519 Chapters 1–6*, 178.
9. Calvin, *Calvin's Bible Commentaries: Galatians and Ephesians*, 24.
10. Cf. Eric Plumer, *Augustine's Commentary on Galatians: Introduction, Text, Translation, and Notes*, Oxford Early Christian Studies (Oxford: Oxford University Press, 2003), 131.

Someone who pleases people in order that they may be saved, not seeking personal glory but God's glory through them, is not in that case pleasing people but God—or at least pleasing God and people at the same time, and not just people.

Eric Plumer, *Augustine's Commentary on Galatians: Introduction, Text, Translation, and Notes*, Oxford Early Christian Studies (Oxford: Oxford University Press, 2003), 131.

pleasure are not ends in themselves without any ramifications for creation. If that were so, the meaning of the incarnation for human beings and for creation (with which Paul ends and begins this epistle) would be discarded and the rhetoric of "pleasing God" would be cut off from all that is life-giving. For Paul, God's glory always includes the flourishing of creation.

1:11–24
Paul's Account of His Call

Paul picks up a theme to which he had already alluded in the introduction: he is the apostolic bearer of a gospel that is not the result of human machinations. His contention is that the gospel that he has been proclaiming, literally "the gospel gospeled (*to euangelion to euangelisthen*) by me" (v. 11) does not derive its entity from humans. Rather, it was received by means of a revelation of Jesus Christ (v. 12). The phrase about reception parallels the statement above (v. 9) about the gospel that the Galatians had received from Paul. The apostle wants to reassure the Galatians about the gospel tradition he passed on to them and establish that its origins are from God and therefore not to be taken lightly. These kinds of affirmations also appear elsewhere in the Pauline corpus. For instance, when Paul transmits the tradition about the Lord's Supper in 1 Corinthians 11:23 he states that he is handing over something that he "received from the Lord." He expresses a related idea in 1 Thessalonians 2:13, when he gives thanks to God that the Thessalonians received "the word of God that you heard from us" not as a human word but "as what it really is, God's word," able to work powerfully in them.

The phrase "revelation of Jesus Christ" (v. 12) could be interpreted as a statement that the gospel of Christ is not a human fabrication because Christ is not just a human being. Jerome reads the passage in that way in order to refute those who might argue that Jesus was not divine: "We do not deny that he assumed human form; we simply reject the notion that he was only a man."[11] The strength of this interpretation is that it focuses on the christological implications of the passage rather than speculating fruitlessly about the exact way in which Paul received the message of the gospel. The problem with such an approach, however, is that in its zeal to defend the divinity of Christ, it too easily veers toward Docetism, emptying Jesus of his true humanity. This tendency is reflected in Jerome's rather weak choice of words to the effect that the Son "assumed human form." Karl Barth, who incidentally thinks that Paul was clearly "not an attractive or congenial person," especially in making statements about his supposed refusal to build his ministry on the foundations of others, makes note of the apostle's "strange awareness of the presence of a wholly different and incommensurable factor—Jesus Christ." The strangeness of Paul himself, he argues, is ultimately "in itself of no importance," but it does become significant inasmuch as it "may bear witness to a strangeness which is wholly different," by which Barth is referring to Paul's Christology.[12]

Paul's declaration is indeed strange: What can he mean by not having received the gospel through human agency (v. 12)? Did the Christians in Arabia and Damascus (v. 17) or Syria and Cilicia (v. 21) tell him nothing of the life and ministry of Jesus? If Paul received the message of the gospel in an apparently disembodied way, how can that gospel be the good news of God's solidarity with creation in the incarnation? The question remains an open one to be tested in the reception of Paul's Christology: to the extent that Pauline reception veers in a docetic direction, it loses its liberating edge and begins to feed into negativity about the body, about women, and about Judaism.

Probably a more fruitful direction hermeneutically is to take his

11. Jerome, *Commentary on Galatians*, 77.
12. Karl Barth, *The Epistle to the Romans*, trans. from the sixth edition by Edwyn C. Hoskins (New York: Oxford University Press, 1968), 533.

point about "human agency" as a jab at the apostolic authority of the apostles based in Jerusalem, especially Peter and James.[13] This points to the fact that our link to the good news of the gospel is guaranteed neither by a human connection to the earthly ministry of Jesus (as symbolized by Peter) nor by some sort of family lineage (as in the case of James, the "brother of the Lord"); it is worked out in the power of the Holy Spirit. This is good news for those of us who are neither related humanly to Jesus nor able somehow to trace our ecclesial genealogy (or, if applicable, our ordination) directly back to Peter. In that case, "apostolicity" is not guaranteed by lineage but rather is to be granted by the Holy Spirit and is seen and verified in its results. Paul argues that his genuine apostolicity is seen in that those who had been afraid of him came to glorify God because of him (v. 24). As Theodoret notes, the wolf began to do what belongs to the shepherds, and so Paul's sudden change became an occasion for singing God's praise.[14]

To illustrate the surprising effects of the revelation of Jesus Christ, Paul depicts his metamorphosis from zealous persecutor of the church to apostle to the Gentiles. Paul wants to make clear his impeccable position in Judaism: he was far more zealous—he remarks—than many of his peers, more intent on keeping the traditions of the ancestors. He hopes to impress upon his hearers that it is his very loyalty to the God of his ancestors that leads him to proclaim the gospel of Jesus Christ to those who are not Jews.

The problem is, of course, that regardless of the depth of his Jewish roots, some of his ideas have been pressed into the service of a kind of Christian chauvinism that is at best dismissive of Judaism and at worst ready to persecute Jews in the name of supposedly Christian values. Galatians 1:13–14 in particular, in which Paul says that his zealousness in Judaism leads him to persecute the church, has no clear disclaimer that reads: "But of course that was a misreading of Judaism" or "Let me make clear that I continue to be a Jew even as I change my course with regard to this matter." The impression is left that zealousness in Judaism does indeed easily connect to violent

---

13. Jerome does so; see *Commentary on Galatians*, 80.
14. "The Letter to the Galatians," in Theodoret of Cyrus, *Commentary on the Letters of St. Paul*, vol. 2, trans. Robert Charles Hill (Brookline, MA: Holy Cross Orthodox Press, 2001), 6.

persecution of Christians, and because Scripture as it stands does not include the later historical record of Christianity (in which it was actually Christians who most often violently persecuted Jews), the passage can serve to affirm a distorted Christian view of Judaism.

From the beginning, Christian interpreters of Galatians have often gone down the path of understanding Judaism as intrinsically vitiated and in enmity with all things Christian, as can be seen in several patristic era commentaries of this passage. Chrysostom, for example, describes Paul's conversion in terms of "shaking off his Jewish prejudices."[15] Jerome states that his own contemporaries who "interpret Scripture according to a Jewish mentality persecute the Church of Christ and devastate it" not because they are zealous for the law but because they have been corrupted by human traditions.[16] Augustine, for his part, thinks that "it is clear that Judaism is opposed to the Church of God," not because the law was bad, but because the Jews had a "carnal and slavish way of life."[17] Though Augustine, like Jerome, wants to defend torah as good, he still resorts to blaming Jews for their reception of it, just as Jerome does. To make a caricature of the Jewish faith in order to contrast it with Paul's understanding of the gospel after his conversion thus became a commonplace of the Christian reception of Galatians. This habit is not easy to break. Even Christian interpreters of Paul who seem to have the best of intentions toward Judaism sometimes in practice end up in hurtful places.

Does Pauline theology inexorably take us in an anti-Semitic direction? One important insight to keep in mind at all times in reading Galatians is that Paul and the Jesus whom Paul proclaimed as good news were who they were *because* they were Jews, not in spite of Judaism. Anti-Jewish Christianity should be a logical impossibility; that it does exist is a sign of a Christian incapacity to deal with its own heritage and internal logic. The Christian faith will never be truly liberating in a Gentile context if it cannot overcome this internal contradiction. That does not mean that Christians are obliged to

---

15. John Chrysostom, *Commentary on the Epistle to the Galatians and Homilies on the Epistle to the Ephesians* (Oxford: John Henry Parker, 1840), 20.
16. Jerome, *Commentary on Galatians*, 82.
17. Plumer, *Augustine's Commentary on Galatians*, 133.

support all policies emerging from the modern State of Israel or to oppose the human rights of present-day Palestinians any more than observant Jews living in Israel or elsewhere today are obligated to do so.

What is often forgotten in the discussion of this passage is that when Paul speaks of his former violent way of life, his Jewish identity should not be the only lens used to understand the way he formerly lived; it is just as important to remember the fact that he was a male socialized to act in certain ways in the context of the Roman empire. Davina Lopez argues that in this text Paul presents himself as formerly "behaving in a manner vaguely reminiscent of a manly Roman soldier," advancing "beyond his own people and defeating others." She links his self-description to "a Roman imperial gender construct of impenetrable masculinity." The life Paul lives before and after his call experience "diverges radically," not because he abandoned Judaism or converted to what later came to be known as Christianity but because he became a different kind of man in his relationship with others—so different, in fact, that he will later describe himself as a "mother" to the Galatians.[18]

Paul places himself in the mold of Old Testament judges such as Samson and prophets such as Jeremiah, who were set apart for ministry even before birth (see Judg. 16:17; Jer. 1:5; in Luke 1:15, a similar image is used of John the Baptist). The apostle believes that the same God who chose him while he was still in his mother's womb and called him by grace also revealed the Son of God "to him" (as the NRSV has it), or more literally "in him" (v. 16). Jerome points out that for Paul to say that Christ is revealed "in me" (*en emoi*) is not at all the same as to state that Christ was revealed "to me." The former means that "the thing revealed was in him already" and later was made known in greater clarity. For Jerome, in other words, "the knowledge of God is innate in all humans," so that all persons, whether or not they are Christians, can act "prudently and uprightly in some respects" and carry within themselves "seeds of wisdom, righteousness and the rest of the virtues."[19]

18. Davina C. Lopez, *Apostle to the Conquered: Reimagining Paul's Mission* (Minneapolis: Fortress, 2008),133–34.
19. Jerome, *Commentary on Galatians*, 85.

The passage has also been at the center of discussions on the doctrine of predestination, since Paul affirms that God chose him even before he was born. Jerome is concerned to defend God's justice in this context by taking into account God's wisdom and different relation to time. He holds that God's foreknowledge allows God to know who will be righteous even before they are born but also that for God "the future has already unfolded," which means that God bases any verdicts on "how things end up, not how they began."[20] Calvin, unsurprisingly, affirms that Paul's calling "depends on the secret election of God," by which "secret purpose" he had been set apart. He also hastens to point out that it was not that Paul had somehow earned such a high honor even before birth but that it was simply God's good pleasure to call him.[21]

Perhaps a more compelling reason for Paul's statement than any developed theology of justice or predestination is simply the expression of a conviction that most people who articulate a strong sense of Christian vocation seem to have: namely, that God was with them, preparing them for their call (whether to ordained ministry or to other forms of service) even before they could understand what it entailed and perhaps even before they were conceived. Paul frames this conviction in the poetic idiom of the Hebrew Bible (see Ps. 139:13–16). The central idea in the verse is that God called him by grace, and the sense of having been "chosen" or "predestined" moves backward from the experience of that grace, weaving together his life narrative and making sense of his varied experiences.

The purpose of Paul's call was for him to proclaim the gospel among the Gentiles (v. 16). His account of the call still doesn't fully resolve the rather ungrounded and disincarnate feel of his claim about "a revelation of Jesus Christ." Paul does not describe that call in detail or even elucidate the content of the gospel he has received. What gives traction to his claim is his contention that he was called in order to proclaim the good news among the nations; conversely, to limit that proclamation or put conditions on it would undermine the reason for his setting apart, call, and reception of the gospel. The urgency of that mission is such that rather than traveling to

20. Ibid., 83–84.
21. Calvin, *Calvin's Bible Commentaries: Galatians and Ephesians*, 30.

Jerusalem to consult with the apostles, he heads immediately to Arabia and later to Syria. By Paul's account, only after three years does he visit Peter in Jerusalem, and then only for a fortnight (v. 18), during which he also sees James the brother of Jesus (v. 19).[22] He then mentions his presence in Syria and Cilicia (v. 21). He points out that the churches in Judea did not know him personally (v. 22), though news of his ministry did come to them (v. 23).

The description of Paul's call and its aftermath in Acts is different from the version in Galatians account, and difficult to harmonize wholly with it.[23] In Acts Paul does indeed go to Jerusalem (Acts 9:26–29) presumably quite soon after his experience on the road to Damascus (a scene that Galatians does not mention). Acts 9:23 states that he had to leave Damascus, "after some time had passed," and moves in 9:26 to his visit to Jerusalem without specifying how much time had elapsed until he arrived. Some interpreters therefore associate that trip with Galatians 1:18. At any rate, Luke seems to depict the formal presentation of Paul to the apostles as a necessary step because the disciples were still fearful of associating with Paul given his past as a persecutor of the young church (Acts 9:26). After that, Acts has him being sent down to Caesarea and afterward to Tarsus (Acts 9:30). The next time he appears in the narrative he is in Antioch (Acts 12:25).

Regardless of the chronology, the Paul of Acts, like the Paul speaking in the first person in Galatians, does not ask the permission of the apostles in Jerusalem to preach the gospel but rather embarks quickly and forcefully on his mission, with the result that many are surprised at the changes evident in him. That some among his opponents cast doubt on his version of the events can be surmised by his exclamation in Galatians 1:20, where he affirms solemnly, "before God," that he is not lying as he tells his story.

---

22. Some interpreters in Christian Antiquity took the fifteen symbolically to mean "complete knowledge and perfect doctrine," without discarding the literal meaning; see Jerome, *Commentary on Galatians,* 90.
23. In his still influential book *Chapters in a Life of Paul,* rev. ed. (Macon, GA: Mercer University Press, 2000), x *et passim,* John Knox sets out the principle that the primary sources for Paul's story are his own letters, and therefore they are always to be preferred to the data in Acts whenever there is implicit or explicit conflict between the two.

FURTHER REFLECTIONS
Jesus and His Siblings

Some patristic Latin interpreters, such as Helvidius, Jovinian, Tertullian, and Marius Victorinus, take James to be a child of Mary of Nazareth and therefore the brother of Jesus according to his humanity, though only Marius does so in the context of a commentary on Galatians.[24] Other Latin interpreters such as Jerome and Augustine consider it "self-evident" that James could not be literally the brother of Jesus; the same tendency can be seen in Greek writers such as Theodoret, Gregory of Nyssa, and Basil. Augustine submits that James is described as the brother of Jesus because "he was one of Joseph's sons by another wife or perhaps one of the relatives of the Lord's mother Mary."[25] Their reticence to imagine Mary as the mother of other children reflects the emerging understanding in the fourth century of Mary's virginity as something she maintained throughout her life: before, during, and after the birth of Jesus. Jerome even wrote a treatise to that effect in 383, *On the Perpetual Virginity of Holy Mary*, also known as *Against Helvidius*, which he quotes in his Galatians commentary. He was convinced that virginity was intrinsically superior to sexual activity in any context and therefore argued that James and the other "brothers" of Jesus were actually his cousins.[26]

Many contemporary interpreters have returned to the company of Helvidius (whose treatise was lost) and Marius in their reading of Galatians 1:19: James was the son of Mary and Joseph, one of several siblings of Jesus. Still, what is worth pondering is that whatever a given interpreter takes to be self-evident and simply part of theological "common sense" (in this case, the perpetual virginity of Mary) always has wider anthropological implications. In the long history of interpreters for whom it was self-evident that James could not be the brother of Jesus, the presupposition was that sexual relations

---

24. Cf. Stephen Andrew Cooper, *Marius Victorinus' Commentary on Galatians: Introduction, Translation and Notes* (Oxford: Oxford University Press, 2005), 266 (on 1:19) and 278 (on 2:12). See also the discussion in J. B. Lightfoot, *Saint Paul's Epistle to the Galatians* (London: MacMillan, 1905) 252–91.

25. Plumer, *Augustine's Commentary on Galatians*, 135.

26. See Andrew Cain, footnote 157, in Jerome, *Commentary on Galatians*, 90–91.

and the bearing of other children would somehow have been inappropriate given Mary's holiness and her special role in the economy of salvation. The assumption presupposes quite a negative view of human sexuality, especially of female sexuality. If Mary's uniqueness is wound up in her perpetual virginity, she is set at a distance from all sexually active females even while she is simultaneously lifted up as the ideal mother.

If James by definition cannot share the humanity of a common mother with Jesus, the link of Jesus to all humanity is weakened. Such indirect forms of Docetism tend to undermine the force of the doctrine of the incarnation. If we add to this particular case the fact that James became the leader of the Jewish Christian path for following Jesus, believing that it is "self-evident" that he could not literally be Jesus' brother (despite Paul's unequivocal words to the contrary), we may begin to brew up an ugly mixture of anti-Jewishness, mistrust of female sexuality, and quasi-Docetism that is not consonant with the heart of the gospel.

2:1–10
Remembering the Poor as a Shared Criterion

Paul first states that after fourteen years he returned to Jerusalem in the company of Barnabas and Titus. The span of years can be understood literally as fourteen years after the events described in the previous chapter or, perhaps, as Aquinas prefers, "in the fourteenth year of his conversion."[27] In verse 2 Paul clarifies that he went up to Jerusalem in response to a revelation (*kata apokalypsin*). This is the second mention of a revelation in the letter (see 1:12). Paul indicates that he is led to put forward his understanding of the gospel that he proclaims (*kēryssō*) among the Gentiles. The setting is a private meeting with "those who are prominent" or "those with a certain reputation" (*tois dokousin*) in the Jerusalem church, or as the

---

27. Thomas Aquinas, *Commentary on Saint Paul's Epistle to the Galatians*, trans. Fabian R. Larcher, Aquinas Scripture Series Vol. 1 (Albany, NY: Magi Books, 1966), 33. Calvin concludes the same thing; cf. *Calvin's Bible Commentaries: Galatians and Ephesians*, 37.

NRSV renders it, with the "acknowledged leaders" of the church (he repeats the idea with varying doses of irony in vv. 6 and 9).

Paul presents the gospel he has been proclaiming for their consideration, in order to make sure, as he expresses it, that he "was not running, or had not run, in vain" (v. 2). This is a metaphor much appreciated by Paul. He uses a similar expression in Philippians 2:16 when he tells the Philippians that he can be assured that he did not run in vain by the fact that they hold fast to the word of life. In Romans 9:16 he uses the image to point out the limits of human exertion and the priority of God's mercy. He will use the figure of speech again in Galatians 5:7 to speak of how the Galatians had "run" well in the past, in the sense of adhering to a given course of conduct. Aquinas takes the phrase in Galatians 2:2 as a reference to the rapidity of Paul's preaching and its expansion from Jerusalem as far as Spain, taking a cue from Psalm 147:15 ("He sends out his command to the earth; his word runs swiftly").[28] Most likely, however, the reference to not running in vain means that Paul wanted to avoid any possibility of not preaching or of not seeming to preach the gospel fully.[29]

Paul's tone in describing the leaders of the Jerusalem church is slightly caustic, as if he were saying that they were at least reputed to be influential dignitaries, though he might have his doubts about their effectiveness. At any rate, they are the "worthies" of the primitive church, and he meets with them in a kind of proto-interdenominational dialogue. In so doing, he grants us insight on how to deal with recognized religious authorities: whatever our opinion of them as leaders, we should neither slight them nor follow them blindly. It is possible that Paul is following some version of the process later described in Matthew 18:15-20 for a situation in which a person feels sinned against by a member of the community, since he underlines the privacy of the meeting and the presence of two witnesses, Barnabas and Titus. Additionally, Deuteronomy 19:15 establishes the need for two or three witnesses in order to sustain a charge of wrongdoing, so Paul's mention of his two companions

---

28. Ibid., 36.
29. See Cooper, *Marius Victorinus' Commentary on Galatians*, 269.

may mean that he is willing, if it is necessary, not only to defend himself but also to bring testimony against his adversaries.

At this point the flow of the account is interrupted by the mention of "intruders" or "spies" (v. 4), whom Paul perceives as "false siblings" in Christ (*pseudadelphous*). By his account, they have bad intentions toward the Gentile churches, because they want to curtail Gentile freedom in Christ. Paul resists them in no uncertain terms, understanding his opposition to them as nothing less than a defense of the truth of the gospel (v. 5). He contrasts their purported desire to "enslave" those who have received his gospel (v. 4) with his own refusal to submit even for an hour to those who would undermine the gospel of freedom for the Gentiles. He implies (vv. 4–5) that the very presence of that gospel of freedom among the Galatians and other Gentiles hinges on his steadfast resistance to the machinations of the "false siblings."

Despite the influence of these adversaries, it seems to Paul that his version of the gospel for a Gentile context is acceptable to the leaders of the Jewish Christian church in Jerusalem. He is admittedly unwilling to concede that he might have received anything at all from these "reputed leaders," whose status he does not hold as particularly special, since God is no respecter of persons (v. 6). This is a reference to the phrase in Deuteronomy 10:17, to the effect that God is not partial and takes no bribes. A similar idea appears in Sirach 35:12–13. This conviction about God is a constant in the New Testament and is quoted with approval by Paul and other writers (see e.g., Rom. 2:11; Jas. 2:1; 1 Pet. 1:17). If God shows no partiality on the basis of somebody's "acknowledged leadership," then Paul finds no need to do so either.

Nevertheless, Paul is not indifferent to the actions of the Jerusalem church leadership. He points out first of all that they do not require Titus to be circumcised (v. 3). This is the first mention of the important theme of circumcision in the letter. Unlike Timothy, whose mother was Jewish, Titus was a Greek without any previous religious or familial ties to the custom, and he is not pressured to be circumcised, even by the leaders of the Jewish Christian church in Jerusalem, regardless of the opinions of the "false siblings." As Augustine points out, Paul's teaching on circumcision is never that salvation is taken away by it, since it can be appropriate in certain cases, but rather to show that it would be contrary to salvation to make hope for salvation dependent on circumcision.[30] That principle is not limited to circumcision but applies to any pious practice, such as fasting; as Luther points out, fasting in itself is not "something damnable" but neither does it serve to "obtain the forgiveness of sins." The same goes for wearing or not wearing a cowl, entering or leaving a monastery, or eating meat or vegetables: such practices are to be carried out in freedom and in charity, but not to atone for sins or to achieve grace.[31]

In the second place, Paul states that the three "pillars," James, Cephas (Peter), and John, seal their acceptance of Paul and Barnabus' ministry with a handshake (v. 9). In antiquity, the handshake symbolized the ratification of a mutual agreement.[32] Strangely, no mention is made of a handshake with Titus. Jerome speculates that "he had not yet reached the point where he could be trusted, along with the elders, with the wares of Christ" so as to become, along with Paul and Barnabas, "a wholesaler of those wares."[33] Too much should not be made on the basis of an argument from silence, but the omission seems suggestive, given the later tensions between Peter and Paul. Could it be that Peter still could not bring himself in good faith to shake the hand of a Gentile convert who was unwilling to become a full-fledged member of the Jewish faith as part of his commitment to the way of Jesus?

At any rate, according to Paul's recollection of the scene, the "pillars" seal their agreement with him and Barnabas so that Peter and his coworkers will continue their ministry in a Jewish context, whereas Paul and his companions are free to spread the "gospel of the foreskin" (*akrobystia*), i.e., of the uncircumcision among the Gentiles (v. 7). Paul's explicit references to the male body are often obscured by translation, though he mentions foreskin, male circumcision, or sperm over twenty times. As Kahl points out, the use of nongendered terms in translation can obscure the fact that the male

---

30. Plumer, *Augustine's Commentary on Galatians*, 139.
31. Luther, *Luther's Works*, vol. 26, *Lectures on Galatians, 1535 Chapters 1–4*, 84–86.
32. See Andrew Cain, footnote 184, in Jerome, *Commentary on Galatians*, 99–100.
33. Ibid., 103.

body is a "major site of theological struggle in Galatians." If this specificity is obscured, then the gender-inclusive statements in chapter three about being clothed in Christ, the subversion of human fatherhood by a messianic spermatology that makes Abraham an ancestor in faith rather than by his literal "seed," and the overturning of gender hierarchies in Galatians 3:28 lose some of their transformative force.[34]

Vitally, the "pillars" and Paul conclude that what is central both for Jewish Christians and for Gentile Christians is to remember the poor (v. 10)—not just the poor in Jerusalem, as has often been supposed, but *all* of the poor and the vulnerable.[35] This is all too often effaced whenever interpreters forget that the concern for socioeconomic injustice is a central biblical theme in all of Scripture. What the agreement in Jerusalem means for Christian churches today is that the remembrance of the poor is at the heart of the message of the gospel. It is not an optional feature or dimension to be decided according to the cultural sensibilities of a given community, as in the case of the application of dietary laws among the Gentiles, but is to be practiced without fail in all Christian congregations. In Paul's ministry his own commitment to this principle can be seen in his encouragement of Gentile Christian churches to share their material resources with the poor in the Jerusalem church (Rom. 15:25–28).

Later, back in Antioch, however, the conflict about what elements of Jewish practice are to be upheld by those Gentiles who now follow Jesus is shown still to be unresolved in practice. Paul therefore publicly reprimands Peter (v. 11) in a way reminiscent of the procedure for resolving church conflict recorded by another strand of the tradition (Matt. 18:17): If a person continues to be recalcitrant even after the offense has been discussed in private and confirmed by the

---

34. Brigitte Kahl, "No Longer Male: Masculinity Struggles behind Galatians 3.28?", *Journal for the Study of the New Testament* 79 (2000): 37–49.
35. Cf. Bruce W. Longenecker, *Remember the Poor: Paul, Poverty and the Greco-Roman World* (Grand Rapids: Eerdmans, 2010), especially chapters 7–9, where he shows that the "consensus" that the poor of Gal. 2:10 only referred to those in Jerusalem is not warranted by the text. The "consensus" has a long history starting in the fourth century (with Ephrem the Syrian, Chrysostom, and Jerome) but was unknown by earlier writers such as Tertullian, Origen, and Athanasius. Longenecker posits that Paul was unconditionally committed to responding to poverty in all places in continuity with Jesus' work of bringing good news to the poor.

evidence of two or three witnesses, "tell it to the church; and if the offender refuses to listen even to the church, let such a one be to you as a Gentile and a tax collector." Paul is quite unafraid to point out inconsistencies in the theology of the church pillars, showing that the principle of *Paulus contra Paulum* can also be expressed if necessary as *Paulus contra Petrum*, with Peter representing established church hierarchies.

Luther imagines Paul's thought processes as follows: "Therefore it makes no difference to me how great Peter and the other apostles have been or how many miracles they have performed. What I am contending for is that the truth of the Gospel be preserved among you."[36] Paul is acutely aware, furthermore, that not all siblings in Christ are truly our brothers and sisters: some are pseudo-siblings or "false believers," as the NRSV renders it, whose intentions are not good. They are the sort of people who for conscious or unconscious motives end up using religious faith to enslave others rather than to liberate them. Paul doesn't hesitate to denounce anything that leads to the constricting of freedom in Christ, no matter what its pious garb.

Today we struggle with the interpretation of Paul, who has himself become an undoubted "pillar" of the church, perhaps—given the variety and weight of his extant letters—even more than James, John, or Peter ever were. Faced with Paul and his complex theological legacy, we can follow the hermeneutical example he gives us in Galatians. In interpreting his message in the epistle, we can approach it with respect, even if admittedly with a sense of irony at times. As we try to wrestle with our own sense of what the good news is, we too try not to "run in vain."

We are free to examine Galatians, to argue with it, and to try to come to some sort of consensus about what is central, keeping in mind the agreement by all parties in Paul's day about the centrality of responding to the needs of the poor for any authentic understanding of the gospel. We are also empowered by Paul's example to call him out on his own inconsistencies, even as he did with Peter. For the sake of our freedom in Christ (v. 4), it may at times be necessary

---

36. Luther, *Luther's Works*, vol. 26, *Lectures on Galatians, 1535 Chapters 1–4*, 93.

to argue with Paul against Paul (*Paulus contra Paulum*), just as Paul argued against the "pillars" and the "false siblings" in Christ. A central hermeneutical principle then, for which Paul himself gives us the warrant, is that whenever he is quoted in a way that leads to the destruction of freedom in Christ, this should be pointed out, not submitted to "even for a moment" (v. 5), lest the gospel be distorted.

In all of this, Paul takes pains to make the point that God "is no respecter of persons" (v. 6) but that God's lack of partiality is expressed, paradoxically, in God's partiality for the vulnerable. In Deuteronomy 10:17–18, the scriptural text quoted by Paul, God's partiality means that God takes no bribes and takes special care to make sure that justice is done to orphans, widows, and strangers, three groups that represent concrete areas of vulnerability. As the Hebrew Bible shows repeatedly, God's greatness and power is manifested in God's love for the weakest. In the context of the emerging Gentile Christian churches, Paul seems to identify the uncircumcised as a vulnerable group whose freedom in Christ must be defended.

It does not seem possible fully to harmonize Paul's version of the events in Galatians with Luke's account in Acts 15, to the point that both Luther and Calvin, unlike most ancient and modern commentators, concluded that the passages refer to two different occasions. In Acts 15, the focus of what Gentile Christians should keep practicing, even though they are not required to convert to Judaism, is not the poor but the avoidance of "things polluted by idols," "fornication," and eating blood or anything strangled (Acts 15:20, 29). In other words, circumcision is not considered necessary for Gentile Christianity in either version of the events, but consideration of the needs of the poor as a criterion for identifying God's justice and God's freedom is absent from Acts 15. There is an account, however, in Acts 11:29, of a collection for the poor among the Christians in Judea in the face of a famine, in

> It is the poor and rejected who keep the church from becoming so comfortably installed in this world that it forgets it is to be in the world but not of it, that its very mission is to constantly challenge unto new life until the final consummation of time.
>
> Virgilio Elizondo, *Guadalupe: Mother of the New Creation* (Maryknoll, NY: Orbis Books, 1997), 59.

which Barnabas and Saul are said to be involved. At any rate, in the version of events remembered by Paul as a direct witness of his conversations with Jewish Christian leaders in Jerusalem, "remembering the poor" is a key issue for interpretation that allows at least for a provisional resolution of conflict between observant Jewish and non-Jewish followers of Jesus.

Paul desires (v. 10) that the Gentile communities "remember" (*mnēmoneuōmen*). Notably, the principle of active remembrance continues to be important in Judaism generally to this day. In Argentina, for example, the Jewish organization *Memoria Activa* continues to insist that the society remember the attacks in Buenos Aires on the Israeli embassy in 1992 and on the *Asociación Mutual Israelita Argentina* (AMIA) in 1994. Among the many dead were both Jews and Gentiles. Because the facts behind the attacks never fully came to light and society is in danger of forgetting about them, *Memoria Activa* points out that a "third attack" is in danger of occurring, that of impunity.[37] In other words, historical amnesia and social forgetfulness easily become tools of injustice. In thinking of the relationship between Judaism and Christianity, between Christianity and other religions, and of the ecumenical relationship among the many different versions of Christianity, we would do well more actively to *remember* the common criterion set out by the Jerusalem "pillars": namely, "that we remember the poor" (v. 10). The linkage between the duty of remembering and the centrality of the needs of the poor keeps the Christian faith honest and is a bridge to interreligious communication, because it is a criterion that is at the heart of the three Abrahamic religions as well as central to many other faiths and to ethical forms of agnosticism and atheism.

FURTHER REFLECTIONS
God's Option for the Poor

Many interpreters of Galatians, from Marius Victorinus and Jerome onward, have limited the meaning of the "poor" in Galatians 2:10 to

---

37. "A 20 años del atentado. Memoria activa: Los actos nos dejan más vacíos," *La Nación*, March 15, 2012, at http://www.lanacion.com.ar/1456667-memoria-activa-los-actos-nos-dejan -mas-vacios.

a group of poor Jewish Christians in the Judean region or alternatively to the "poor in spirit."[38] Nevertheless, the priority of addressing the needs of the vulnerable as a criterion of the authenticity
of the gospel can be traced through Christian history. It is a clear
theme in both the Greek and Latin Fathers in the Middle Ages, in
the Renaissance and Protestant Reformation, in the Catholic Reformation, and on through to modernity. It can be found especially in
the homiletical tradition, from Gregory of Nyssa's *Homily on Love for
the Poor* to Ambrose's sermon on King Ahab's greed.[39] The theme
was rearticulated in the twentieth century by many Latin American theologians and placed at the center of their theological and
ecclesial imagination.[40] Consistently, in all these various theological
strands, God's concern for the poor is a reflection of the character of
God, the protector of the poor, rather than a reflection of the moral
worthiness of the oppressed. It is not a matter of the poor being
somehow more saintly but a matter of God's justice and faithfulness
in the face of inequity.

Roberto Goizueta makes the point that one reason God's option
for the poor is often misunderstood in English-speaking North
America is that the individualism of the dominant culture leads
people to imagine it as an option for some individuals (the poor)
against other individuals (the privileged). To exclude a group from
God's grace would mean that such grace would cease to be a common good. God's option for the poor, however, does not exclude the
privileged but rather calls them (us) urgently to conversion.[41] To be
indifferent in the face of inequality is not a sign of being unbiased
but a decision to privilege those who have power and privilege over
those who do not. God's emphasis on responding to the needs of
the vulnerable as manifested in the Hebrew Scriptures and later in
the New Testament opens a path for the transformation of all.

---

38. See Cooper, *Marius Victorinus' Commentary on Galatians*, 277; Jerome, Galatians, 104.
39. See the excellent anthology covering all of these periods compiled by José Ignacio González
    Faus, *Vicarios de Cristo: Los pobres en la teología y la espiritualidad cristianas* (Madrid: Trotta,
    1991).
40. Cf. Julio Lois Fernández, *Teología de la liberación: Opción por los pobres* (Madrid: IEPALA,
    1996).
41. See Roberto Goizueta, *Caminemos con Jesús: Toward a Hispanic/Latino Theology of
    Accompaniment* (Maryknoll, NY: Orbis, 1995), 173–74.

2:11–14
The Difficulty Inherent in Consistency

In this section we run head on into what is sometimes termed "the Antioch incident," something that James Dunn, who has written a book about the theology of Galatians, believes has been insufficiently stressed in the history of the epistle's interpretation. Dunn thinks that the conflict between Paul and Peter is central because it allows "issues which had been submerged" to rise to the surface of theological discussion, and with them the "beginning of the explicitly distinctive features of Paul's theology."[42]

Perhaps even more pointedly, the matter underlying the "incident" is not so much the particular contour of Pauline theology but the distinctiveness of the gospel itself: What exactly *is* the good news of Jesus Christ, and how is it to be appropriated and lived out concretely in diverse cultural and ethnic settings? More specifically, what does it mean for non-Jews to follow a Jewish rabbi in faith and practice? How can such a thing be done? For Peter, such questions are not at the forefront of ministry, but Paul's main focus— one might call it his specialty as well as his calling—is answering this very question, and he sees it as a matter of life and death for the nascent Gentile churches that are at the center of his concern. It may be impossible to make sense of Galatians without entering imaginatively into the tensions that make the events at Antioch into an "incident" worth noting.

According to Paul's account, when Peter (Cephas) goes to Antioch, he acts inconsistently. Sometimes he insists on a strict Jewish Christian dietary regimen, and at other times he eats kosher and nonkosher foods indiscriminately. Though in 2:3 Paul has introduced the matter of male circumcision for Gentile converts and will later return to the topic, what comes to the fore in this section is the matter of commensality. As many communities of faith have found through the centuries, eating together is an effective way to coalesce groups and to pass on traditions, but it also can lead to tensions and divisions.

42. James D. G. Dunn, *The Theology of Paul's Letter to the Galatians* (Cambridge: Cambridge University Press, 1993), 72–73.

Peter is caught here (v. 11) in a dilemma as he tries to work out his practices as a Jewish follower of Jesus in a Gentile context. Elsewhere in his epistles we see that Paul is pressed by local congregations to come up with guidelines about food as it relates to faith practices. In dealing with food sacrificed to the gods, for example, he proposes a flexible attitude, depending on how such dietary customs affect the faith of the people in the community who witness what is eaten (1 Cor. 8:1–13). In Antioch it could be said that Peter likewise tries to be flexible, but according to Paul he is doing so in a way that is not helpful to the Gentile churches, because it is inconsistent and hypocritical (Gal. 2:13).

It is worth keeping in mind that some degree of hypocrisy is always present in any religious practice, or indeed, in any sort of ethical practice whatsoever. Who of us is entirely consistent? Perhaps the principle should be for us to point out our mutual inconsistencies in a spirit of love. In that case not only would Paul be right to point out Peter's inconsistencies in the matter of commensality, but we also would be correct to point out Paul's own inconsistencies when necessary.

The crux of the matter is that in a given symbolic universe, if a specific group (in this case, Jewish followers of Jesus) is to share in faith practices such as eating in a ritual setting on equal footing with a group that formerly was not on equal terms (for instance, Gentile followers of Jesus), both the practices and the symbolic universe will inevitably shift. This can be profoundly disconcerting to all the parties involved but especially to those long invested in practices that help frame their particular identity as a people beloved by God. Any shift in such practices will lead to new challenges. How then is it possible to respect particularities and not to flatten out differences, while at the same time respecting each other and treating each other as equals? Not only Peter, but also Paul, and each of us, have to struggle with this question.

> If Peter fell, I, too, may fall; if he stood up again, so can I.
>
> Martin Luther, *Luther's Works*, vol. 26, *Lectures on Galatians, 1535 Chapters 1–4*, 109.

Paul affirms (v. 11) that he resists Peter's inconsistency openly, to his face (*kata prosōpon*), presumably in contrast to the sneaking around of the "false siblings" (v. 4). It seems to him that Peter's self-contradictions speak for themselves (v. 11). As a series of well-chosen verbs in the imperfect tense suggest, first Peter regularly eats with the Gentile Christians, but when James' envoys arrive, he begins to withdraw and then habitually to cut himself off from fellowship at meals with Gentile Christians. He does so, in Paul's view, for fear of offending the Jewish Christians who have arrived, but he drags along with him the rest of the Jewish Christians in the community—even Barnabas—into that same separation at meals. What Paul perceives, however, is that they end up participating together less in table fellowship than they do in hypocrisy.

Paul sees that they have fallen away from orthopraxis (v. 14), or as he puts it, that they have ceased to walk in a straight course (*orthopodousin*), uprightly, according to the truth of the gospel. They are not giving glory to God in their actions because they are choosing to divorce themselves from the joys of commensality with Gentile Christians. This is a serious matter not least because commensality functions as a sign of eschatological hope and as an anticipation of the great banquet in the very presence of God. Are Gentile and Jewish Christians not to share together in that celebration? The presumed solution—namely, that Gentile Christians are welcome to sit at the table if they adhere to a Jewish Christian dietary regimen—is not in accordance with what had been pledged by a handshake in Jerusalem (v. 9).

Once again Paul states that he confronts Peter in front of everyone, meaning most likely in the presence of the envoys from James, Barnabas, and the Jewish and Gentile Christians from Antioch (v. 14). The public nature of the reprimand is important because it is an opportunity for the entire community to learn from the situation: in Augustine's words, "It was necessary for him to say this to Peter in front of everyone so that by Peter's rebuke everyone might be put right."[43] Paul therefore poses a rhetorical question to Peter: If you as a Jewish Christian do not consistently live as a Jew, how can you compel Gentile Christians to adopt Jewish customs? The answer expected by a question posed in these terms would of course be: "I cannot and I humbly repent of my hypocrisy."

The freedom that Paul feels to point out Peter's inconsistencies,

---

43. Plumer, *Augustine's Commentary on Galatians*, 145.

his instructions elsewhere for Gentile Christians to imitate him as he imitates Christ (1 Cor. 11:1), and his command to distrust anything he might say that might distort the gospel of freedom in Christ (Gal. 1:8) open up remarkable hermeneutical possibilities, as already intimated above (see on 1:8–9). Implicitly, he again invites us to apply the dialectic of Paul against Paul. Specifically, Paul's interpretation of the gospel as a glorious possibility of freedom tends inherently to oppose any interpretation of the gospel—among them a number of interpretations that identify themselves as Pauline—that push us into bondage. The possibilities of this hermeneutical move are quite exhilarating if we think, for instance, of their potential in confronting "Paul" or "Pauline theology" whenever these are used to restrain the voices and the ministry of women. In those situations, we are to treat Paul as Paul himself treated Cephas, opposing him to his face for not "acting consistently with the truth of the gospel" (v. 14).

Along these same lines, we should be reminded that it would be a mistake to understand this passage primarily as a polemic against Judaism or against Jewish Christianity. It should be seen, rather, as an attempt to focus on what is central to the Christian faith: how the gospel of Jesus Christ allows (and indeed requires) the freedom to express itself in particular cultural contexts. A given particularity, however, is not to be imposed on other cultural contexts. As Augustine points out, Paul's aim is to avoid taking away any local custom whose observance does not hinder the kingdom of God, while at the same time making sure that people do not place their hope for salvation in inessential or superfluous things.[44]

The adherence to a given set of dietary guidelines, as valuable as such guidelines might be in themselves, is not of ultimate importance. Clearly, specific practices of commensality have served Judaism well across the centuries and helped it maintain its traditions in adverse circumstances, besides bringing much pleasure. They are not objectionable in themselves and it is not surprising that Jewish followers of Jesus might wish to preserve them. The problem that Paul wants to underline emerges in a context where some Christians are Gentiles and don't keep kosher, whereas other Christians are

44. Ibid., 143.

of Jewish origin and do keep kosher: How are they to eat together? They will run into insoluble conflict unless the rules of commensality are treated as penultimate. The passage is therefore not a discussion of Judaism per se, but rather of Jewish followers of Jesus and their relations with non-Jewish followers of Jesus and how to respect the particularities "in Christ" of each group.

Paul is irritated with Peter because he believes that Peter is acting inconsistently. If indeed Peter wants to keep kosher, then he should do it all the time, not only to preserve appearances under pressure from Jewish Christians linked to James. Regardless of his own dietary principles, it is unprincipled to make them central for Gentile Christians who are neither Jews nor Jewish Christians or for Peter to drag along (*synapēchthē*) other Jewish Christians, including Barnabas, in his rather inconsistent and uneven wake (v. 13). In short, Paul resists Peter face to face because he thinks Peter's attitude is reprehensible.

These tensions between Paul and the Jerusalem "pillars" generally and between Paul and Peter specifically, have made many commentators nervous through the centuries. Chrysostom proposes the idea that in reality there were no tensions at all, but that the apostles planned the apparent dispute as a stratagem. He furthermore manages to frame this idea, as he so often does, in a manner pejorative toward Judaism: namely, as a condescension to its "infirmities."[45] In Chrysostom's mind, Peter acts as if he embodied a version of Jewish Christianity, but in reality he is participating in a farce. Paul, for his part, acts in public as if he were contradicting Peter, but in reality he does not. Jerome also follows this pattern, stating that Peter is not in error and Paul does not rashly rebuke his elder and defending the expedient of "temporary deception" of the people for their own good.[46] Such an interpretation hides two problems: first, a defense of a hierarchical leadership that must by definition always see eye to eye on all matters; and second, an anti-Jewish bias that presupposes that a consistent Jewish Christianity is somehow of lesser value than the Gentile versions of the Christian faith.

There is another strand of the tradition, however, represented by

---

45. Chrysostom, *Commentary on the Epistle to the Galatians*, 36–40.
46. Jerome, *Commentary on Galatians*, 104–10.

Marius Victorinus and Augustine, that feels free to discover differences and mutual correction among the apostles and is not worried about upholding some sort of apostolic infallibility.[47] This approach holds that to posit a stratagem in order to explain away tension between the various apostles is paramount to making both Peter and Paul into liars, which would be much worse than simply admitting that Peter acted in an inconsistent manner and that Paul pointed it out. Augustine engages in a famous epistolary dispute with Jerome over this very matter.[48] Augustine thinks that Peter did indeed make a mistake, but that very fact allows him to exercise humility, as Jesus had taught him: "he was willing to endure this rebuke from a junior shepherd for the salvation of the flock."[49] Origen had earlier noted that Peter tended to outbursts and thought that his silence in the face of Paul's reproof meant that he had made progress toward spiritual maturity and self-mastery.[50]

Even more significantly, perhaps, is that already Marius Victorinus holds up the principle of the congregation's right and responsibility to reprimand even the apostles.[51] He translates the phrase in verse 11 that the NRSV renders as "he [Peter] stood self-condemned" as "he had been reprimanded," that is, he had undergone correction by the congregation in Antioch. In other words, Marius finds precedent in Pauline theology for a mutual correction not only between apostles but also between leaders and their congregations in accordance with the interpretive principle of *Paulus contra Paulum* and *Paulus contra Petrum* mentioned above. This is a profoundly antihierarchical approach. Luther and the Reformation would inherit this exegetical tradition and apply its principles freely in the critique of the existing church hierarchy, though not always consistently to themselves, once they were in positions of ecclesial and civil authority.[52]

---

47. Cf. Cooper, *Marius Victorinus' Commentary on Galatians*, 277.

48. See Augustine, "Epistola 28," in *Epistolae. Opera Omnia Editio Latina, Patrologiae Latinae Elenchus* 33, http://www.augustinus.it/latino/lettere/index2.htm.

49. Plumer, *Augustine's Commentary on Galatians*, 145.

50. See Stephen Andrew Cooper's footnote 121 in Cooper, *Marius Victorinus' Commentary on Galatians*, 277, quoting Origen's *Commentary on John* 32.63 and *Contra Celsum* 2.1.

51. Cooper, *Marius Victorinus' Commentary on Galatians*, 277.

52. See Cooper's discussion of Marius's influence on later exegetes in ibid., 203–12.

FURTHER REFLECTIONS
On Not Sharing the Lord's Supper with Other Christians

Peter's wavering on the matter of commensality in the church and Paul's reaction to his vacillation both bring to mind another important question related to eating in the church: how different Christians celebrate the Eucharist. In the Baptist churches in which I grew up in Argentina, eyebrows were often raised even if a Baptist from another congregation participated in the Lord's Supper. To invite a Methodist or Lutheran not baptized by immersion to the table was unthinkable. Roman Catholics were often not even considered members of the same faith. The celebration of the Lord's Supper was interpreted squarely in the "remembrance" tradition of Zwingli, as an ordinance and not as a sacrament. Ironically, however, Zwingli himself would not have been welcome to share the bread and the wine at that table (or more exactly, the crackers and small cups of grape juice that were handed around by the deacons). Later, as an adult, while visiting Argentine Methodist and Lutheran congregations, often as an invited preacher, I was always generously invited to partake in the celebration. I was also told quite often, by many people and in no uncertain terms, that the refusal by "my people" to share the Lord's Supper with them on the occasions in which they had visited Baptist congregations had been hurtful to them.

Baptist identity in that context and at that time was tied into "eating" a certain way and only with certain people. It was part of the discipline of being a well-defined, countercultural religious minority, committed to a pattern of "believer's baptism" in contradistinction to Constantinian understandings of Christendom. To share the Lord's Supper in that particular way was thought of as a badge of being willing to share also in the ridicule doled out by society to a minority religious group. In time, ecumenical experiences, often with other religiously non-hegemonic groups, led me to ask: Is it not possible to share the Lord's Supper with others without diluting the meaning of a counter-hegemonic identity? Could it actually serve to strengthen it? Communal, contextual particularities are not fixed but continually under negotiation and flux, as communities of faith seek to discern how best to be faithful to the rhythms of God's Spirit of transformation.

2:15-21
Justification and Transformation of Life Now

Paul now switches from the first person singular (which he had used in his account of the conflict with Peter in Antioch) to a wider first person plural (vv. 15–17). By doing so he places himself firmly in the community of Jews who have come to follow Jesus. "We ourselves are Jews by birth," he states, meaning that he was born into Judaism, no differently than were the "pillars" of the Jerusalem church. He contrasts that condition with being born from among "Gentile sinners" (v. 15). Because a "sinner" is one who deviates from the straight path of virtue, this construction may be an ironic nod to the previous section, where Jewish Christians such as Peter are actually those who are meandering off the path (v. 14).

Whatever his birthright, and whatever his convictions about the privileges that such a heritage entails, Paul states that he now acts as he does knowing that a human being is not justified (*dikaioutai*) by the "works of the law" (v. 16). With this statement, he introduces explicitly two important themes of the letter: the "law" and "justification." Paul hammers away at the latter in verse 16, mentioning the same idea three times with slight variations and contrasting it with the "works of the law" to form almost a poetic structure:

> A person is not justified by the works of the law (but through the faith of Christ).
> We are justified by the faith of Christ (and not by works of the law).
> Nobody will be justified by the works of the law.

With the metaphor of justification Paul introduces a legal image into his discussion. "To justify" refers to being "rendered just" in the sense of being held as guiltless or acquitted and therefore cleared of all wrongdoing. As Luther puts it, "A Christian is not someone who has no sin or feels no sin" but rather someone to whom God, thanks to faith in Christ, does not impute that sin.[53] However, though it is rooted in the legal imaginary, the image implodes any notion of straightforward and reasonable human justice, because it draws from a notion of divine justice that is quite different from and often opposed to the distributive or retributive justice of human courts.

"Justification" in Paul's sense consists of God's work.[54] God makes someone just, not rewarding or punishing a person on the basis of merits or demerits, but as a reflection of God's own transformative justice. That is why the "works of the law," inasmuch as they consist of righteous deeds or actions, cannot lead to "justification" in this sense, because they are human endeavors. Paul is speaking of an agency or creative "work" that by definition only God can carry out, in contrast to human "works." This does not mean that human conduct is irrelevant, as Paul's own concerns about Peter illustrate. It means rather that just as human creativity is related to God's work of creation but qualitatively different from it or human love is related to God's love yet different from it, so also human justice is derived from God's justice yet is not equivalent to it. God's justice transforms and justifies us as human beings in order to empower us to walk along a path that appreciates others in their many differences while not excluding them because of their particularity. "Justification" as Paul describes it in Galatians is not an abstract phenomenon but a transformation that is manifested and tested out in the life of the concrete community of faith made up of people of many different backgrounds.

Because "justification by faith" became such a central tenet of the Reformation, it is difficult, particularly for Protestants, to think of "justification" outside of the parameters etched out so clearly by Luther, for whom the doctrine was pivotal and constituted a restatement of the gospel. However, as Paul Tillich points out, although Luther's message "has the truth of Paul," it is "by no means the full Paul; it is not everything which Paul is," in part because Luther does

---

53. Luther, *Luther's Works*, vol. 26, *Lectures on Galatians, 1535 Chapters 1–4*, 133.
54. Martyn prefers to translate the term as "rectification" rather than as "justification:" God makes right what was wrong; cf. J. Louis Martyn, *Galatians: A New Translation with Introduction and Commentary*, Anchor Bible (New York: Doubleday, 1997), 246–80.

not take sufficiently into account two other central dimensions of Pauline theology: pneumatology and eschatology.

According to Tillich, Paul has three main centers in his thinking: first, "his eschatological consciousness, the certainty that in Christ eschatology is fulfilled and a New Reality has started;" second, his "doctrine of the Spirit, which means for him that the Kingdom of God has appeared," and that "the New Being, in which we are, is given to us in Christ;" and third "the critical defense against legal-ism" constituted by Paul's understanding of justification by faith.[55] In Galatians, though justification is an important theme, it is but one of several ways that Paul uses to speak of the work of God in Christ by the Spirit. The theme of justification is not an end in itself but part of a larger argument about how the good news of the gospel is to be lived out in concrete situations, in this case by those who follow Jesus among the Galatians.

The lens of the life of specific congregations can help us see why Paul rejects a way of understanding the "law" that allows it to become an end in itself rather than a means for God to exercise grace. When that happens, it becomes distorted and can be used to hurt and exclude rather than to guide and to bless. This is what Paul is afraid would be the outcome of Peter's waffling on the matter of dietary guidelines for Gentile Christians. He makes the point that precisely those followers of Jesus who (like Peter and Barnabas) have been born into the Jewish faith should know that being made just in rela-tion to God and to other people cannot be a fruit of anything but of the grace of God. They of all people should not confuse what is peripheral with what is central to pleasing God.

As Jewish followers of Jesus, familiar both with the Torah and with the way that Jesus embodied God's law of grace and love, Paul thinks that Peter, Barnabas, and the rest of the Jewish Christians involved in the dispute in Antioch should have particular clarity about how God makes people just. They have experienced in their own lives that by faith in Christ or through the faith of Christ (v. 16) the way of the Torah intersects with the good news of the gospel, so that all people,

---

55. See Paul Tillich, "Lecture 31: The Reformation: Luther and Catholicism," in the transcription of his lecture series from the spring of 1953, *The History of Christian Thought*, at http://www.religion-online.org/showchapter.asp?title=2310&C=2336.

regardless of their heritage, are invited to be made just or "justified" in the eyes of God.

Though Paul is indeed speaking of the Torah as a Jewish Christian, what he understands by the "law" and its function in Galatians is not at all what most non-Christian Jews would mean when they think of the Torah. He is, in a sense, answering a question ("Can a person be justified by the works of the law?") that they are not asking. Whereby Paul insists that justification in the eyes of God cannot be achieved by the works of the law, many observant Jews both past and present would find such a statement not just offensive but also nonsensical.[56]

What Paul does is imagine the law almost as a metaphysical entity, as a "power" that can take on a life of its own and thereby become no longer an instrument of grace, but of alienation. What makes the matter of interpretation difficult is that we need to read Paul in all of his Jewishness (for he cannot be understood except in the light of his Hebrew roots), without making him into a paradigm for ancient or contemporary Judaism (even though he himself would seem to have us do so, as in 1:14). His inflation of the law into an agent with ontological status and power is compelling in many ways (as is the similar move that he makes with the ego in Rom. 7:14-25), for it allows for sharp insights into the human condition, but it cannot stand as the definitive interpretation of the Torah. The distortion of the law as Paul lays it out is not the inevitable outcome of living according to the law as it is understood in Judaism. For Christians, the force of this argument should be driven home by the very life of Jesus, who is depicted in the gospels as an observant Jew.

Augustine suggests that one way to understand verse 19 is that Paul contrasts the function of a "carnal" or "fleshly" (*carnaliter*) interpretation of the law with a "spiritual" (*spiritualiter*) one: "through the law understood spiritually he died to the law in order that he might not live under it carnally."[57] Central to Paul's logic is that when the law (whether explicitly religious or not) becomes an end in itself it can easily be co-opted by dominant common sense,

56. Cf. Amy-Jill Levine, *The Misunderstood Jew: The Church and the Scandal of the Misunderstood Jesus* (New York: HarperOne, 2006), 126–27.
57. Plumer, *Augustine's Commentary on Galatians*, 149.

something that has nothing to do with the Torah's defense of the weak. That is when it becomes allied with "sin, death and the devil," as Luther liked to put it.[58] The law becomes an enshrinement of the privilege of those who have money and power in a given society, as in the Jim Crow laws in the United States, which worked to preserve white privilege; the "New Jim Crow" system of incarceration; or the anti-immigrant laws in many U.S. states that serve to push undocumented immigrants into the shadows, where they can be used as cheap labor and then discarded at will. If such laws constituted "justice," Christ would indeed have died in vain (v. 21).

As Paul's hearers would have known, Jesus was executed under a Roman legal system that was meant to keep colonial subjects, both Jews and Gentiles, securely subjected. But though he was killed by an imperial common sense that mocked the supposed "king of the Jews," that was not the end of the story: Christ rose, and by the Spirit's resurrection power, the grace of God continues to work to transform society.

Whenever the Pauline argument about the "law" is used in an anti-Jewish manner, not only is it hurtful to Jews, but it also becomes an instrument of the very sort of "law" that it is meant to critique. If we can keep the possibility of a life-giving observance of the Torah in mind, it actually helps us understand Paul better as he argues passionately against the consequences of the distortion of the law. An ongoing human problem, as he sees it, is that the penultimate (in this case, God's law) can often pass for the ultimate (God), to the detriment of human relationships with God. There is surely some degree of autobiography here: Paul himself had attempted to live out the Torah zealously and presumably had not found peace with God in that way. It therefore makes sense to him to contrast the attempt to be justified in relation to God by living out the law perfectly, with the way of Christ, in which he has found grace and freedom. Paul is working out the simultaneous continuity and discontinuity between the faith of Jesus (the Jewish faith) and faith in Jesus as the "end" or fulfillment of the law. He now "knows" (v. 16) that God works in Jesus Christ to make human beings just.

---

58. Cf. Luther, *Luther's Works*, vol. 26, *Lectures on Galatians, 1535 Chapters 1–4*, 134.

Paul's christological conviction about God's work of justification in Christ brings with it a possible complication, however, which he develops in verse 17. If "we" are seeking (*zētountes*) to be justified in Christ, what are we to make of the fact that we are also found to be sinners? The "we" of the sentence could mean Jewish Christians, who find that they are no different than Gentiles, in that they are also found to be "sinners." It could also mean all Christians, both Jewish and Gentile followers of Jesus. The conviction of justification in Christ does not change the fact that all Christians are "found to be" (v. 17) continually missing the mark, regardless of our profession of faith. Where, then, does that place Christ and his work? Does it not make him a "minister of sin" or a "servant of sin" (*hamartias diakonos*)? In other words, is not the work of Christ shown to be ineffective as one in whom God makes human beings just, if the lives of Christians are so easily shown to be unjust? The question, though it is meant by Paul as a rhetorical one to be answered negatively, is worth pondering on its own merits. What is the point of Christ's ministry or work on our behalf, if we clearly continue so often to walk in paths of injustice? The question is an open wound in the history of the Christian church, and one that festers. It points once again to the ambiguity of religion as a force that often does not seem to work for the good.

Paul, although he admits the ambiguity both of religion as a phenomenon generally, and the imperfections of those who profess faith in Jesus specifically, answers his own rhetorical question about Christ as a servant of sin with a stalwart: "Of course not!" "By no means!" "God forbid!" or—as the NRSV has it—"Certainly not!" It is the same expression he uses several times in Romans in a similar vein (see Rom. 3:4, 3:31, and 9:14). His certainty hearkens back to the Old Testament idea that God is faithful, just, and upright, without deceit (Deut. 32:4) as well as to his conviction that it is the God of justice and no other who acts in Christ. His conviction, in other words, is based not on theological anthropology but on God, who in Christ serves justice and not sin.

For Paul, an exchange of attributes takes place that has a positive effect rather than a negative one, because followers of Jesus die to the old life (and are "crucified" with him) in order to live anew with

Christ, so that sin and alienation might die, but life and grace prevail. Key to this dynamic is that the exchange is an unequal one: grace and love prevail over sin and death, because Christ, though entirely human and in solidarity with the human condition, is at the same time so much more than that and able to call life and justice into being. In other words, Paul's logic depends on the full humanity and the full divinity of Jesus Christ.

Nonetheless, his explanation in verse 18 about why Christ is not a servant of sin is not easy to follow. He moves once more to the first person singular, so that he is speaking again forcefully and directly on the basis of his own life and trajectory. His argument is that if he were to build up the way of life characterized by injustice that he had previously torn down, then he would not be able to blame Christ for that. He would in that case be showing or constituting (*tanō*) himself as a transgressor rather than participating in the marvelous exchange whereby Christ becomes as we are that we might become as Christ is. What actually has happened in his life, however, is quite different: "through the law" (*dia nomou*) he has "died to the law" in order to live for God (v. 19). The law (manifesting God's grace) led him to the place where he was able to die to the law (inasmuch as it is a penultimate force) in order to be able to live for God or "to God" (v. 19). It is important to note here that the law itself also participates in the dynamic of the marvelous exchange in a way that no mere law-gospel or law-grace antithesis could convey.

In verse 20, Paul delves even more deeply into the economy of the exchange: he has been co-crucified with Christ (v. 19) and has died to his old life. In this scheme, neither the ego nor the law is destroyed, but rather they are transformed in dying and being raised along with Christ. Once again, this cannot be grasped through binary or antithetical thinking. It is not that the law is either good or bad, to be embraced or to be rejected. For Paul, we are not made just in and through the law, and yet the law is not annulled but rather is involved in our justification, inasmuch as it is transformed through Christ. The law is an entity which, like the ego, is not bad in itself; rather, both law and ego are "made just" in a material fashion ("the life I now live in the flesh") according to the way of Jesus Christ. Both the law and the ego cease being an end in themselves, participating faithfully and fruitfully in God's economy of grace. In short, Paul does not want to tear down, abrogate, or nullify the grace of God that he has discovered in Christ, as would be the case if he mistakenly made the law into an end in itself (v. 21).

Though Paul speaks of having been "crucified with Christ," the passage is not a celebration of death, for the theme of the verse is life. He uses the verb "to live" four times to underline how Christ lives "in him" and so vivifies him entirely. Life "in the flesh" (*en sarki*), that is, in the midst of the injustices of hegemony, is now transformed. The expression points to a powerful embodied existence justified in Christ. Followers of Jesus experience justification by being "made just" in the flesh, in Christ, in faith, and in grace.

For the vulnerable and the marginalized—for those who are identified with the basest materiality in the logic of predominant common sense—this can be very good news; according to this christological pattern of exchange they are not abjected but justified: they are given agency and made visible to a society that would rather not acknowledge them. For Paul, the Son of God "gave himself" (*paradontos eauton*) in order that this might happen, an expression that echoes what he had said in the beginning of the letter in 1:4: namely, that the "Lord Jesus Christ" gave himself (*dontos eauton*) in order to set us free (v. 20).

The text also underlines Christ's love and agency "for me" (*hyper emou*), reflecting a personal connection to God thanks to God's work of justification in Christ. This personal dimension is not individualistic but rather has wider implications for the immediate community of faith and for society. Concretely in the context of Galatians, life "in the flesh" is now lived "in faith" (*en pistei*) in a way that permits Paul and others to continue to build up the young churches rather than to tear them down through infighting and struggles for power.

The phrase "it is no longer I

> We are enclosed in the Father, and we are enclosed in the Son, and we are enclosed in the Holy Spirit. And the Father is enclosed in us, the Son is enclosed in us, and the Holy Spirit is enclosed in us, almighty, all wisdom in goodness, one God, one Lord.
>
> Julian of Norwich, *Showings*, trans. Edmund Colledge and James Walsh, The Classics of Western Spirituality (Mahwah, NJ: Paulist Press, 1978), 285.

who live, but it is Christ who lives in me" (v. 20) is an intriguing one. It could be taken to mean anything from a mystical dissolution of the self or an annulment of the ego to a mutual indwelling between Christ and his followers. Luther speaks in this context of being entirely conjoined or cemented together.[59] For Calvin we are "engrafted" into the death of Christ and "derive from it a secret energy, as the twig does from the root."[60]

The implications of an intimate union between Christ and his followers have been explored particularly by the mystical tradition. Julian of Norwich (late fourteenth century), who loves homely images, speaks of being "knitted together" and being made one with God "in bliss" through the work of Christ and the power of the Holy Spirit.[61] We yearn deeply for that "substantial union" and "can never have love or rest or true happiness" until no created thing comes between us and God.[62] Indeed, the fruit and the end of our prayer are to be united with Christ and to be like Christ in all things.[63] At the same time, Christ has a "spiritual thirst" and a "longing in love" to "gather us all here into him, to our endless joy."

Julian understands our union with Christ as something that has now already begun and nevertheless will not be completed until the end comes at the appointed time: "For we are not now so wholly in him as we then shall be." God's longing and thirst for us come from God's everlasting goodness, and the power of the longing of Christ enables us to respond to his longing.[64] For Julian our mystical union with Christ always has an ethical, material manifestation, always entails union not only with God but also with other persons, and is a matter of great joy and bliss, both now and in the age to come.[65] In all of this she is thoroughly Pauline.

---

59. Cf. Luther, *Luther's Works*, vol. 26, *Lectures on Galatians, 1535 Chapters 1–4*, 168.
60. Calvin, *Calvin's Bible Commentaries: Galatians and Ephesians*, 60.
61. Cf. Julian of Norwich, *Showings*, trans. Edmund Colledge and James Walsh, The Classics of Western Spirituality (Mahwah, NJ: The Paulist Press, 1978), 246 and 284.
62. Ibid., 131.
63. Ibid., 250.
64. Ibid., 230.
65. Cf. Ibid., 318–19.

FURTHER REFLECTIONS
The Faith of Jesus Christ

The "faith of Christ" or "faith in Christ" is a theme that appears numerous times in Galatians. In 2:16 Paul states that a human being is justified through or by means of the faith of Christ or by means of faith in Christ (*dia pisteōs Christou*). He adds that he and others have believed in order to be justified by faith in Christ or by the faith of Christ (*ek pisteōs Christou*). In 3:22 he states that the promise has been given to those who believe "through the faith of Jesus Christ" or "through faith in Jesus Christ" (*ek pisteōs Iēsou Christou*). Even in Galatians 5:5-6 there is an oblique reference to the matter when he speaks of waiting for the hope of righteousness "through the Spirit, by faith" as well as of "faith working through love." Does the "faith of Jesus Christ" mean for Paul the act of professing faith in Jesus Christ (objective genitive) or the faithfulness manifested by Jesus Christ in relation to God (subjective genitive)?

The phrase in 2:16 is perhaps most often translated "faith in Christ;" in this case, the faith of the Galatians in Jesus Christ. This interpretation can be seen in many translations into modern languages and is defended by Galatians specialists such as James Dunn, who holds that the "most straightforward" way to understand these passages "is surely as references to the act/attitude of (human) believing."[66] However, I suspect that an even stronger argument can also be made that it refers to the faith or the faithfulness *of* Jesus Christ.[67]

Richard Hays, in his extensive study of the passage, remarks that "Paul's gospel presents Jesus Christ as the protagonist sent by God whose faithful action brings deliverance and blessing to humanity."[68] If the phrase is understood as the faith (in the sense of the faithfulness) of Jesus Christ, it is important to remember

---

66. James Dunn, "Appendix 1: Once More, PISTIS CHRISTOU," in Richard Hays, *The Faith of Jesus Christ: The Narrative Substructure of Galatians 3:1–4:11,* 2nd ed. (Grand Rapids: Eerdmans, 2002), 271.

67. J. Louis Martyn argues forcefully for the "faith of Christ" as well, from the perspective of a "high" Christology by which the work of Christ is the work of God; cf. Martyn, *Galatians,* 263–75.

68. Hays, *The Faith of Jesus Christ,* 162.

that an emphasis on the fidelity and persistence manifested by Jesus Christ goes beyond the idea of Christ as a "model," particularly if it is read from the perspective of a "high Christology from below."[69] Hays tries to address this by noting that "Jesus' faith is not merely exemplary, as in nineteenth-century liberal theology, but vicariously efficacious."[70] To put it this way may weaken his position, however, since by underlining vicarious efficacy it seems to move the argument back in the direction of abstraction and of Anselmian atonement, even though Hays does also mention the Irenaean idea of recapitulation and the notion of participation in Christ, both of which are congruent with the Pauline Christology of exchange. What is perhaps most compelling about Hays's argument is that he grounds his understanding of Paul's theological language in the "narrative substructure" constituted by the *story* of Jesus Christ and therefore indirectly leads us back to the concrete materiality of the way of Jesus.

Theologically, what seems central here is that in the faithfulness manifested by Jesus, we see the very character of God in solidarity with our human condition and God's initiative in pulling us out of our entanglement with hegemonic systems of dominance. Paradoxically, interpretation of the phrase as our "faith *in* Jesus Christ," which at first glance seems to try to avoid the idea of Christ as a model of faithfulness (and therefore of a works-righteousness trap), can end up putting so much emphasis on human faith that it can seem to weaken God's initiative and weigh humans down with one more impossible obligation (faith). The main distortions of faith language occur when it is divorced from the language of love, grace, and justice. In the life of Jesus Christ we recognize God's faithfulness, love, and justice, which by grace renew and transform us in order for us to also learn the way of faithfulness.

Perhaps ultimately it is not necessary to choose exclusively between one interpretation or the other (though I prefer to translate the phrase as the "faith of Christ"), because they actually co-inhere if

---

69. See for instance the treatment by Thomas N. Finger, *A Contemporary Anabaptist Theology: Biblical, Historical, Constructive* (Downers Grove, IL: IVP, 2004), 139–42.
70. Hays, *The Faith of Jesus Christ*, 210.

the pneumatological dimension is sufficiently taken into account. In our own faith in Christ, the faith of Christ is made active in us by the work of the Spirit so that we become not only co-laborers in Christ, but co-believers with Christ.

C. 3:1–27
Walking by Faith in Freedom

3:1–5
The Gift of the Spirit

At this point, giving vent to his frustration, the apostle famously exclaims, "You foolish Galatians!" The word translated "foolish" (*anoētoi*) conveys the idea of a lack of sense or of discernment, and Paul uses it twice in this section, here in verse 1 and again in verse 3. Luke puts the same expression in the mouth of Jesus ("Oh, how foolish you are, and how slow of heart to believe . . . !") in his account of the disciples who encounter the risen Lord on the road to Emmaus and at first do not recognize him (Luke 24:25). As in that situation, here the Galatians are unable to see what is before their very eyes: the crucified Jesus Christ. Paul himself, publicly and graphically, has presented Christ to them as the crucified Lord who has made possible the marvelous exchange described in the previous passage, yet they are at present unable to discern the meaning of the good news.

The detail given here by Paul about the nature of Jesus' death is noteworthy: to be "publicly exhibited" or "clearly presented" (*proegraphē*) as crucified (v. 1) means that he was "proscribed" or listed as an outlaw, being made subject to public notice. Similarly, the Latin *proscriptus* refers to the banishment or death of the accused as well as to the sale of the confiscated property of such a person.

Building on this Latin notion of confiscation, Marius Victorinus and Augustine further portray the confusion of the Galatians metaphorically as an "expropriation." They imagine the Galatians as the "inheritance," the "property," and the "goods" of Jesus, in whom he dwells by grace and faith.[1] Now, however, the Galatians seem willing

---

1. Eric Plumer, *Augustine's Commentary on Galatians: Introduction, Text, Translation, and Notes*, Oxford Early Christian Studies (Oxford: Oxford University Press, 2003) ,151 (see

to allow themselves to be "expropriated." Augustine is careful to note that such an expropriation or proscription does not harm Christ (by virtue of his divinity) but rather harms "the possession itself, which is deprived of the care of his grace."[2] Nonetheless, given that in Christ God enters intimately into human reality, even experiencing the "proscription" devised by an unjust imperial legal system and the "expropriation" of God's beloved creation by the forces of the present evil age, any harm to God's creation is felt deeply by God.

Paul expresses the fear that the Galatians have fallen into a kind of bewitchment. The verb he employs (*baskainō*) is unusual, used only this one time in the New Testament. Perhaps he is referring to the evil eye (i.e., an attitude of envy or an intent to harm) or to some other sort of evil power capable of blinding them. Jerome rejects the idea that Paul suspects the "involvement of witchcraft" and makes reference to how the "bewitching of malice obscures good things," quoting the Wisdom of Solomon 4:12.[3] Luther identifies the bewitchment roundly with the work of Satan.[4]

It may also be that Paul's rhetorical question ("who has bewitched you?") evokes Deuteronomy 28:53–57 (LXX), which describes the curse resulting from forsaking the way of God's commandments. That passage horrifically portrays how starving parents, in a city under siege by its enemies, "cast the evil eye" on their own families, even engaging in cannibalism. According to Deuteronomy 28:54, "even the most refined and gentle of men" will "cast the evil eye" (*baskanei tō ophthalmō*) on his brother, his wife, and his children, and in verse 56, even the "most refined and gentle" of women will do the same with her husband, son, and daughter, even secretly eating her newborn child and its placenta.

Susan Eastman suggests that Paul alludes to this passage to

---

also Plumer's footnote 62 on page 150) and Stephen Andrew Cooper, *Marius Victorinus' Commentary on Galatians: Introduction, Translation and Notes* (Oxford: Oxford University Press, 2005), 286. Perversely, Marius blames "the Jews" for this expropriation; as Cooper points out, he ignores the Roman agency in the crucifixion (see footnote 154 on the same page).

2. Plumer, *Augustine's Commentary on Galatians*, 153.

3. Jerome, *Commentary on Galatians*, in *The Fathers of the Church: A New Translation*, vol. 121, trans. Andrew Cain (Washington, DC: The Catholic University of America Press, 2010), 119.

4. Martin Luther, *Luther's Works*, vol. 26, *Lectures on Galatians, 1535 Chapters 1–4*, ed. Jaroslav Pelikan (Saint Louis: Concordia Publishing House, 1963), 190–94.

develop his argument about blessing and curse in Galatians 3:1–14 and that the vivid imagery about the evil eye underlies his use of positive familial imagery for the church in contrast to the curse of the law brought on by the teaching of his opponents.[5] If these intertextual resonances are indeed in play, Paul also might be implying that his opponents are greedy and miserly "parents" avid for the "flesh" of the Galatians (6:12–13), whose teachings lead to siblings in Christ who bite and devour each other (5:15), in contrast to himself, a loving "mother" to the Galatians (4:19) who embodies in his actions the motherly compassion of Christ.

The result of this "bewitching" is to delude the Galatians and to lead them to forget the public, material nature of Christ's execution and its aftermath, the resurrection. Though they have been the beneficiaries of the public proclamation of the good news of the gospel, having experienced it with their sense of hearing and of sight, they are in danger of losing their focus and becoming distracted by what is peripheral. Sensory experience is important for Paul when it comes to faith, as his frequent references to "hearing" and "seeing" illustrate. Only the work of the Spirit can bring back into focus what is truly central to the good news. He therefore challenges them to answer a simple question: How did they receive the Spirit? Was it through the "works of the law" or through the "hearing of faith?" Whereas in the previous chapter he set up the contrasting pair of "works of the law/faith in Christ," here the pair is "works of the law/ hearing of faith."

In these five verses, Paul mentions the Spirit three times. Notably, he assumes that the Galatians can recall the receiving of the Spirit as something perceptible that marked the beginning of their lives as Christians.[6] They have received the Spirit by believing what they have seen and heard of the gospel, which is symbolized by the publicly crucified Jesus Christ. At first glance, the Spirit, received by faith, seems to be set up in stark opposition to the "works of the law" and to the "flesh." Yet we should always keep in mind that Paul does

5. Cf. Susan Eastman, "The Evil Eye and the Curse of the Law: Galatians 3.1 Revisited," *Journal for the Study of the New Testament* 83 (2001): 69–87.
6. Cf. James D. G. Dunn, "Toward the Spirit of Christ: The Emergence of the Distinctive Features of Christian Pneumatology," in *The Work of the Spirit: Pneumatology and Pentecostalism*, ed. Michael Welker (Grand Rapids: Eerdmans, 2006), 21–22.

not reject either the law or the flesh in the sense of materiality but rather believes that they are transformed by the same gospel as the Galatians. What makes the Galatians "foolish," ignorant, or lacking in understanding is to forget the pattern of their own conversion, which entails the transformation of their experience of the flesh and the law by the work of the Spirit. If they set aside the memory and the perception of the continuing work by which Christ is made present to them, they will prove that they lack perspicuity and spiritual discernment.

As is clear in the preceding section, for Paul the law is necessary but penultimate. The same is true of the "flesh" in the sense of our mortality. The law and the flesh cannot by themselves bear the weight of glory and of God's immortality but rather are transformed by the Spirit, who has indeed worked powerfully among the Galatians (v. 5). Paul speaks similarly in Romans 8:2 of the liberating Spirit of life in Christ Jesus. The law and the flesh are transformed by the power of the Spirit, therefore, in a manner that allows them gloriously to carry out their respective vocations of guidance (the law) and materiality (the flesh) in mutually empowering ways. Although an anti-Jewish or a dualistic reading of Paul can be used to justify scorn both of the law and of the flesh, neither law nor flesh are discarded by Paul.

Admittedly, in understanding Paul's use of "flesh" we should remember that the expression has a variety of meanings in his letters, ranging from simple mortality and materiality to a negative sense, where it is a synonym of a life that tries to ignore the ways of God's Spirit. He uses the word in the latter sense several times in his writings, for instance in Romans 7:5; 2 Corinthians 1:17; and Philippians 3:3. His fear in this passage is that the Galatians are falling into a pattern that ignores the dynamic of grace and focuses on what is secondary to the detriment of what is primary.

Many theological and ethical problems emerge from assuming that this negative use of the multifaceted expression "flesh" implies that the flesh in the sense of materiality or bodily existence is an enemy of the Spirit of God. When "fleshly" embodiment is seen as sinful in itself, religious weight is lent to the disparagement of all that a given culture associates with materiality: subaltern subjects such as women and nondominant men, human bodies in general, and nonhuman nature. The truly human nature of Jesus and the doctrine of the incarnation are incompatible with this negative view of the "flesh." That is why it is important to interpret Paul's comments about the flesh very carefully. The contrast in verse 3 between "Spirit" and "flesh" is not between "Spirit" and "body" but rather between the invigorating and liberating work of God's Spirit in our lives and the "flesh" understood as our human tendency to disregard God's grace and to become idolatrous. We do

> Thus when the Spirit is poured into diverse instruments, the Spirit does not immediately extinguish the vices of nature; but throughout life he goes on purging the sin that inheres, not only in the Galatians but in all people of all nations.
>
> Martin Luther, *Luther's Works*, vol. 26, *Lectures on Galatians, 1535 Chapters 1–4*, 189.

so by putting things that are good in themselves in the place of God. To do so, as Paul points out for a second time in verse 3, is foolish, lacking in discernment and wisdom—or, said otherwise, lacking the Spirit.[7]

It is Paul's pneumatology, then, that provides the key that allows us to appreciate the liberating aspect of his theology and to find the rightful and productive places for the flesh and for the law in his understanding of grace. The God-given "supply" of the Spirit mentioned in verse 5 is an abundant and inexhaustible one; Paul uses the same expression in 2 Corinthians 9:10 in reference to the way God not only provides abundant seed to those who plant the land and bread for them to eat but also works to multiply the fruit of justice in the lives of those who are generous with people in need. In Galatians 3:5, Paul reminds the Galatians how God has worked powerfully by the Spirit in their lives through the "hearing of faith" (*akoēs pisteōs*), or as the NRSV has it, "by your believing what you heard." By the Spirit all humanly imposed barriers are overcome bountifully, and

---

7. Charles H. Cosgrove, *The Cross and the Spirit: A Study in the Argument and Theology of Galatians* (Macon: University of Georgia Press, 1988), 178, concludes that what makes the Galatians "foolish" in Paul's opinion is precisely that they have failed to understand "the link between the Spirit and the crucified Christ."

God's children are called to freedom and renewal, to the glory of
God and the transformation of creation.

FURTHER REFLECTIONS
National Character

From the earliest times, one of the issues of interpretation surround-
ing Galatians 3:1 has been whether Paul admonishes the Galatians
as "foolish" because they have let themselves be distracted from
what was central to the gospel (as I have argued) or whether their
foolishness is a matter of national character, a kind of "national vice,"
as Jerome puts it. The latter is based on the theory that each cultural grouping has a specific character and therefore tends both
to develop virtues and to make mistakes in ways characteristic of
that culture. For instance in the case of the Galatians, it would be
manifested as a tendency to be "unteachable, senseless and slow-
minded in their quest for wisdom."[8]

For early Christian writers, this was a way to wrestle with the
problem of human particularity without abandoning the idea of the
universality of the gospel message. In *A Treatise on the Soul,* building
on classical tradition, Tertullian develops a list of national peculiarities to depict how local customs lead individual people from a given
culture to develop specific traits: cowardice (the Phrygians), levity
(the Moors), cruelty (the Dalmatians), and so on. Jerome models his
own discussion of Galatians 3:1 on Tertullian's catalogue, as well as
on classical sources such as Cicero.[9] For his part, in his exposition of
the text, Luther favors the idea that "we distinguish among nations
on the basis of their vices" and mentions the search of novelty
among Germans and the arrogance of Italians as examples.[10] These
examples can easily sound like grotesque generalizations and can
function very negatively, especially when national or cultural ste-
reotypes are racialized and are not used as a tool of self-discovery

8. Jerome, *Commentary on Galatians,* 118.
9. Cf. Tertullian, *A Treatise on the Soul,* in *Latin Christianity: Its Founder, Tertullian. The Ante-
Nicene Fathers,* vol. 3, ed. Alexander Roberts and James Donaldson (repr., Grand Rapids:
Eerdmans, 1989), 200–201.
10. Luther, *Luther's Works, vol. 26, Lectures on Galatians, 1535 Chapters 1–4,* 188.

(as Luther seems to propose) but rather as a pretense for attacking particular groups of people (as in the negative depiction of "Jews," "Gypsies," "Blacks," "Chinese," "Mexicans," and so on).

The distortions inherent in this sort of racialized stereotyping, however, should not blind us to the possibility that there is such a thing as the collective personality of a nation, which is not fixed ontologically but nevertheless functions at a given time and given place in conscious and unconscious ways. For example, the tendency in the United States for the citizenry to applaud its role as a "shining city on the hill" and as an example of freedom and democracy for the world hides the country's penchant for collective amnesia about the violent way in which it acquired its land and maintains its military power globally, with hundreds of military bases and installations outside of its own territory. To this is added the control of its population (especially of people of color) through its prison-industrial complex at home.

This tendency toward self-deception operates at a religious level as well, always pushing to turn the Christian gospel into an ideological justification for U.S. "greatness." If we take into account a national tendency toward self-deception (one that can be seen in all nations, though its characteristics and lethal potential vary greatly), Paul's rebuke to the "foolish Galatians" can serve as a reminder that the gospel of Jesus Christ disputes any sort of justification by national prowess as much as it challenges any kind of condemnation by national provenance.

3:6–14
Covenant Relationship with God: Abraham

At this point Paul embarks on a piece of reasoning that is both alien and familiar by contemporary standards. On the one hand, as many of us do today, he defines family in a way that goes much beyond genetic relationships. On the other hand, the categories that he uses are not common currency for most of us. What Paul wants to underline is that for Abraham to be counted as one's ancestor, what is needed is not genealogical proof of a biological connection but rather a stance similar to that of the venerable patriarch: unwavering faith in God's fidelity and capacity to fulfill God's promises, even when the circumstances do not seem to warrant that confidence.

Though according to the Genesis narratives Abraham's faith did have its ups and downs (for example as he tried to manipulate the way in which God might make good on the divine promises), his attitude of faith was constant enough to allow him, along with Sarah, to become the ancestor of a great people chosen by God to be a blessing to all nations. According to Paul, then, Abraham was made just in the eyes of God because he put his confidence in God and likewise all people—whether Jews or Gentiles—who put their confidence in God are made just in God's eyes and can be called children or descendants of Abraham.

In verse 6 Paul quotes Genesis 15:6. In that context, what justifies Abraham in the eyes of God is Abraham's confidence in God's promise: namely, that Abraham's descendants will be as numerous as the stars in the sky. By making faith in God the operative element in Abrahamic lineage, Paul grafts all Gentiles of faith onto Abraham's family tree (v. 9). He finds scriptural warrant for this move in Genesis 12:2–3, where even before his name is changed to Abraham, or "father of a multitude," Abram receives the divine promise that all the families or nations of the earth will be blessed through him. Trust in God's promises, as represented by the great ancestor Abraham, takes precedence for Paul over all subsequent actions of God, even over the mighty acts of the liberation of the children of Israel from Egypt and the gift of the law.

In recent decades theologians both from west Africa and central Africa have underlined the importance of the theme of ancestors to Christian theology. They posit the figure of Christ as Ancestor. The Bible does not mention any physical descendants of Jesus, but as these theologians point out, besides being a Brother and a Friend, Jesus can be recognized as an Ancestor in the faith who corporately represents all past, present, and future members of the communion of saints. John Pobee therefore speaks of Jesus as *Nana Yesu* in the Akan language of Ghana, that is, "the Great and Greatest Ancestor."[11]

11. John Pobee, *Toward an African Theology* (Nashville: Abingdon, 1979), 94.

Bénézet Bujo presents Jesus not only as a Proto-Ancestor and a life-giving source for the community but indeed as the "privileged locus for a full understanding of the ancestors."[12]

In Pauline fashion, Bujo reads the ancestors both literally and metaphorically through the lens of Christology. There are flesh and bone ancestors to whom we are deeply indebted, for without them we would not exist. Through Christ other ancestors can also be ours even if we are not their physical descendants. For Paul the fact that those who follow Christ in faith are "in Christ" means that all the benefits of Christ, including his connection to Abraham, are given over to the family of the faith: in this sense also "to know Christ means to know his benefits."[13]

Paul makes two important discursive moves in this passage. First, without mentioning Moses by name, he shifts him and the law which he embodies into the background, placing Abraham in the symbolic center of the story of God's dealings with Israel. Second, he puts Christ into the foreground by identifying him as the primary heir or "seed" of Abraham. For Paul, God's pact with Abraham takes center stage, and that pact is ratified not primarily in the Torah, but in the person of Jesus Christ. The law is not dismissed or abrogated, however. Rather, once again, the logic of the marvelous exchange comes into play, by which Christ does for us what we cannot do for ourselves in upholding the law.

Paul first quotes (v. 10) Deuteronomy 27:26, the last in a series of curses (listed in Deut. 27:11–26) on those who do not respect the Torah, particularly its provisions having to do with incest and social justice. Departing from mainstream Jewish tradition, Paul takes this passage to mean that nobody can fulfill the law and that therefore all persons, even those who follow the law scrupulously, come under a curse. This Pauline interpretation is not warranted by the actual context of Deuteronomy; it only makes sense if the "law" is understood in a peculiarly Pauline way as a metaphysically inflated entity that

---

12. Bénézet Bujo, *African Theology in Its Social Context*, trans. John O'Donohue (Maryknoll, NY: Orbis, 1992), 83; for the context of the concept see 75–92 .

13. Philip Melanchthon, *Loci communes theologici*, trans. Lowell J. Satre, in *Melanchthon and Bucer*, ed. Wilhelm Pauck, Library of Christian Classics (Philadelphia: Westminster Press, 1969), 21.

has become an end in itself, deflecting people from reconciliation with God rather than leading them to God as it should.

His conception of the law as something that has become distorted is what allows Paul to conclude (v. 11) that nobody can be justified by the law but rather only by faith, since "the one who is righteous shall live by faith" (a reference to Hab. 2:4). Only a grossly distorted version of the law could possibly be contrasted with faith, since normally faith—as understood both in Jewish and Christian contexts—would guide a person in the process of learning to fulfill the spirit of the law, and conversely the law would help guide a person along the path of faith. Jesus himself is quoted in the Sermon on the Mount as saying that he did not come to destroy the law but to fulfill it (Matt. 5:17; see also Luke 16:17).

Luther famously believes that with his statement about Abraham in verse 6, Paul "makes faith in God the supreme worship, the supreme allegiance, the supreme obedience and the supreme sacrifice."[14] Luther's understanding has deeply marked Protestant sensibilities of all stripes. Certainly faith in the God of Jesus Christ is a central component of what came to be called Christianity, and a genuine faith will reflect a deep trust in God and God's compassion, grace, and love. As Calvin puts it, faith enables human beings to rest and trust in God.[15] However, faith is not in itself a "work" that makes us deserving of God's grace but rather, as Calvin points out, merely an "instrumental cause," a kind of path given by God's grace, by which we come to know and enjoy God's justification.[16]

The problem arises when such faith is interpreted in opposition to "works" or to the "law" in a way that it becomes a wholly internalized act of mental assent with few positive ethical consequences. Luther himself, despite his many hyperbolic formulations contrasting faith and the law, did not reflect in his life this sort of fideism; many of his later direct or indirect descendants, however, have been tempted by an easy antinomianism in the name of faith,

---

14. Luther, *Luther's Works*, vol. 26, *Lectures on Galatians, 1535 Chapters 1–4*, 226–27.
15. Calvin, *Calvin's Bible Commentaries: Galatians and Ephesians*, trans. John King (Forgotten Books: 2007), 72.
16. Ibid., 70.

or as Dietrich Bonhoeffer memorably put it, by "cheap grace."[17] By contrast, to live by faith as in the context of the Habakkuk passage quoted by Paul means actively to live out a way of justice that pleases God and reflects God's character.

In fact, Habakkuk 2:6–8, the passage directly after the "righteous live by their faith" text, is an impassioned polemic in God's own voice against economic and social injustice and the idolatry intrinsic to materialism. One of the important balancing acts we must keep in mind in interpreting Galatians, then, is to avoid the cheap grace of antinomianism while simultaneously maintaining a Pauline awareness of the possible distortions of central religious categories, including both the law and the gospel.

Paul continues his polemic against a puffed up and distorted law in verse 12, where he quotes Leviticus 18:5, a passage which in its Old Testament context states clearly that anyone who follows God's statutes and ordinances will live. Paul makes the exact opposite point: that nobody is justified in God's eyes through the law. That the law does not "rest on faith" (*ek pisteōs*) is "evident" (*dēlon*). Here again, this would not be "evident" at all from a non-Christian Jewish perspective and only makes sense if we keep in mind that for Paul "law" is understood here as shorthand for a distortion of the spirit of the Torah.

It might be helpful to remember that Paul also thinks that false gospels can masquerade as true gospel; in other words, not only the law can be distorted but so can the good news of Jesus Christ. For Paul, religious insight or truth is not ever safe from distortion, and therefore Christians must be vigilant about its misuse. This Pauline sensibility is in continuity with the prophetic and Jesuanic critiques of religion and should consistently be applied to his own writings if they seem to lead in hurtful directions (as in the principle of *Paulus contra Paulum* described above).

Anyone caught in the throes of the secular legal system when it functions to protect the privileged rather than the weak can understand the kind of legal distortions pointed to by Paul, whether or not one accepts his contention that Old Testament law can become

---

17. Dietrich Bonhoeffer, *Discipleship*, Dietrich Bonhoeffer Works, Vol. 4, trans. Barbara Green and Reinhard Krauss (Minneapolis: Fortress Press, 2001) 43–44.

a curse rather than a blessing. One example of this is the contemporary mass incarceration of African Americans in the United States, which functions as a "New Jim Crow": that is, a method of racialized caste control that combines laws, policies, institutions, and economic interests to maintain racial hierarchies while at the same time purporting to be colorblind.

Young black men in the United States are often locked up as a result of selling illegal substances, as part of the "War on Drugs," even while many of their white drug-consuming customers continue their recreational drug use without penalties as they study and work. Even if they are able to get out of prison, the employment opportunities of these young black men will be limited by their lack of access to higher education and by the social and legal penalties imposed on those who have incurred prison time.[18] To such young men, the "law" as they have experienced it bodily has a distorted, "puffed-up" logic that is detrimental to life and flourishing and has no sympathy for the transforming power of grace but rather is often diametrically opposed to it. This is the kind of distortion of the "law" that Paul's polemic can help us understand, if we unlink his discourse from harmful Christian anti-Jewish habits of mind, as well as from simple antinomianism. Paul is not against the function of the law per se but rather is distressed about the distortions of the law when it becomes either an end in itself or a means to the wrong kind of end (as in the United States, where it often functions simply to shore up the economic interests of a privatized prison-industrial complex).

Paul's following move once again links his argument to the christological logic of the marvelous exchange: Christ becomes a curse in order that we might be blessed (vv. 13–14). The language Paul uses is first of all that of redemption. The verb "to redeem" (*exagorazo*) is used frequently in the Septuagint in the sense of paying a ransom or of delivering someone from slavery in a way that involves effort and cost.[19] The background of this metaphor of redemption, of literally buying a slave out of the marketplace, therefore has both economic

18. Cf. Michelle Alexander, *The New Jim Crow: Mass Incarceration in the Age of Colorblindness*, rev. ed. (New York: The New Press, 2012), 178–220.
19. Kenneth S. Wuest, *Galatians in the Greek New Testament* (Grand Rapids: Eerdmans, 1944), 96–97.

and political implications. For those suffering from the unjust and racist system of incarceration in the United States, by which more African American men are now in jail or in prison than were entangled in the nets of slavery in the past, the text can take on a strongly liberating sense: Christ became as we are (captive to an unjust system) that we might be free (no longer bound by that unjust system). He became a curse, that is, a person on whom condemnation falls, that we might live by grace.

Paul hammers away at the idea of "curse," mentioning it three times: those who depend on the distorted law are under a curse (v. 10); Christ has been made a curse for us (v. 13), and Christ has redeemed us out from under the curse (v. 13). To say that Christ literally became a curse has been disturbing to many interpreters, especially because it seems to imply that the First Person of the Trinity is willing to curse the Second Person.

Jerome, for instance, wants to avoid any whiff of a Marcionism that would imply that the Creator is a bloodthirsty judge. Rather, following the logic of the marvelous exchange, he carefully underlines that Christ was not born a curse, but became one in our place. In the same way, Paul writes that Christ became sin (2 Cor. 5:21) and assumed the form of a servant (Phil. 2:7) in order to bridge the separation suffered by humans as a result of our alienation from God.[20] That Christ becomes a curse, then, does not mean that God is one whose vocation it is to curse, but rather that God pursues a way to bless creation by identifying in Christ fully with the human condition in order to reverse the curse

> He died so that we might live. He descended into Hades so that we might rise to heaven. He became foolish so that we might become wise. He emptied himself of the fullness and forms of God and assumed the form of a servant so that the fullness of divinity might dwell in us and so that we might go from being servants to masters. He hung on a tree so that by means of a tree he might erase the sin we had committed through the tree of knowledge of good and evil.
>
> Jerome, *Commentary on Galatians*, 144.

---

20. Cf. Jerome, *Commentary on Galatians*, 139–44.

and bring the blessings promised to Abraham to all people. In the end, as Augustine points out, the curse is overcome by the curse: "death is cursed, sin is cursed, the serpent is cursed, and all these things are triumphed over in the cross."[21]

Paul bolsters his description of the way Jesus takes on the "curse" by quoting Deuteronomy 21:23, where we find a description of what happens to the bodies of those condemned to the death penalty by stoning. Their bodies are to be strung up onto a tree, presumably as an object lesson, though not left there all night, since they are cursed and would contaminate the area if left hanging. This reference to the death penalty has many painful resonances, from the stoning of women accused of adultery to the "strange fruit" of abused and tortured black bodies lynched and left hanging on display from Southern trees.[22] Such cruelty has often been justified biblically and religiously, a fact that in itself reflects the truth of Paul's worry about the distortion of the law. Though Christians have often projected such distortion onto other faith traditions, both Jewish and Muslim, or onto "godless" atheists and agnostics, it is the *Christian* alteration and misrepresentation of spiritual law that should be our particular concern.

In Paul's account, Christ identifies with those condemned and strung up on a tree, allowing himself to be condemned and hung up on the cross, which he subverts by his dying and rising to become for the accursed a tree of life. By this exchange, that is, by Christ taking on death in order to give life, the blessing of Abraham is extended by faith to those who are not genealogically connected to him, namely to the Gentiles, and sealed by what was promised, the Holy Spirit (v. 14). Paul thus picks up the pneumatological thread of the letter here once again: it is the work of the Holy Spirit to enliven the wonderful exchange and make it relevant to those who follow Jesus today.

As is quite usual in Paul, the meaning of the Spirit in verse 14 is tightly wound up with Jesus Christ, in whom the blessing of Abraham comes to the Gentiles. We are up against an example of Paul's pneumatological Christology or christological pneumatology,

21. Plumer, *Augustine's Commentary on Galatians*, 163.
22. The haunting song "Strange Fruit," written by Abel Meeropol in 1937 about the lynching of black people in the U.S. South, was interpreted most famously by Billie Holiday.

by which the work of the Spirit always is conjoined to the work of the Son, and the work of the Son is always completed and actualized by the work of the Spirit. The christological dimension, which makes reference to the incarnate reality of Jesus of Nazareth, always anchors spirituality to concrete history and materiality, whereas the pneumatological dimension, which points to a future with hope, opens up history and materiality to new possibilities.

The point of Paul's argument is not to set up an antithesis between the law and faith but to underline the centrality of the Spirit. By using the powerful conjunction *hina* ("in order that") twice in verse 14, he sets up concentric circles with the Spirit at their center: Christ has redeemed us *in order that* the blessing given to Abraham might come to the Gentiles, *in order that* (or "so that") we might receive the Spirit. The Spirit is the operative agent here and indeed is the Subject of the action that allows the covenant promise to Abraham to be received by his descendants in Jesus Christ.

3:15–18

Speaking in Human Terms

Paul now proceeds to show what he means "according to human norms" (*kata anthrōpon*) or (as the NRSV has it) by using "an example from daily life." Paul is quite fond of this expression and uses it for instance in Romans 3:5 ("I speak in a human way"), Romans 6:19 ("I am speaking in human terms because of your natural limitations"), and 1 Corinthians 9:8 ("Do I say this on human authority?"). The tone of the expression communicates that he is making a bit of a rhetorical concession to speak so simply, perhaps implying that at other times he speaks more "divinely" or in a way more directly linked to God's revelation. As Chrysostom puts it, Paul uses human examples "to temper his discourse and render it more acceptable and intelligible to the duller sort."[23] Perhaps we should take Paul at his word and understand that he is about to embark on one of his weaker theological arguments.

23. John Chrysostom, *Commentary on the Epistle to the Galatians and Homilies on the Epistle to the Ephesians* (Oxford: John Henry Parker, 1840), 56.

He starts out by affirming that a contract or pact that has been ratified should not be arbitrarily tampered with. The kind of pact or covenant mentioned here (*diathēkē*) most often refers to a will that disposes of property (see, for instance, Heb. 9:15). However, since the word is used in the Septuagint to translate the Hebrew word for "covenant," in New Testamant Greek it has a cultic resonance as well, so that it means will, testament, and covenant simultaneously. The ritual dimension can be seen for instance in Jer. 34:18–20 where the ratification of the pact is accompanied by an animal sacrifice. In the story in Genesis 15, where there is likewise an animal sacrifice, the pact or covenant is connected to a particular promise that God makes, specifically that Abram's descendants will be plentiful and will inherit the territory in which Abram finds himself at that moment.

In the conceptual genealogy that Paul draws on, pact or covenant is always linked to promise; it is therefore not surprising that in the space of this short section, Paul should mention "covenant" twice and "promise" three times. By doing so, he underlines the primacy of divine agency in the Abrahamic covenant: God is the one who both makes and keeps promises, above and beyond our human capacities to keep our vows and commitments. If a will or pact made in human fashion is to be respected, then how much more will this be the case if the ever-faithful, ever-merciful, and ever-loving God is the guarantor of a promise?

In the case of Abraham, God's promise was made even before the Torah was given, and therefore, for Paul, it takes priority over the law (v. 18): the inheritance comes from the promise that God made, not from any later developments. For him, then, the law is important but derivative, whereas the promise is primary, as he will further explain in the following section (Gal. 3:19–27). Logically, he will need to connect Christ to that original promise, or Christ also would be placed in a secondary or derivative place, something Paul would not allow.

As a way to insert the Christological theme into the Old Testament story of the Abrahamic covenant, in verse 16 Paul accordingly moves to a discussion of the "seed" of Abraham, which he will then graft onto the legal image of the testament, will, or covenant. In the

New Testament, the word *sperma* can refer to botanical seeds, to human semen, or figuratively to the descendants or posterity of a given individual, usually a male, though not always (see Rev. 12:17, where it refers to the children of the woman clothed with the sun). The NRSV tactfully suggests "offspring" as a possible translation of *sperma* but runs into the confusing "offsprings" when it attempts to render the plural "seeds." The distinction between the singular and plural noun is important in the context of the verse precisely because Paul is intent on building his argument based on the difference between "seed" and "seeds." He does so by zeroing in on the "seed" of Abraham, an expression that appears several times in the Genesis Abram/Abraham cycle in reference to the promise God makes both to Abraham and to his descendants (see Gen. 12:7; 13:15; 17:7–8; and 24:7). Paul boldly—or recklessly, depending on the point of view—identifies that "seed" with a single person, Christ. His argument only makes sense if Christ functions as a representative figure for a collective that includes both Jews and Gentiles. At the end of the chapter he will indeed open up the concept to cover a plurality of persons who, because they are "in Christ," also can be counted as "seed" of Abraham and heirs to the promise (v. 29).

God's promise in Gen. 13:15, 17:8, and 24:7 is to Abraham's "seed." In the context of Genesis, the promise is always linked to the land. With a certain hermeneutical sleight of hand, dealing quite freely with the Old Testament text, as is his wont, Paul makes two important interpretive moves, one implicit and one explicit. First, he implicitly unlinks the promise given to Abraham from the land, simply by ignoring that aspect of the Abrahamic covenant, though in the Genesis narrative (as in contemporary Zionist movements, both Jewish and Christian) it is a central component of the pact. Second, in explicit contradistinction to the Genesis texts, he interprets the "seed" of Abraham as a reference to only one person, namely Christ, rather than to a multitude. He does so by arguing that "seed" is singular and not plural. Given that elsewhere (in 1 Cor. 15) he understands Christ in a corporate and representative way, as the "new Adam" or "new human being," this is not as strange a move as it might seem at first glance, since he includes a multitude "in Christ." And yet it must be admitted that his interpretation is hardly warranted on the basis of the Genesis text alone; it is only Paul's desire to link Christ to the Abrahamic promise that leads him down this rather forced path.

Though Paul may be trying to argue in a way convincing to his Jewish Christian opponents who already agree with him on the centrality of Christ, it would be difficult for a non-Christian Jewish interpreter to accede to this reading of the Abrahamic covenant. Amy Jill Levine, for instance, concedes that his "interpretation is clever" but points out that it flies against the plain sense of the Old Testament context (for instance, Gen. 12:7, where "seed" is clearly a collective, not individual, noun).[24] Christian interpreters have likewise noted the weakness in the argument: Calvin hints at this when he states that the apostle "does not make his argument rest on the use of the singular number."[25]

We would probably do well to take Paul at his word when he says that he is speaking humanly (v. 15), understanding the expression along the lines of what he says in 1 Corinthians 7:12 and 2 Corinthians 11:17: he is speaking not with the "Lord's authority" but as a human being—or even as a bit of a fool for God. Jerome seems to take the passage this way, saying that Paul, who was willing to be all things to all people, became a fool for the sake of the Galatians, whom he had earlier called fools. He argues that Paul uses everyday and even trivial meanings in speaking to these Gentiles, such that their use "might have displeased the erudite if he had not said first, 'I speak in the manner of men.'"[26]

In verse 17 Paul makes a reference to 430 years, probably a nod to Exodus 12:40–41, where it refers to the lapse of years spent by the children of Israel in Egypt. Paul is pointing out that during those centuries, and without the benefit of the law, the Abrahamic covenant and promise functioned and indeed informed a way of life. Nothing in the later giving of the law through Moses voided that previous relationship and commitment between God and Abraham's descendants. As Theodoret puts it, the promise made to Abraham "could

---

24. Amy-Jill Levine, *The Misunderstood Jew: The Church and the Scandal of the Jewish Jesus* (New York: Harper One, 2006), 79.
25. Calvin, *Calvin's Bible Commentaries: Galatians and Ephesians*, 80.
26. Jerome, *Commentary on Galatians*, 146.

undergo no addition, diminution or cancellation through the giving of the Law, which happened a long time later."[27] Rather, the law built on the inheritance and promise already granted by God. Abraham was indeed justified before the law, by the promise that he received by faith, and likewise all those justified in ancient times (before the giving of the law) were justified also by faith.[28] In fact, the law is "something fashioned and produced by faith."[29] Up to here, we are on sound footing. The problem emerges, however, when Christian commentators frame the Mosaic law as somehow "contrary" to the faith, the promise, and the gospel of Jesus.

Christian interpreters have indeed all too often set up the "bad" law against the "good" gospel, or in Augustine's words opposed living "carnally" by the works of the law to living "spiritually" by faith.[30] It is all too easy to forget that it is possible by the same token to follow the Torah "spiritually" and to live out the gospel "carnally!" Furthermore, the carnal/spiritual contrast can easily derive into a harmful dualism whereby the body is related to the "flesh" and to the "law," whereas the will, the soul, or the spirit are imagined in contradistinction to the body and at war with it. Such dualism has intrinsic difficulties in taking over Christian theology wholesale because of the centrality to the Christian confession of faith of the doctrine of the incarnation and the belief in the bodily resurrection of Christ. Nevertheless, it does appear in various forms and at times finds a warrant in Paul (and in Galatians specifically) for doing so.

It is worth remembering that an alternative tradition in theology uses this passage to defend the closeness between the law and the promise (and therefore the gospel). We see this, for example, in Irenaeus, who quotes Galatians in order to argue against Marcionism and for continuity in God's work, which can be seen both in Abraham and in Christ. Significantly, Irenaeus unites Abraham and those who are his descendants in Christ in a common eschatological hope, not fully realized in either case: Abraham "believed in things

---

27. "The Letter to the Galatians," in Theodoret of Cyrus, *Commentary on the Letters of St. Paul*, vol. 2, trans. Robert Charles Hill (Brookline, MA: Holy Cross Orthodox Press, 2001), 12.
28. See *Augustine's Commentary on Galatians*, 165.
29. Thomas Aquinas, *Commentary on Saint Paul's Epistle to the Galatians*, trans. Fabian R. Larcher, Aquinas Scripture Series Vol. 1 (Albany, NY: Magi Books, 1966), 84.
30. Plumer, *Augustine's Commentary on Galatians*, 165.

future, as if they were already accomplished, because of the promise of God," and likewise, "because of the promise of God," we look
forward to the full unfolding of our inheritance in the realization of
God's reign.[31]

One of the ways in which Christian theology can safeguard itself
against supersessionism and against triumphalism of any kind is precisely to remember the coexistence of present and future eschatology: though much has happened through grace already that can be
celebrated, God's reign is not yet fully realized. We await the fulfillment of God's promises alongside others, many of whom are not
Christian and may not use the language of faith, but with whom we
can nevertheless share an expectation of justice with peace and of
life abundant for all of creation.

FURTHER REFLECTIONS
Paul and the Palestinian Question

One of the most difficult conundrums for present-day interpreters
of Paul who want to break away from the bad habits of Christian
supersessionism and anti-Judaism is how to think about the modern state of Israel. For many conservative Christians, the answer
is clear: "We stand with Israel." However, Christian Zionism is not
necessarily a bulwark against an anti-Jewish reception of Paul; it
is perfectly possible to endorse the annexation of Palestinian territories by Israel as part of a necessary chain of events that bring
history closer to the "end of days" while simultaneously railing
against those who do not recognize in Jesus the promised one of
Israel. To make matters even more complicated, especially in the
United States, anyone who questions the modern state of Israel's
prerogative to build walls that harm Palestinian villagers or even
preemptively to bomb Muslim-majority neighbors can be accused
of anti-Semitism. This happens even to observant Jews. According
to this logic, questioning the prerogative of the modern state of

---

31. Irenaeus, *Against Heresies*, in *The Writings of the Fathers down to A.D. 325: The Ante-Nicene
Fathers*, vol. 1, ed. Alexander Roberts and James Donaldson (repr., Grand Rapids: Eerdmans,
1993), 492.

Israel to take whatever bellicose measures it desires to ensure its "security" becomes tantamount to denying the historicity of the Holocaust and to repeating abuses toward Jews that in the past have been a pattern in Christian-majority countries. Sometimes it is forgotten that Judaism is not identical to the modern state of Israel, and for that matter that not every person living in Israel is Jewish. There is a very long history of Jews, Christians, and Muslims living alongside each other and cooperating in various ways in what is now Israel-Palestine.

As Christians, in trying to make sense of how to discern the best path along this treacherous ground, it is important to listen to the voices of thoughtful Jewish scholars (both Israelis and non-Israelis) who are concerned with *shalom* and approach the question of the rights of Palestinians with justice and peace in mind. It is also important to listen to the voices of Palestinians. One pivotal declaration written by an ecumenical group of Palestinian Christian leaders is the Kairos Palestine document, titled *A Moment of Truth: A Word of Faith, Hope and Love from the Heart of Palestinian Suffering.*[32] In it, they describe the suffering of the lives of Palestinians under occupation and remind us that a theology that legitimizes such a reality is a sin against God and against humanity.

Is it possible for Jews, Christians, and Muslims, as "children of Abraham" and heirs of the promises of God, as well as for nonbelievers and adherents of other world religions, to find ways to share space and resources, not forgetting the poor and vulnerable in the land? It might be helpful to try to imagine how the theology of Paul in Galatians could shed light on this particular situation, not because Paul could have imagined present-day political circumstances but because his priority is always for both law and gospel to be life-giving rather than distorted. In the measure that various theologies (including Christian Zionism) have become toxic rather than life-giving for Palestinians and also for many Israelis, Paul gives us warrant to question them vigorously. Indeed, it may be a matter of life and death for us to do so.

32. It can be downloaded in several languages from http://www.kairospalestine.ps/.

3:19–27
Being Clothed with Christ

If the promise to Abraham has priority over the law, why even bother with the law at all? As in Romans (7:7–12), where he vigorously defends the law as holy, Paul wants to make clear that the law is not opposed to God or to God's promises. The law was added and was indeed "ordained by angels" and given by the one God, through a mediator, as a way to guide and comfort human beings. It was added "for the sake of" or "because of" (*charin*) our transgressions (Gal. 3:19). The word translated "transgression" (*parabasis*) conveys the image of somebody stepping off a path. Though meandering off a path can be very pleasurable and desirable, in certain circumstances—for example, in mountaineering—it can be the difference between life and death. To have the added guidance that allows a person to find the correct pathway is merciful. The sense one gets from the verse is not of rigidity or legalism but of the graciousness of God's provision.

The notion that the law was "ordained by angels" appears in several biblical texts, starting with the blessing of the children of Israel before the death of Moses, where there is a description of "myriads of holy ones" alongside God in the giving of the law (Deut. 33:2). In Stephen's speech as recorded in Acts 7:53, he speaks of the reception of the law "as ordained by angels." In Hebrews there is likewise a reference to "the message declared through angels" (2:2). Jerome comments that in the Old Testament, whenever an angel is reported to have spoken, and those words are later understood as a message from God (as in Exod. 3:6), "the angel who appears is one of a multitude of ministers," but the one who speaks in the angel is Christ, the mediator.[33]

By his reference to a mediator in verse 19 Paul clearly means Moses, but early Christian commentators such as Origen, Jerome, and Augustine identified the preexistent Christ as the mediator who gave the law.[34] From a Trinitarian perspective, the giving of all good

33. Jerome, *Commentary on Galatians*, 148
34. Cf. Jerome, *Commentary on Galatians*, note 101 on page 147 and Plumer, *Augustine's Commentary on Galatians*, 165–67.

gifts, including the law, comes from the Triune God (the one God of v. 20), so that there is a sense in which it can be said from within the logic of the Christian confession that the eternal Son and the Spirit of Life were coinvolved with the First Person in the giving of the law. As Augustine puts it, the Holy Spirit was active and "the Word of truth himself, though not yet incarnate, never withdrew from any true administration."[35] This idea need not stand in opposition to the understanding of Moses as the human mediator meant in the passage.

The law is in itself good and in accordance with God's good promises (v. 21), though it cannot be said to be in itself equal to God. As a result of our profound alienation from God and our constant history of transgression against others, that is, given the extraordinary power of sin in our world (v. 22), the law has its limits. Paul believes that it cannot vivify or enliven us (*zōopoiēsai*). "Making alive" is a creative act that only the one God can carry out directly. That creative work of vivification is characteristic of the Holy Spirit but also describes the work of the Father and the Son.

Paul's implicit premise in the passage is that Jesus Christ is not only the representative of humans as the promised "seed" of Abraham (v. 19) but also that Jesus Christ is the representative of God. Christ has divine agency and can do what only God can do: vivify us and overcome the power of sin in the cosmos. Whereas the law was mediated through the angels and Moses, for Paul the work of God in Christ is direct and immediate: God with us. It is not a matter of disparaging the law but rather of celebrating the economy of God that leads to justification by faith. For Paul the law cannot be expected to do what only God can do: the law is penultimate by nature, and not ultimate, and yet it is a good and holy thing, given by God, even if it is not in itself God.

The reservoir of meaning in the image of justification by faith (v. 24) has been tapped almost to the point of exhaustion since the Reformation. When thought of in isolation, it can lead to a limited notion of God's work in the lives of human beings; it is worth nothing that Paul does not narrow his focus only to justification in this passage but rather speaks also in terms of inheritance, vivification,

35. Plumer, *Augustine's Commentary on Galatians*, 167.

filiation, and even clothing. As Elsa Tamez points out, justification has to be understood primarily from a theocentric perspective, not from a legal one, so that the justice in question is God's justice, not that of a particular legal system. In her view, justification is an out-working of God's liberation and forgiveness so that all are able to live as persons of worth and practice justice. Justification by faith has to be liberation from structural sin, including patriarchal structures that heap guilt on women simply because they are not men. The gift of grace invites people to follow a logic different from that of a patri-archal logic of sin and death, allowing them to become subjects of their own lives rather than subjected to the rule of injustice.[36]

If the law is not in itself God, but rather points the way to God, it cannot have a role other than an intermediate one. Accordingly, Paul holds that it serves to prepare the way for Christ's coming and for the way of faith in him. In other words, the law functions as part of God's merciful involvement with us, "so that" or "in order that" (hina) we might be ultimately justified by faith (v. 24). To try to make his point he uses the analogy of the law as a guide (paidagōgos), able to steer humans in the right direction (v. 24). In that cultural context the "pedagogue" was not a teacher but rather a man, usually a slave, who accompanied a young male of privileged social status to school and back, watching over his conduct as a custodian or supervisor (hence the NRSV translation "disciplinarian").

The pedagogue is sometimes depicted in ancient plays in a comic role but for the most part was a figure that commanded a good deal of respect and was well-known not only in Hellenistic or Roman circles but also in Judaism. Plato and Aristotle both mention the custodial functions of pedagogues in the rearing of sons, as does Josephus, who makes reference to his own son's pedagogue. In rab-binical writings, the term appears in parables relating to the supervi-sion of a king's son, and in the Talmud, Moses is depicted as Israel's pedagogue.[37]

---

36. Cf. Elsa Tamez, "Justification by faith," in Dictionary of Feminist Theologies, ed. Letty Russell and J. Shannon Clarkson (Louisville, KY: Westminster John Knox Press, 1996), 162–63.
37. Cf. Richard N. Longenecker, "The Pedagogical Nature of the Law in Galatians 3:19–4:7" in Studies in Paul, Exegetical and Theological (Sheffield: Sheffield Phoenix Press, 2006), 54–56, which includes the quotes from Plato (Lysis 208C), Aristotle (Nicomachean Ethics 3.12.8), Josephus (Life 76, §429) and the Talmud (Exodus Rabbah 21.3 and 42.9).

Paul uses the image with an unusual twist when he applies it to the Law itself, but he is drawing from a familiar trope to construct his analogy. When the young man comes of age, Paul argues, he no longer requires a pedagogue. Paul's point continues to be that it is not Moses (or the law given by God through Moses) who has priority but rather faith symbolized by the older figure of Abraham. The law is our kind and helpful guide, in place to nudge us along the path toward our teacher, in whom we are "made just." We are thus "justified by faith," that is to say, we as humans are pronounced righteous and treated as just by the God in whom we place our confidence.

As in much of this epistle, given the sad history of Christian anti-Semitism, it can be difficult to find a balanced way to read and interpret Paul's ideas. Jewish scholars have pointed out repeatedly that they don't perceive the "law" as a fearful and heavy burden or as something appropriate for an earlier stage of moral development now to be outgrown; they find it useful as a guide today, and judging by the ethical consciousness and contributions of many strands of contemporary Judaism, rightfully so. They certainly do not appreciate or deserve being described (as they are by Augustine and many other Christian commentators) as haughty and prideful because of the law and in need of being humbled.[38]

Paul himself seems almost of two minds on this issue: he states that he does not want in any way to reject the worthiness of the law, but at the same time he sets up an understanding of the law that easily leads to its rejection, or to the rejection of those who continue to give priority to the Torah for their faith practices. As emphasized already above, the main point to remember in trying to unravel Paul's dilemma is the penultimate nature of the law. Paul fears (and it is tempting to imagine that this fear is a reflection of his own past zeal) that the law can take on an ultimate character that properly belongs only to God. To this must be added his belief in the divine character of Christ. If Jesus Christ is indeed both human and divine, as Paul believes, not just a guide who points the way to God, then his life and work take on a centrality for Paul that takes priority over all other possible ways.

38. For example, Plumer, *Augustine's Commentary on Galatians Augustine*, 167.

The question that then emerges is whether to confess Christ in the way that Paul does necessarily leads to a sense of superiority toward other expressions of faith and even to doing violence to those who do not share that conviction. It would seem that whenever Christians hold a modicum of social or political power, the latter temptation is magnified. Is it possible for Christians who share Paul's high Christology to follow Jesus without disparaging the law, Judaism, or for that matter those fellow Christians who cannot see their way to a Pauline Christology? At the heart of the matter is the need to unlearn the dismal practice of the condemnation of the other, a habit that is contrary to the good news of the gospel and to Jesus' explicit command to his followers not to judge others (Matt. 7:1–5). A condemnatory attitude toward one's neighbor ultimately makes all talk of justification meaningless.

If someone's Christology is truly "high," then it should give traction to the way of nonviolence lived out by Jesus. When the nonviolent pursuit of justice and peace does not have a grip on a person's Christology, then arguably what is being upheld is a docetic Christology that doesn't take the incarnation seriously and misses the main emphasis of Pauline Christology. Whenever a "high" Christology resorts to violence toward others, or even to an attitude of systematic disdain toward "low" Christologies, it is sowing the seeds for its self-destruction. For followers of Jesus who want to engage Paul's Christology seriously, then, the task at hand is to be faithful to the inner logic of the love and grace of God shown to all in Christ, which is what Paul believes makes possible his own ministry to the Gentiles in the first place. Such fidelity to God's grace should question any temptation to project negativity outwards onto Judaism or elsewhere in order to preserve a spurious sense of Christian superiority.

The coming of faith or "now that faith has come" (*elthousēs*) in verse 25 therefore is best understood as a movement in tandem with the work of God's grace and love. This opens up new horizons of possibility rather than limiting access to God to certain prescribed and authorized gestures of faith. On the contrary, as Christopher Morse argues, "[i]f the coming of faith (Gal. 3:25) occurs only as the coming of grace, then no time limits of this passing world can be set upon when faith shall arrive in any human destiny."[39]

Paul assures the Galatians in verse 26 that through the faith of Jesus Christ they are all children of God, or quite literally, that they (both men and women) are all "sons" of God, inasmuch as all have the full rights that only male heirs received in that context. From this male-centered filial metaphor Paul then switches to a more inclusive image: inasmuch as we are baptized in Christ, we put on Christ as a garment and are propelled in the right direction by virtue of Christ's work of justification in us. In putting on Christ, we are in Christ and Christ in us, in a mutual indwelling that echoes the perichoretic dynamic of the Triune God.

Melchior Hofmann contends that those who have "in truth put on Christ Jesus through faith and baptism in such a way that they are in Christ Jesus and Christ Jesus in them" cannot be condemned: "[t]he law has no sovereignty over them anymore."[40] Read in the context of a counter-hegemonic approach to the message of the gospel such as that of Hofmann and other sixteenth-century Anabaptists, the idea that the "law" (as the tool of the religiously and politically powerful in a given society) no longer has power over those who put on Christ is a profoundly subversive insight. It should not be surprising, therefore, that Hofmann died in prison after years of incarceration, something that shows the paradoxical nature of liberation in Christ from the "law of sin and death;" there is no guarantee that the person who puts on Christ will be able to avoid persecution and suffering in this "present evil age."

There is also an implicit pneumatology in this movement of being clothed with the virtues and characteristics of Christ. As the medieval commentator Robert Grosseteste put it, "A bodily garment is fitted for the one who wears it, whereas a spiritual garment shapes its wearer."[41] Even more to the point is Jerome, who writes that this

39. Christopher Morse, *Not Every Spirit: A Dogmatics of Christian Disbelief*, 2nd ed. (New York: Continuum, 2009), 340.
40. Melchior Hofmann, "The Ordinance of God" (1530), in *Spiritual and Anabaptist Writers*, ed. George H. Williams and Angel M. Mergal (Louisville, KY: Westminster John Knox Press, 2006), 188.
41. Robert Grosseteste, in *The Bible in Medieval Tradition: The Letter to the Galatians*, ed. and trans. Ian Christopher Levy (Grand Rapids: Eerdmans, 2011), 241.

garment shines with the "intense brightness of the Holy Spirit."[42] The metaphor of clothing appears numerous times in the New Testament and in extracanonical literature. In Colossians 3:14, in a similar context, the admonition is to be "clothed in love," which binds everything together. In Romans 13:14, Paul writes "put on the Lord Jesus Christ." In Ephesians 4:22–23, we read about putting away our old selves, our former way of life, and clothing ourselves with the new self, "created according to the likeness of God in true justice and holiness." The image is also used for pulling off or stripping off the old self with its practices and clothing ourselves with the new self, "which is being renewed in knowledge according to the image of its creator," meaning that we are clothed with compassion and humility (Col. 3:9–12). In the Shepherd of Hermas, a similar idea is expressed about being clothed in the Holy Spirit.[43]

Likewise, to be a child of God means to receive the Holy Spirit, and to have the Holy Spirit is to be set with Christ in the transition from death to life.[44] One final pneumatological dimension of putting on Christ as the justified children of God that emerges from this text is its relation to Wisdom. In what amounts almost to a throwaway comment, Augustine suggests that to put on Christ as in this passage means to put on Wisdom: to be clothed with Wisdom, to participate in Wisdom, and to perform Wisdom.[45] This is an intriguing possibility, especially from a liberationist and feminist perspective: putting on Christ is not dependent on social status or gender, and as a garment it brings with it new performative possibilities opened up by the Spirit of Life, so that, as Serene Jones puts it, we "wear the garb of forgiveness and new life that Christ embodies for us." Clearly, as Christian history generally and our own particular experiences show us, "this does not mean that we stop performing sinful roles at the same time that we are acting as if we are forgiven," yet our

42. Jerome, *Commentary on Galatians*, 152.
43. Cf. Shepherd of Hermas, Similitude 9.24, trans. J. B. Lightfoot, in Early Christian Writings, http://www.earlychristianwritings.com/text/shepherd-lightfoot.html.
44. Karl Barth, *Church Dogmatics*, I.1, *The Doctrine of the Word of God* (Edinburgh: T. & T. Clark, 1975), 458.
45. Cf. Plumer, *Augustine's Commentary on Galatians*, 173.

wrongdoing and stumbling about are "not the final word about who we are before God."[46]

FURTHER REFLECTIONS
Uses of the Law

In the Old Testament, the "law" is much more than a collection of legal codes found in the Pentateuch, such as the Ten Command-ments. The law, or *torah*, refers to instruction about how to live in accordance with God's will. In the New Testament, law (*nomos*) usually also means "instruction." After the shift symbolized by Con-stantine's conversion and the slow formation of Christendom, the predominant theological understanding of *nomos* became marked profoundly by the codified understanding of the law inherited from the Roman Empire, a legacy that still survives in Roman Catholic canon law. Such perceptions about the law in turn deeply shaped Christian interpretations of the meaning of the Pauline understand-ing of the "law." The Magisterial Reformers, especially Luther, were mesmerized by the insight that justification came by God's grace, not by the law. Excessive reliance on the law meant self-justification and self-righteousness, something that by definition could not be pleasing to God. Neither could the gospel simply be defined as *nova lex*, a new kind of law. What then was the purpose of the law? Their answers to Paul's rhetorical question in 3:19 often led the Reform-ers to discuss the use of civil law and to what extent it should be implemented and acknowledged by Christians, since they did not want to undo most of the laws that regulated life in their societies.

In his commentary on Galatians 3:19 Luther holds that there is a "twofold" or "double" use of the law. The first use of the law came because God ordained civil law in order to "restrain transgressions" and "hinder sin." Magistrates, parents, ministers, and "all civil ordi-nances" serve to "bind the devil's hands." It is roughly equivalent to "natural law" or the innate sense of what is right and wrong shared by all human beings. However, Luther thinks that Paul is not talking

---

46. Serene Jones, "What's Wrong with Us?," in *Essentials of Christian Theology*, ed. William C. Placher (Louisville, KY: Westminster John Knox Press, 2003), 156–57.

of that first use of the law in Galatians 3 but rather of a "theological or spiritual use" of the law, one that paradoxically leads humans to "increase transgressions."[47] There is deep psychological insight in this counterintuitive statement: as Augustine had pointed out long before, prohibition increases desire for illicit action."[48] Centuries later, Freud took the idea even further in *Totem and Taboo*, when he explored the notion that desire was instituted by prohibition.[49] As any person in charge of enforcing rules soon discovers, the very act of making a given fruit forbidden does indeed seem to heighten its desirability. On the other hand, the law is not only about prohibition but also about positive actions and gestures of compassion. To focus too strongly, as Luther does, on a view of the law as the mighty hammer of God that serves primarily to reveal human unrighteousness overlooks the basically positive reception of the torah by Jesus as depicted in the Gospels.

Despite the habitual flashes of deep insight in Luther's hyperbolic formulations about the dynamic of the law, then, the need for a positive view of the law as an ethical guide remained. Luther rejects any third use of the law in instructing both believers and nonbelievers in Christ about how to live. He thinks faith is enough of an incentive for people to fulfill the demands of any sort of law, whether "natural" or "divine." Nonetheless, having had time to observe the ethical shortcomings even of the most ardent proponents of justification by faith, Luther's colleague and friend Philip Melanchthon goes beyond the binary of the *duplex usus legis* and points to a third use of the law, which is not soteriological but pedagogical, providing necessary guidance also to those who are acquainted with the grace of the gospel.[50]

In Calvin's understanding of the three-fold function of the law, the first use is a pedagogical function (*usus pedagogicus*): it serves to show human beings God's justice and is a kind of mirror able to reflect back to people their lack of righteousness. The second

---

47. Luther, *Luther's Works*, vol. 26, *Lectures on Galatians, 1535 Chapters 1–4*, 308–9.
48. Cf. Augustine, *City of God* (XIII.5), trans. Henry Bettenson (New York: Penguin, 2003), 514.
49. Sigmund Freud, *Totem and Taboo: Resemblances between the Psychic Lives of Savages and Neurotics*, trans. A. A. Brill (New York: Moffat, Yard and Company, 1918), 58 et passim.
50. This was especially the case after 1535 but can be glimpsed even in the earlier versions; see Melanchthon, *Loci communes theologici* , 49–70.

function is a political use (*usus politicus*), helping those who do not respond to God by threatening them with earthly punishments in order to prevent them from doing evil. However, it could be said that the third use of the law (*tertius usus legis*) is for Calvin the most important of all. It is a positive means for knowing concretely what the will of God might be in daily life.[51] It is meant specifically for Christians and aids the process of sanctification, pointing back to the Ten Commandments and to the natural moral law of humanity that became distorted as a result of human alienation from God.[52] The notion of a third use of the law in some ways seems to sell pneumatology short, as it can easily push aside the Holy Spirit and put in its place a codified "law" to govern Christian life. On the other hand, the understanding functions as a bulwark against antinomianism by allowing theologians to argue that the law does after all have a positive function in the lives of Christians.

Perhaps the most useful distinction of all is the one made by Martin Luther King Jr. in his 1963 "Letter from Birmingham Jail."[53] He holds simply that there are two types of law, just and unjust. According to King we have a legal and a moral responsibility to obey just laws, but likewise we have a moral responsibility to *disobey* laws that are unjust. The way to determine whether a law is just is to see whether it "squares with the moral law or law of God," by which King means that it "uplifts human personality." By contrast, if it "degrades human personality" it is unjust. It further helps to understand the power dynamic behind a given law: if it is used by a majority group to compel a minority group to act in ways that are degrading, and if the majority group does not apply such norms to itself, then it is unjust. He gives as examples of unjust laws not only segregation and Jim Crow but also the indirect and "devious

---

51. Cf. Karl-Heinz zur Mühlen, Robert E. Shillenn, Steven Rowan, John E. Lynch, "Law," in *The Oxford Encyclopedia of the Reformation*, ed. Hans J. Hillerbrand, vol. 2 (Oxford: Oxford University Press, 1996), 404–14.

52. John Calvin, *Institutes of the Christian Religion* 2.7.6–7; ed. John T. McNeill, trans. Ford Lewis Battles, Library of Christian Classics (Philadelphia: Westminster Press, 1960), 354–56.

53. For a version of the letter than includes textual criticism see appendix 3 in S. Jonathan Bass, *Blessed Are the Peacemakers: Martin Luther King Jr, Eight White Religious Leaders, and the "Letter from Birmingham Jail"* (Baton Rouge, LA: Louisiana State University Press, 2001), 237–56.

methods" that make it difficult for African American U.S. citizens
to become registered voters and exercise their rights at the ballot
box.[54] The civil rights leaders knew that specific laws and the rule
of law generally are important and necessary and can be a force for
positive change as was the case in the Supreme Court decision of
1954 that declared school segregation unconstitutional. Nevertheless, laws can also become distorted and a force for injustice and
evil and must be confronted and disobeyed if necessary.

An extreme version of the law-gospel dialectic has never been
very practical for everyday Christian life. Although "grace alone" suf-
fices at one level, it need not be in enmity with the "law" if the latter
does not become "puffed up," distorted, and harmful. When it does,
it has to be confronted. Paying attention to the way the law-gospel
dynamic actually works in the Christian life can be helpful for pro-
moting understanding between Catholics and Protestants, as illustrated in the Lutheran-Roman Catholic agreement on justification.[55]
It can also help Christians learn to avoid the narrative practices that
strengthen an anti-Jewish mindset by portraying practicing Jews in
the New Testament (such as the Pharisees) as representatives of the
"law" in stark contrast to Jesus or his disciples as purveyors of "grace."
As many Christian and Jewish New Testament scholars have underlined, this is a gross distortion both of Judaism and of the message
of Jesus, who was profoundly Jewish and explicitly engaged the law
in respectful ways. Civil laws and the "laws of God" can both inform
and be informed by the glorious freedom of the children of God.

54. Bass, *Blessed Are the Peacemakers,* 243–44.
55. See the "Joint Declaration on the Doctrine of Justification" (1999) by the Lutheran
    World Federation and the Catholic Church at http://www.vatican.va/roman_curia/
    pontifical_councils/chrstuni/documents/rc_pc_chrstuni_doc_31101999_cath-luth-joint
    -declaration_en.html.

X. 3:28–4:7

The Trinitarian Dynamic at the Heart of God's Relationship with Creation

3:28
Equality in Christ

The verse has a rhythmic quality reminiscent of poetry or of a hymn; it may be part of a baptismal formula used in the primitive church. There are several similar listings of pairs in the Pauline corpus, but none are identical to Galatians 3:28, as they subtract pairs (1 Cor. 12:13 lacks male/female) or add other pairs (Col. 3:11 includes circumcision/uncircumcision and barbarian/Scythian but omits male/female). Our verse is composed of three parallel clauses, each of which start with the phrase "there is not," "there is no," or, as the NRSV has it (inserting a temporal dimension that is not necessarily to be found in the Greek text), "there is no longer" (*ouk eni*). All three clauses conclude with a contrasting pair.

The first two contrasting pairs, "Jew or Greek" and "slave or free," are separated by a negative conjunction translated "and not" or "nor" (*oude*). However, in the case of the third contrasting pair, "male and female," Paul introduces a slight variation by using the connective conjunction "and" (*kai*), perhaps echoing the wording in the Septuagint version of Genesis 1:27. It uses the same words for man and woman, *arsen kai thēly*, in the context of God's creation of male and female in God's image. The verse ends with an affirmation about unity in Christ, expressed in the second person plural: "for all of you are one in Christ Jesus."

Each of the contrasting pairs offers a glimpse into a web of complex power relations. Different people with diverse ethnicities, social status, and genders are invited to relate in new ways in Christ. They are not forced into sameness: to be equal does not mean to be identical. In other words, equality in Christ as envisioned by Paul does not negate cultural, sexual, social, or religious differences. As Davina Lopez puts it, "Physical differences—marked on and by the body—are lurking under the 'clothing of Christ' that all of the (Galatian) children are to put on. . . ."[1]

In theory, we can affirm with Ernst Käsemann that such "difference no longer separates; it rather serves the advancement of each and is the presupposition for the universal priesthood of all believers, in which each is directed toward each and gives freedom to each for service."[2] At the same time, we need to realize that the three pairs point respectively to very different dimensions affecting relationships within the church and in society. While stressing the "border-transgressing unity" that all of these groups have in common, Brigitte Kahl suggests paying close attention to the categories nation/culture/religion (Jew or Greek), class/social status (slave or free) and biological sex (male and female).[3] Each of the pairs need to be examined in turn, without the presupposition that they overlap precisely with the categories of "race, class, and gender" familiar from recent anthropology and sociology.

The first sphere, "Jew or Greek," relating to nation, culture, and religion, probably makes reference to the two main forms of living out the Christian faith at the time the epistle was written: the Jewish-Christian "Way," deeply rooted in Jewish practices, and its rapidly growing offshoot, Gentile Christianity. These would have been Jews and Gentiles "in Christ." There is a sense in which this category of Jew/Gentile overlaps with "race," inasmuch as to be a Jew was to inhabit a given human "family," but this dimension should not be exaggerated, since from the beginning the children of Israel included many "strangers" who became not only sojourners among the Jews but officially part of the family. Many Gentiles belonging to what

1. Davina Lopez, *Apostle to the Conquered: Reimagining Paul's Mission* (Minneapolis: Fortress, 2008), 149.
2. Ernst Käsemann, *On Being a Disciple of the Crucified Nazarene* (Grand Rapids: Eerdmans, 2010), 106.
3. Brigitte Kahl, "No Longer Male: Masculinity Struggles behind Galatians 3.28?," *Journal for the Study of the New Testament* 79 (2000): 37–49, especially 38.

modern people might call different "races" were proselytes or admirers of the Jewish faith, such as the Ethiopian official (Acts 8:26–40) and the Roman Centurion Cornelius (Acts 10:1–48), both of whom were later baptized as followers of Jesus.

There were Hellenistic Jews and Gentile proselytes long before the emergence of the Christian movement, so the Gentile/Jew binary is not "racially" as clear-cut as some might imagine. It is worth keeping in mind that "race" in the context of a codified racism directed against darker-skinned people for the economic benefit of lighter-skinned people, as still exists in the United States, is a modern phenomenon arising in its present form alongside the European conquest of the Americas, the seizure of land from its indigenous peoples, and the enslavement of Africans to work in the newly acquired territories. Though they were not "raced" in the distinctly modern way with which we are familiar, the reality of two distinct paths of discipleship, a Jewish-Christian way and a Gentile-Christian way that at times come into conflict with each other, is a theme of Galatians that should not be occluded. The categories of gender and sexuality should likewise not be forgotten in considering the "Jew/Greek" contrasting pair: "Jews" and "Greeks" are not to be imagined only as a heterosexual male collective but as a rainbow of many different women and men. Though accounts of church history have often all but erased women from the story, in both Jewish and Gentile Christianity women have tended to comprise the majority of the faithful.

Daniel Boyarin has warned that Paul's project as seen in Galatians 3:28 is aimed at overcoming human difference but that as a result of this emphasis, the apostle confuses sameness and equality, erases difference, and opens the door to a devaluation of Jewishness. Boyarin conceives of Paul as a Hellenistic Jew, "motivated by a Hellenistic desire for the One," predicating human unity based on a human essence that goes beyond differences. Such unity, however, is for Boyarin based on a duality that debases materiality and celebrates the universal human spirit.[4]

Clearly, there is a wide stream in the history of Pauline reception

4. Daniel Boyarin, *A Radical Jew: Paul and the Politics of Identity* (Berkeley: University of California Press, 1994), 7 et passim.

that does exactly what Boyarin describes. However, I do not discover in Paul himself the evidence to convict him as one who erases
difference or devalues the Jewish tradition. He is too committed to
what would later be called the doctrine of the incarnation to fall into
Hellenistic spirit-body dualism. Furthermore, he clearly sees his role
as a Jew as a position of privilege. As Pamela Eisenbaum points out,
"Paul did not relegate Jewishness to a lower order of being; it is his
interpreters who do that." She adds that Boyarin is right in highlight-
ing a tendency in Christian Pauline interpretation that persists even
among scholars who try to avoid an anti-Jewish slant: "Jewish law is
still seen as an obstacle to the goals that Paul is trying to promote."[5]
At any rate, the liberating meaning of "no longer Jew nor Greek"
will never emerge if the text is read as an excuse to obliterate Jewish
particularity, whether as a particularity within the Christian church
(Jewish followers of Jesus) or outside of it (Jews *tout court*).

The second sphere, "slave or free," relating to class and social status,
refers to economic and social inequalities caused by human injustice
and requiring immediate action and transformation. Domestic slaves
were sometimes held in Jewish and Jewish-Christian households as
well as in Gentile and Gentile-Christian households. Among Jewish Christians, if the instructions in Genesis 17:12–13 were upheld,
male slaves were circumcised.

A review of ancient Jewish literature shows that though slavery
was a part of economic and domestic life, slavery was not considered
an ontologically fixed feature of some groups, as was the conviction
among some Greek and Roman philosophers. Jewish legal writings also reflect the fact that (as in Gentile households) the boundaries between slave and free were often somewhat blurred, since
some slaves were better educated than their free counterparts and
some female non-slaves, as well as boys or girls who were underage,
sometimes lived in conditions of dependence that amounted to a lack
of freedom. On the other hand, it should not be forgotten that female
slaves in particular (though not exclusively) often had to endure
sexual exploitation and humiliation without any sense that they pos-
sessed "honor" or merited respect. Though Jewish legal tradition

5. Pamela Eisenbaum, "Is Paul the Father of Misogyny and Antisemitism?," *Cross Currents* 50
(Winter 2000–2001): 517–18, 514.

(unlike Roman law) did not allow the owner unlimited power of life and death over a slave, the buying and selling of slaves was a common transaction at the time in both Gentile and Jewish contexts.[6] It was therefore part of the culture into which the gospel of Jesus made its way.

Any strong association of slavery with Africans or with "blackness" emerged long after Antiquity and biblical times. However, given the history of slavery in the Americas, it would be problematic to read Galatians 3:28 through a lens that ignores that experience. Despite the legend about the "curse of Ham" (derived from a faulty reading of Gen. 9:18–25 in order to justify the enslavement of Africans) and persistent white ethnocentrism and racism evident in much of the history of Christian exegesis, there is no indication of antipathy toward black-skinned peoples in the biblical text itself. Nonetheless it is possible that though sub-Saharan Africans were a minority among people enslaved in the first centuries of the Common Era, the darker skin color of Africans in a lighter-skinned environment created in some an association of blackness with slavery in Greece, Rome, Arabia, and Palestine.[7] Whatever the origins of the sin of white racism, Galatians 3:28 subverts any distortion of ethnocentrism or sense of innate superiority based on social class, income, or any other characteristic that might be prestigious in a given culture and time: in Christ such hierarchies are to have no traction.

The third sphere, "male and female," points both to biological and morphological differences between and among the sexes and to how those differences are interpreted and constructed as gender roles. As mentioned above, the reference to "male and female" may well be a nod to the *imago Dei* in Genesis, which has been an important trope for feminist theologians or others interested in equality between men and women: neither male nor female is alone the "normative" human being created in the image of God. God's image is found in human community, which encompasses men and women. To state that in Christ "there is no male and female" should not mean an

6. Cf. Catherine Hezser, *Jewish Slavery in Antiquity* (Oxford: Oxford University Press, 2005), 105–15 and 217–20

7. Cf. David Goldberg, *The Curse of Ham: Race and Slavery in Early Judaism, Christianity, and Islam* (Princeton, NJ: Princeton University Press, 2003), 195–99.

erasure of human particularities as sexual beings but rather the realization that a gender hierarchy is inconsistent with the gospel. As
Brad Braxton points out, what Paul asserts is not "the obliteration of
difference but the obliteration of dominance."[8]

The doctrine of the incarnation of the eternal Second Person of
the Trinity in the specific (fully) human being Jesus of Nazareth suggests that God is profoundly committed to particularity, to the point
of becoming (a particular) one of us, in order that we might (in all
our particularities) become as God is. To suggest that some humans
with specific characteristics (such as a particular skin color or gender or sexuality) should lord it over all the others deeply opposes the
liberating message of the gospel, as does the attempt to use violence
to enforce domination and hierarchy.

The classical narrative arc of the Christian account of God's
involvement with humanity starts with creation in God's image,
then moves to human alienation from God and its violent consequences, and continues with God's fidelity and love despite human
sin. That love is shown concretely in many ways, particularly in the
incarnation and work of the Son, which leads to a reversal of human
alienation and the burnishing of God's image in humanity by the
power of the Spirit. If gender inequality is a consequence of sin and
alienation from God, as seem to be implied in the description of
Eve's plight in Genesis 3:16 ("your desire shall be for your husband,
and he shall rule over you"), then undoing gendered and other social
hierarchies should be a consequence of the grace and reconciliation
with God described lyrically in Galatians 3:28. Theologians have
long held that this is so, but too many of them have used futuristic
eschatology to posit that equality will only be possible in a very distant heavenly future.

Augustine, for instance, states with regard to Galatians 3:28 that
inequalities between Jew and Greek, free and slave, men and women
will be overcome eschatologically. Yet he quickly adds that at present we only have the "first fruits" of what is to come. In practice, he
says, this means "that difference, whether of peoples or of legal status
or of sex, while indeed already removed in the unity of faith, remains

---

8. Brad Braxton, *No Longer Slaves: Galatians and African American Experience* (Collegeville, MN:
The Liturgical Press, 2002), 94.

in this mortal life." The existing hierarchical order "is to be observed on this life's journey."[9] The push toward futuristic eschatology on this matter for fear of social change or upheaval needs to make way for the dimension of realized, present eschatology: gender equality that can begin to be experienced today, even as we live into the hope of the new creation in its full splendor.

FURTHER REFLECTIONS
Paul and Apocalyptic Eschatology

In considering the dialectic between realized and future eschatology in Paul it has become indispensable among readers of Galatians to take into account what J. Louis Martyn calls Paul's "cosmological apocalyptic eschatology."[10] This refers to the notion that in this "present evil age" (Gal. 1:4), powers contrary to God have sway over the cosmos and are able to influence and enslave human beings. The need for redemption goes beyond the dimension of the forgiveness of sins, because humans have become so deeply entrenched in an unjust reality that drastic measures are needed. God therefore carries out an apocalyptic war against the evil powers, in order to deliver God's elect from them. Specifically, by sending Christ into the world, God has "invaded" it in order to liberate the world through the work of Christ and of the Spirit, "striking the decisive and liberating blow against the power of the present evil age," though the struggle against the powers and principalities is not yet finished.[11]

Martyn's "apocalyptic" approach to Paul is helpful in that it pushes us to take very seriously the apostle's complex understanding of the human condition (one that goes much beyond the need for a forensic "justification") as well as God's energetic response to our plight. Without falling into dualism, Martyn also provides a way

---

9. Eric Plumer, *Augustine's Commentary on Galatians: Introduction, Text, Translation, and Notes*, Oxford Early Christian Studies (Oxford: Oxford University Press, 2003), 175.

10. Cf. J. Louis Martyn, *Galatians: A New Translation with Introduction and Commentary*, Anchor Bible (New York: Doubleday, 1997), 97–105 et passim. Martyn is in turn influenced by Martin C. de Boer, notably by his essay "Paul and Jewish Apocalyptic Eschatology," *Apocalyptic and the New Testament: Essays in Honor of J. Louis Martyn*, ed. Joel Marcus and Marion L. Soards (Sheffield: JSOT, 1989), 169–90.

11. Martyn, *Galatians*, 105.

of grasping conflict and duality in Paul (for example, how to address the tensions between the present evil age and the age to come, or between the "flesh" and the Spirit). What Martyn does not specify is precisely how the powers functioned in Paul's time and continue to function today through historic phenomena such as empire and colonialism, the literal enslavement of human beings, gender ineq-uities, entrenched economic disparities, environmental destruc-tion, or institutional racism. As a result, the material, liberating implications of Paul's eschatology are left somewhat up in the air. Apocalyptic perspectives, including those of Paul, are always best understood when interpreted from the perspective of the most vul-nerable in a given society; whenever apocalyptic notions are read from a place of privilege, they can easily be co-opted into a justifi-cation for violence (as when God's "invasion" and "war" on this "evil age" become closely identified with the wars of particular empires).

Another detour that theologians have used to move away from the subversive implications of this verse is to spiritualize it, that is, to move it exclusively to the realm of individual faith without work-ing out its social implications. Jerome makes the important point that "slaves and free men are distinguished by faith and not by social standing," so that it is not someone's social standing that determines his or her worth. The same holds for Jews and Greeks and for men and women. However, Jerome does not tease out any material con-sequences for the life of the church or of society from that criterion: he leaves social hierarchies intact.[12]

Luther provides a glimpse of another approach in his commen-tary, when he works through the theme of our oneness in Christ. He continues to build on the logic of the wonderful exchange and, hark-ing back to Galatians 2:20, posits that we are fully joined together with Christ, to the point that "we must be in heaven, and Christ must live and work in us." This happens "not speculatively but really, with presence and with power."[13] The sociological and ecclesiologi-cal ramifications of the liberating presence of Christ can be glimpsed

---

12. Jerome, *Commentary on Galatians*, 152.
13. Martin Luther, *Luther's Works*, vol. 26, *Lectures on Galatians, 1535 Chapters 1–4*, ed. Jaroslav Pelikan (Saint Louis: Concordia Publishing House, 1963), 357.

in his statement, even though Luther does not relate them to the social hierarchies of his time for fear of anarchy. The fear of unleashing destabilizing social changes has led Christians, especially those with something to lose, to try to build retaining walls around this text. Its great force, however, pushes back constantly through the history of theology.

It is also important to push back at interpretations that use the verse in order to erase particularities and absorb everyone into a single way of being "in Christ." The doctrine of the incarnation with its assumption of particularity questions homogeneity and sameness, even in the eschatological realm. Interpretations that push equality in Christ far into the future, and sustain social asymmetries and injustice in the present in the name of order, have no Christological warrant and reflect only the fears of the powerful.

The concluding phrase in the verse, "for you are all one" (*eis*) stresses the unity of the whole, in contrast to the parts of which the whole is made up. Such unity is a key Pauline notion, often related to the metaphor of the body, functioning at once ecclesiologically and christologically. We see this for instance in Romans 12:5 ("we, who are many, are one body in Christ") and 1 Corinthians 12:12 ("all the members of the body, though many, are one body"). Unity in this simultaneously Trinitarian and ecclesiological sense is also a theme in Johannine theology, as in John 10:30 ("The Father and I are one") and 17:11 ("Holy Father, protect them . . . that they may be one, as we are one"). In the Galatians passage, the "oneness" or unity of verse 28 echoes the earlier statement of verse 20 that "God is one," and it is anchored there. Unity in Christ is predicated on the common union of the Triune God, by which being "in Christ" also means to be "in the Spirit" and "in the Father."

Lopez suggests that perhaps we are to take Galatians 3:28 as part of a broader Pauline argument of "a transformed consciousness and solidarity among the defeated" in the face of a Roman imperial ideology intent on conquering and enslaving all its "others"—including, presumably, the people represented in the three contrasting pairs, inasmuch as they are part of the way of Jesus.[14] A hermeneutical

---

14. Lopez, *Apostle to the Conquered*, 150.

key that ties Lopez' insight together with Paul's constant theme of the "wonderful exchange" is to understand that he is working with what could be called a high liberationist Christology from below. In other words, he believes in the preexistence and the divinity of the Son while simultaneously linking the manifestation of that divinity inextricably to Jesus of Nazareth, who lived in a specific time and place, was executed by the Roman Empire, and was resurrected from the dead. This allows Paul to exalt Jesus Christ as the Son of God in the most sublime terms possible while never negating Christ's true humanity, particularity, and solidarity with the least of society nor forgetting that the way of Jesus Christ is dangerous, for it questions imperial and hegemonic structures as well as religious certitudes whenever they begin to harden into idolatry.

A dynamic, liberationist, subversive high Christology from below allows Christian theology to steer clear of the aporias of binary thinking that lead to adoptionism (a purely human Jesus) or Docetism (a purely divine Jesus) or to Christologies that are purely ascending from "below" or conversely purely descending from "above." The traditions about Jesus—whether Markan or Johannine—never fit into a simplified scheme. The notion of a high Christology from below also allows theology to avoid a static, formulaic approach to the Chalcedonian definition according to which Jesus Christ is "truly God and truly human" and "complete in Godhead" as well as "complete in humanity." That definition should be understood as shorthand for a long, involved story of God's relationship with creation rather than a kind of algebraic equation that shuts down conversation.

The fact that such a Christology is one of the central insights of much of Latin American Liberation, as well as of Latino/Latina theologies in North America, is sometimes lost in their reception in the Anglo-American realm. Usually when such theologies speak of the "historical" character of Jesus, they are not referring to the "search for the historical Jesus" in its various German and Anglo-American waves but rather to the concrete, particular, and historical specificity of the message, which by the work of the Spirit can be actualized and continued today. Latino/Latina approaches to theology in the U.S. context find a basis on a high liberationist

Christology from below to struggle against cultural imperialism, ethnic prejudice, and racism.[15]

Joerg Rieger points out that Paul indeed manifests both a "high ecclesiology" and a "high Christology" but not in the sense of a hierarchy where power flows down from above, as in the Roman Empire, but rather in contraposition to it. "High" in this sense leads to the exaltation of what society considers "low," in church (1 Cor. 12:24) and also in society. It also leads to the being "made low" of those who formerly were "uplifted," as can be seen in Paul's own life. He became a fool, a victim of torture, weak, poor, and homeless (2 Cor. 11:21–27), not in order to glorify such conditions but as part of his adherence to the way of Jesus, "in which the way of being in solidarity with the powerful is by being in solidarity with the lowly."[16] According to this logic, what it means to be "lord" or to be "from above" radically reverses the expectations of the dominant systems of power, prestige, and distribution of privilege.

FURTHER REFLECTIONS
Equality in Christ as a Feminist Possibility

The notion that in Christ there is no "male and female" (Gal. 3:28) has been read by women through the centuries as a positive, egalitarian theme with liberating possibilities. Quakers Priscilla Cotton and Mary Cole, imprisoned in Exeter, England, for a decade in the mid-seventeenth century for exercising the gift of prophecy, quote the verse in their tract *To the Priests and People of England* (1655). They use Galatians 3:28 in order to shift and subvert the meaning of 1 Corinthians 14:34–35 ("women should be silent in the churches"), which had been used to try to silence them. They argue that because in Christ there is "no male and female," the injunction to be silent, if it is to apply to anyone, will have to apply to both women and men, just as the statement in 1 Corinthians 14:31 that

---

15. See Benjamín Valentín, "Who Do We Say He Was and Is? Jesus and Christology among Latino/a Theologians," in *In Our Own Voices: Latino/a Renditions of Theology*, ed. Benjamín Valentín (Maryknoll, NY: Orbis, 2010), 85–111.

16. Joerg Rieger, *Christ and Empire: From Paul to Postcolonial Times* (Minneapolis: Fortress, 2007), 52; see also 45–54.

all in the church may prophesy one by one must apply to women and men equally. They concede that "woman" at times represents "weakness" in the Scriptures, but both males and females are to be understood as "women" in this sense, if they cannot endure sound doctrine (2 Tim. 4:3) or if they are limited to "the wisdom of man" (1 Cor. 2:4–5:13). "Here mayst thou see from the Scriptures, that the woman or weakness whether male or female, is forbidden to speak in the church," they state; but it is equally plain that women do not always represent weakness, as is made clear by the example of the instruction of Apollos by Priscilla, the four prophesying daughters of Philip, Mary Magdalene's proclamation of the resurrection, the women who labored with Paul in the gospel (Phil. 4:3), and many other cases. Cotton and Cole conclude that not they, but their priestly male accusers, are the ones who should be silent: "Indeed, you yourselves are the women, that are forbidden to speak in the church. . . ."[17]

As Rosemary Radford Ruether points out, although it is encouraging that such themes and readings can be found throughout Christian history, they cannot gain traction in the church unless certain cultural and social conditions are present that allow the recognition that the meaning of theological symbols, including those in Scripture, is socially constructed rather than frozen eternally as a God-given "order of creation" ordaining the subjugation of certain groups, including women. She points out that one way that the shift of consciousness about these symbols happens is when women gain education and agency in the church, learning, speaking, and being heard as theologians.[18] In the seventeenth century, Cotton and Cole made good use of their literacy skills and their rhetorical abilities, in order to make their voices heard and to propose a hermeneutical shift toward gender equality on the basis of their reading of Galatians 3:28, in conjunction with their convictions about the empowering nature of the gospel. Theologically speaking, it is

17. Priscilla Cotton and Mary Cole, *To the Priests and People of England, We Discharge Our Consciences, and Give Them Warning,* in *Radical Christian Writings: A Reader,* ed. Andrew Bradstock and Christopher Rowland (Malden, MA: Blackwell, 2002), 147–52.
18. Rosemary Radford Ruether, "The Emergence of Christian Feminist Theology," in *The Cambridge Companion to Feminist Theology,* ed. Susan Frank Parsons (Cambridge: Cambridge University Press, 2002), 3–4.

no coincidence than alongside their christological understanding of equality in Christ we find the strong implicit pneumatology of the Quaker movement of the time.

Christian movements tend to tear down gender inequalities along with other injustices when they recognize that the Holy Spirit is no respecter of persons and that the Spirit annuls all social hierarchies of class, education, and gender.[19] Unless the Christology of "equality" is fueled by a pneumatology open to do "a new thing," even as the pneumatology is challenged toward sociopolitical concreteness and particularity by the doctrine of the incarnation, the feminist force of Galatians 3:28 remains no more than a distant eschatological possibility. Said otherwise, the Word has to be received under the power of the Spirit in order for the churches to be able to see and hear the Bible in new ways and for passages such as Galatians 3:28 to take hermeneutical precedence for church doctrine over male-centered texts (such as 1 Tim. 2:11–15).[20]

3:29–4:5
Adoption as God's Children

After speaking of the role of the law and giving his readers a glimpse of what it means to be "in Christ," Paul returns to the theme of promise and inheritance (3:29). Who are these "heirs" (*klēronomoi*)? The expression is not exclusively Pauline. In Hebrews, it is used christologically, referring to the Son as the one whom God has appointed heir of all things (1:2) and then by extension to those who became heirs of God's promise (Heb. 6:17). In the fifth Parable or Similitude of the Shepherd of Hermas (probably written early in the second century), "heir" is used in the context of an apparent Spirit-Christology,

---

19. Such was the view of Cotton and Cole's contemporary Mary Cary; cf, Rosemary Radford Ruether, *Women and Redemption: A Theological History* (Minneapolis: Fortress, 1998), 135–45.

20. Dawn DeVries argues that this leads in essence not only to ecclesiological changes such as the ordination of women but also to a canon that is in practice more "open" than closed. See her article "'Ever to Be Reformed according to the Word of God': Can the Scripture Principle Be Redeemed for Feminist Theology?", in *Feminist and Womanist Essays in Reformed Dogmatics*, ed. Amy Plantinga Pauw and Serene Jones (Louisville, KY: Westminster John Knox Press, 2006), 54–55.

referring first of all to the preexistent Holy Spirit, who is willing to share God's inheritance with a faithful servant, the Son of God, who then also becomes an heir.[21] Paul tends to use the term to describe those who have believed in the gospel and have become followers of Jesus, children of God and heirs of the kingdom (cf. Rom. 8:17 and Gal. 4:7).

For Jerome, the child-heir as described by Paul is a symbol of the entire human race, while the "guardian and trustees" (Gal. 4:2) of humanity are the prophets, just as its pedagogue or disciplinarian is the Law of Moses. Jerome parts from the supposition that "the advent of Christ has reference to the maturation of the human race."[22] Though increasing human maturity would seem desirable, the apparent logical corollary that if Christ brings the possibility of maturity, Judaism must be a religion of the "immature," is a flawed conclusion too easily reached, especially whenever the Jewishness of Jesus himself is obscured or denied.

Calvin, who sees the problem, is concerned that someone might use this passage to treat the great figures of the Old Testament as childish or immature. In the face of the "matchless faith" of Abraham and the "vast intelligence" of the prophets, "with what effrontery shall we dare talk of such men as our inferiors? Were not they rather the heroes, and we the children?" He tries to resolve the tension by pointing out that the figure of the child-heir is not a description of particular persons but rather "the universal condition of both nations."[23] This is somewhat helpful in avoiding a facile supersessionism but moves toward another trap: that of an abstraction that flattens out the specificity of the adoption and inheritance of each particular child of God, according to God's mercy and grace.

Within the Christian church, as José Ignacio González Faus reminds us, we often forget what it should mean for our common praxis that according to Paul God considers us fully as God's heirs. By doing so, God lifts up humanity in its dignity and potential as made up of particular, unique persons with whom God desires to

21. Cf. Shepherd of Hermas, Similitudes 5.2.6–8; 5.6.5–7, trans. J. B. Lightfoot, in Early Christian Writings, http://www.earlychristianwritings.com/text/shepherd-lightfoot.html.
22. Jerome, Commentary on Galatians, 154.
23. Calvin, Calvin's Bible Commentaries: Galatians and Ephesians Galatians, 98.

be in communion both individually and as a collective. Nevertheless, some church structures seem to put a brake on what this could
mean for human development and growth rather than encouraging
it.[24] We see this when church leaders insist on treating many of the
members of their denominations as unripe and incapable of moving
into maturity and responsibility.

A classic example of such treatment is when women are considered structurally or ontologically unworthy of certain forms of
pastoral calling or incapable of exercising certain gifts of the Spirit
publicly. This stance is usually accompanied by forms of comple-
mentarian theological anthropology, often purportedly based on
Pauline strictures. Paul himself seems to have wavered on this front
(cf. 1 Cor. 11:5 and 14:35). Perhaps he was conscious that taking
filiation and inheritance seriously in practice does indeed destabi-
lize longstanding patriarchal structures, and sometimes it made him
nervous.

**Then that little man in black there, he says women can't have as much rights as
men, 'cause Christ wasn't a woman! Where did your Christ come from? Where
did your Christ come from? From God and a woman! Man had nothing to do
with Him.**

**If the first woman God ever made was strong enough to turn the world
upside down all alone, these women together ought to be able to turn it back
and get it right side up again! And now they is asking to do it, the men better
let them.**

Sojourner Truth, "Ain't I a Woman?" (speech, Women's Rights Convention, Akron, Ohio, 1851),
http://www.nps.gov/wori/learn/historyculture/sojourner-truth.htm.

The very viability of the church as a living, growing organism is
at stake in this matter. From the beginning women have found good
news in the gospel of Jesus, despite the many barriers that have made
it difficult for women to live out its implications fully and concretely.
Women have often seemed to constitute a captive church audience,
faithful despite the patriarchal posturing of its formal leaders. In the
present, however, it is becoming increasingly clear that if women are

---

24. José Ignacio González Faus, *La humanidad nueva: Ensayo de cristología*, Séptima edición
(Santander: Sal Terrae, 1984), 606–9.

treated as constitutionally immature, then they may not only move to churches more open to their interests but simply move away from church life altogether. Such desertions are already happening not only in the secularized regions of Western Europe or North America but also in the global South. To understand the church as made up of children of God who are God's full heirs, taking Paul's insights in Galatians seriously, has implications for the very survival and continuance of church communities. It means that the church needs to learn to exercise respect for the growing maturity of *all* human beings—male and female—in concrete ways. To speak of filiation and inheritance as abstract categories is not enough.

Though sin and injustice certainly continue to mar the lives of all human beings, God's willingness not only to adopt us as children but to make us into full heirs of the divine life and legacy is empowering and transformative. The church should function as a laboratory for the possibilities inherent in our relationship with God as heirs and with each other as siblings of equal worth in God's eyes, not as a space to stifle, discipline, and punish those who want to do a "new thing" as heirs to God's promises.

Whenever the church becomes fearful of its own transformative potential and retreats toward rigidity, ecclesiology is in danger of becoming cut off from a life-giving pneumatological Christology or christological pneumatology, and the concrete treatment of human beings (theological anthropology) suffers. The many voices skeptical or fearful of "church" in our societies may well caricature ecclesiological reality, but they also remind us that many of our churches have indeed become sites of repression rather than laboratories for transformation and gardens for the flourishing of abundant life. Teasing out the implications of what it means for every follower of Jesus to be an heir of God's promises of liberation and transformation is one way to remind the church of its genuine calling.

Paul's argument, then, is that if Christ is the "seed" of Abraham, by extension those who are "in Christ" and belong to Christ are likewise Abraham's offspring and heirs of the promises of God. If someone's heirs—even God's heirs—are not yet of age, then they are not in a condition to inherit but remain under tutelage and guardianship: the time has to be ripe for the heirs to come into their inheritance.

The "guardians and trustees" appointed to look after the heirs until they come of age (v. 2) are terms that were used for estate managers in Asia Minor in early imperial times. In Roman legal practice, multiple guardians and administrators were often appointed by the testators of wills to supervise heirs not yet of age, along with their properties.[25]

Paul is piling metaphor on metaphor here, not writing an allegory, so he can posit the heir as an orphan in need of guardians and trustees for the purposes of his argument, even as he immediately moves back to the image of filiation and adoption by the living God. At one time, he holds, the proper conditions were not yet in place for the unveiling of God's desire to incorporate all who wish it into a filial relationship with God. God's future heirs were therefore for a time in bondage to the "elemental spirits of the world." However, when God determined that the proper time had come, God put into place a particular manner for their liberation. It required the Son of God to take on a life circumscribed by the time and space of creation, in order to open up God's promise of inheritance to all.

The elemental "spirits" or "rudiments" (*stoicheia*) of the world that enslave humanity (v. 3) are not easy to render understandably. The expression can mean the basic bits required for learning something, for example, the letters of the alphabet. It can also make reference to the elements that compose the world, in classical antiquity most often identified with earth, air, fire, and water.[26] Many ancient writers (such as Empedocles, Philo, and Plutarch) feared that the soul might be unable to pierce through these elements and be trapped in "the ceaseless rotation of the four elements."[27] Finally, the expression can be used to speak of the heavenly bodies represented by the zodiac. Both the earthly elements and the heavenly bodies were sometimes regarded as personal divine beings, hence "elemental spirits."

---

25. Cf. John K. Goodrich, "Guardians, Not Taskmasters: The Cultural Resonances of Paul's Metaphor in Galatians 4:1–2," *Journal for the Study of the New Testament* 32 (2010): 251–84.

26. Walter Bauer, *A Greek-English Lexicon of the New Testament and Other Early Christian Literature*, trans. and adapt. William F. Arndt and F. Wilbur Gingrich, 2nd ed. (Chicago: University of Chicago Press, 1979), 769.

27. Eduard Schweizer, "Slaves of the Elements and Worshipers of Angels: Gal. 4:3, 9 and Col 2:8, 18, 20," in *Journal of Biblical Literature* 107 (1988): 455–68.

In early Christianity it was quite common to take over elements of the pagan philosophical polemic against astrological fatalism. Along those lines, Marius Victorinus describes the liberation that comes from not having to do "as the stars have commanded and the course of the world has ordained." Those who are now serving Christ do so with "liberty in their actions under the Spirit's ruling," as opposed to being controlled by "elemental forces."[28]

What seems important here is that Paul argues that without Christ, even under the kind tutelage of the law and of God's tender mercies, humans were "enslaved" by the reigning logic of the system, the common sense by which good things become ends in themselves and thus distorted. In this sense, the "elements" can be related to the idea of the "principalities and powers" that in this "present evil age" have become hostile to the welfare of creation, an idea we find elsewhere in the Pauline corpus. Even—or perhaps especially—religious precepts, such as the law, in themselves quite good and necessary, run the risk of becoming taskmasters who enslave us. Paul does not state explicitly in this passage that messages that purport to be the gospel of Jesus Christ can also become distorted and function as "rudiments" gone haywire, but given the context of his disagreement with his Jewish Christian colleagues, that possibility is present as well. Paul continually tries to ensure that the gospel of Jesus Christ itself not be distorted and made into a force of enslavement that would be no gospel at all.

As a safeguard against such distortion, Paul puts forward a proto-Trinitarian theology that encapsulates the concrete dynamic of God's desire to live in harmony with human beings. The first point he makes in this regard is that God sent forth the Son (v. 4). The verb here (*exapesteilen*) is the same one that he will repeat in verse 6 to say that God has sent the Spirit of the Son into our hearts. In both instances the implication is that the sending is not a one-time event but the sending of a pervading presence and influence. It is used elsewhere of the divine sending of higher beings (Wis. 9:10), of God's angel (Ps. 151:4 LXX), and of Paul himself (Acts 22:21).

28. Stephen Andrew Cooper, *Marius Victorinus' Commentary on Galatians: Introduction, Translation and Notes* (Oxford: Oxford University Press, 2005), 303; see also Cooper's footnote 32 on the same page.

Such sending is always linked to a divine mission. In fact we find in this text a hint of the *missio Dei*, the sending of God by God, that should be at the heart of any theology of mission or of sending. The gospel of John posits a similar idea from the perspective of the resurrected Christ, who was sent and now also sends us out in the power of the Holy Spirit: "As the Father has sent me, so I send you" (John 20:21).

When a certain misguided Christian missionary zeal tries to "spread the gospel" by any means possible, and by so doing forgets the grounded, down-to-earth character of Jesus, it becomes unfaithful to the sending of the Son in the fullness of time. On the other hand, to ignore Christianity's identity as a missional movement would also be a mistake. At the core of the Christian story is the God who sends, the God who is sent, God who is in both the sending and in the being sent. To believe in this God is to participate, at one level or another, in that sending, along with the angels, the apostles, and all of God's creation.

Though it is brief, verse 4 is packed with meaning, or as Calvin puts it, "these few words contain much instruction."[29] The sending "of God by God" happens in "the fullness of time" (*to plērōma tou chronou*). There is often talk in Christian circles about the *kairos* concept of time as indicating the proper time or season in which God acts, as for instance in Romans 5:6 where Paul states that "at the right time (*kairos*) Christ died for the ungodly." Here, however, Paul speaks of God's engagement with humanity in chronological time. A similar thought can be found in Ephesians 1:10. This unabashed entering of the eternal God into time is a remarkable idea, though the relation of God to time is difficult to think through.

As Augustine remarks in the *Confessions*, it is not "in time" that God precedes time. There was not yet "time" when God had not made something; God created time itself. As creatures, we are conditioned by time and have an expectation of a future in God, even though we do not know in the end what we are measuring when we speak of present, past, and future.[30] Augustine thinks of God's

29. Calvin, *Calvin's Bible Commentaries: Galatians and Ephesians*, 101.
30. Cf Augustine, *Confessions* (XI.13.16–17; XI.25.32–33; XI.30.40), trans. Henry Chadwick (Oxford: Oxford University Press, 2008), 230–1; 239–40; 244–45.

engagement with time as a created entity, not as an everlasting and closed cosmic process or as a mere succession of days defined by astronomical calculation. This opens up the possibility of particularity, creativity, and uniqueness within time.[31]

If God, who is eternal, chooses to enter into the time-space continuum to develop an eternal relationship with God's creation, then it is not absurd to speak of God in a human idiom necessarily tied to time, even as we know that "time" cannot contain God. It is helpful to keep this insight in mind whenever we ponder eschatology: what is most important is God's commitment to us both in our time and beyond the constraints of time as we know it. We cannot fit the dynamic nature of God's life fully into a time imagined on the basis of the rotation of our planet around our small sun, nor can the "future" imagined for us by God accommodate itself fully into human conceptions of time, whether they be cyclical or linear. What we can know on the basis of Paul's statement is that God was not willing for our time to reach its fullness without God's full and timely commitment to human life as we know it now.

God enters into our historicity and materiality, into our particular time-space continuum, and this is attested to by the fact that the Son was "born of a woman, born under the law" (v. 4). The verb used here to express that Christ was begotten or born of a woman (*genomenon ek gynaikos*) is the same one Paul chooses in the prologue to Romans when he states that the Son of God was "descended from David according to the flesh" (Rom. 1:3). The verb is then repeated to make the point that the Son was "born under the law" (*genomenon hypo nomon*). In these parallel phrases, Paul is safeguarding against two related tendencies that would later do a good deal of harm to the Christian faith and that continue to reappear today in various guises: namely, Docetism (the tendency to regard Jesus as only apparently, but not fully, human) and anti-Judaism (the tendency to forget that Jesus was Jewish). To efface Jesus' Jewishness is to erase a central aspect of his humanity as a person of faith in a given time and place; to efface his humanness is likewise to erase his particularity, including his faith in the God of Abraham, Hagar, and Sarah.

31. Cf. Henry Chadwick, *Augustine: A Very Short Introduction* (Oxford: Oxford University Press, 1986), 75–76.

Conflating the two safeguards, we might paraphrase Paul to say that when the time was ripe, God's Son was born of a Jewish mother, in a particular time and a particular place. Notably, in patristic exegesis it was common to understand this passage as a protection against a Christ imagined as not entirely human. Cyril of Alexandria, for example, quotes it to argue against Apollinarianism, saying that in this passage Paul clearly means that Jesus was born of his human mother Mary, not "through" Mary as if she were a channel from which he took nothing.[32] Nevertheless, the patristic interpreters often missed the explicit connection between the true humanity of Jesus and his Jewishness.

Though Paul does not mention Mary by name, it is likely that her story was not unknown to him. The "born of a woman" is not only a generic way to say that Jesus came into the world the usual way, as a baby rather than as some sort of adult apparition, but a nod to a particular young woman, of a specific culture, religious faith, time, and place, who physically birthed and nurtured him in all ways, including in the way of the torah. It takes many hours of attention and much physical labor to raise any child well, and Mary did so alongside her community and family, while she simultaneously bore other children and did her part to provide the economic surplus that would allow a family in Nazareth to feed and educate itself despite heavy tax burdens and an imperial yoke.

The observance of the law is so central to Jewish piety that Paul's phrase to be born "under the law" (v. 4) can be taken to mean essentially that Jesus was born into the "Jewish religion" or the Jewish way of life.[33] Indeed, Jesus was raised, lived, and died as an observant Jew, came from an observant Jewish family, and chose his disciples from among other observant Jews. An anti-Jewish version of the Christian faith is therefore necessarily a docetic version of Christianity, one that forgets the specificity and materiality of the life of Jesus, who lived "under the law" as one of the children of Israel of his time. Docetism always effects an erasure of the very particularity,

---

32. Cf. Lucas F. Mateo-Seco, "'Envió Dios a su Hijo, nacido de mujer (Gálatas 4,4–5 en el pensamiento patrístico anterior al Concilio de Éfeso)," in *Scripta Theologica* 32 (2000): 13–46, especially 34–37, where Mateo-Seco discusses Cyril's interpretation of Galatians 4:4 in the latter's commentaries and homilies.
33. Walter Bauer, *A Greek-English Lexicon of the New Testament*, 542.

materiality, and humanity of Jesus that for the Christian faith is the key to God's salvific and liberating solidarity with humanity. In consequence, to erase the Jewishness of Jesus paradoxically destroys the very basis of the Christian faith.

In verse 5 Paul boldly explains why he thinks the Son was sent to live in our material reality in this very specific way, by using the forceful conjunction *hina* ("so that" or "in order that") twice, to underline that Christ came in order to liberate us and that we might be adopted into God's family. Two images are juxtaposed: an economic and social one (redemption) and a familial and legal one (adoption). We were bought by God and rescued from slavery, a theme already touched on in 3:13, and we "received adoption" or were placed by God in the condition of full-fledged "sons" with all the rights and privileges corresponding thereto, a theme dear to Paul's heart (he uses the same noun, *huiothesia*, in Rom. 8:15 and 23 in reference to Christians and in Rom. 9:4 in reference to Israel).

Here again, as in the case of the sending of God by God, we are invited into the very heart of God's life; as Augustine puts it, "For we receive adoption because the only Son did not scorn participation in our nature."[34] We are adopted as God's children, or more literally, as "sons" of God, because we are all (regardless of gender) given the full legal rights and status that in Paul's time were conceded to free male children.

FURTHER REFLECTIONS
Born of a Woman: Galatians 4:4 and Chalcedonian Christology

Calvin posits that if the Son was sent, it means that the Son existed before the sending, before the incarnation, and that "this proves his eternal Godhead." Putting this notion together with Paul's mention of the Son's birth from a woman in the fullness of time, he finds a warrant for the Chalcedonian idea of the two natures of Christ in this passage.[35] The text may well serve as one of the scriptural roots for

---

34. Plumer, *Augustine's Commentary on Galatians*, 179.
35. Calvin, *Calvin's Bible Commentaries: Galatians and Ephesians*, 101.

that later dogma, but the leap Calvin makes in reading Chalcedon into Paul is not without problems. The main one arises whenever Christ's "humanity" and "divinity" are thought of in abstract terms, so that the humanity elides the specificity of the way of Jesus as portrayed in the Gospels and presupposed by Paul and is absorbed almost entirely into a triumphal, exalted conception of the divine, symbolized by the exclusively vertical connection of humans with the eternal divine.[36]

In this approach, which always has a docetic flavor, the materiality and particularity of the life of Jesus is flattened out or left out altogether, as indeed is the case when Calvin comments, regarding the expression "born of a woman," that "the word woman is here put generally for the female sex."[37] In a single aside, the historical figure of Mary of Nazareth is diluted, along with the prophetic and political voice she is given by Luke in the Magnificat (Luke 1:46–55). Even worse, the "woman" or "female" in this text can become a generic representative for the "female principle" representing all that is imperfect, passive, and unformed and indeed particularly subject to corruption. In such cases "woman" is often linked to the figure of Eve. Marius Victorinus, for example, holds in his commentary on the passage that "even in the first human being there was no sin except from a female," and conversely links maleness to perfection: "all things that are perfect are said to be a man (*vir*) and all things that are imperfect, a female."[38]

Abstract readings of "woman" or "female" forget that the particular woman in this passage should be understood from two directions at once: as the concrete and historical woman Mary of Nazareth and also as a representative of humanity. Mary's role actually serves to shift emphasis away from a patriarchal genealogical model and toward a new kind of adoptive relationship with God: her unconventional maternity subverts and denies human and patriarchal notions of fatherhood, including that of "father Abraham."[39]

---

36. Cf. Jürgen Moltmann, *Der Weg Jesu Christi. Christologie in messianischen Dimensionen* (München: Christian Kaiser, 1989) 70–74.
37. Calvin, *Calvin's Bible Commentaries: Galatians and Ephesians,* 101.
38. Cooper, *Marius Victorinus' Commentary on Galatians,* 305–6.
39. Cf. Mercedes Navarro Puerto, "Nacido de mujer (Gál. 4,4): Perspectiva antropológica," in *Ephemerides Mariologiae* 47 (1997): 327–37.

Perhaps that is why it is all too easy for some to lose sight of her uncomfortable specificity and read her role abstractly simply as the human "material" used to make the incarnation possible.

Jon Sobrino suggests that a theology that too eagerly allows itself to be shaped by the logic of the Chalcedonian formula tends to be marked by three weaknesses: a lack of concreteness, a lack of historicity, and a lack of relationality. The best way to avoid those traps is to be guided hermeneutically by the Jesus of the Synoptic Gospels, and particularly by his praxis. Expressed positively it means that Jesus walked in the ways of the reign or commonweal of God. Expressed negatively, his praxis was directed against the "anti-kingdom" and against all forces of idolatry.[40] It is this historical particularity of struggle and fidelity that gives concrete shape to the humanity of the eternal Son and to the divinity of Jesus of Nazareth. As Sobrino points out, the specific epistemology that emerges from continuing to follow Jesus in new historical situations by the grace and power of the Spirit allows the Chalcedonian formula to become a holistic tool that safeguards both the humanity and the divinity of Jesus in our theologies.

4:6–7
The Spirit of the Son

As Paul's language reminds us, the Spirit sent by God and received by us as God's adopted children and heirs is not just any spirit, but the Spirit of the Son. To name the Holy Spirit explicitly as the "Spirit of the Son" anchors the work of the Spirit in the history of Jesus of Nazareth. The Spirit is able to connect us to that story and to actualize it in our particular historical and cultural circumstances, to the point that by the Spirit we are able to utter in a meaningful way the very words of the Markan Jesus in his prayer in the Garden of Gethsemane (Mark 14:36): "Abba, Father!" The phrasing of verse 6 implies that the Spirit, sent by God into our hearts, is the One who cries out in supplication in our stead: deep cries out to deep.

40. Jon Sobrino, *La fe en Jesucristo: Ensayo desde las víctimas* (Madrid: Trotta, 1999), 424–39.

The privilege of addressing God as "Abba," or as "Father," is the result of an adoption that is carried out at God's own initiative at all levels. Paul therefore encourages the Galatians—and by extension all followers of Jesus—to address God with the same intimacy and familiarity that Jesus did. Perhaps even more importantly, by God's Spirit God empowers and impels us to do so. That is why Basil of Caesarea uses the language of familiarity (*oikeiosis, oikeiotes*), both in the sense of familial ties and in the sense of closeness, to speak of the intimacy we have with God as a result of the Spirit's work.[41] That "familiarity" of the Spirit with us (Basil would say "with our soul") in turn leads us to be transformed into an ever greater likeness with God, manifested in many ways: enjoying spiritual gifts, understanding the "mysteries" of God's economy, dancing with angels, experiencing interminable joy, remaining in God, being assimilated to God, and finally becoming as God is (*theōsis*).[42]

It becomes apparent through this close relationship to God that—whatever we may have

> Behold the full array of these three Powers, operant through their own power and one Godhead. For God, says Paul, who is the Father, sent the Son, who is Christ. Christ in turn, who is himself the power of God and is God himself, Christ *sent (God sent,* says Paul, for now God and Christ are conjoined, especially with Christ's sanctification after the Mystery), Christ *sent the Spirit of the Son* (...).
>
> Cooper, *Marius Victorinus' Commentary on Galatians,* 308–9.

been before—we are no longer (*ouketi*) slaves or servants but rather children of God. Our experience of the Holy Spirit is therefore both an experience of liberation and an experience of filiation. Paul argues further than if we are God's children, then each of us is an heir of God "through God" (*dia theou*). This construction, although it is well-supported in the manuscript tradition, is rather curious. Indeed the many textual variants of the expression bear witness to the different ways in which copyists

41. Cf. Basil of Caesarea, *On the Holy Spirit,* XIX.49, trans. David Anderson (Crestwood, NY: St. Vladimir's Seminary Press, 1997), 76–79.
42. Ibid., (IX.23), 44.

tried to modify it in order to make sense of it. Among their altera-
tions were "heir on account of God," "heir through Christ," "heir
of God through Christ," "heir through God in Christ Jesus," and
even (following Rom. 8:16) "heir of God and joint heir with
Christ."[43] If, however, God works in a Trinitarian way, and the
work of Christ and of the Spirit is the very work of God, not of a
demigod or demiurge, it makes sense for Paul to say that we are
heirs "through God." All that the later tradition would parse out
as the Trinitarian economy of God appears in condensed fashion
in these two short verses.

Because we are God's adopted children, God sends the Spirit
of the Son into our hearts. The Trinitarian dynamic is what weaves
together Paul's notion of "sending" or of "mission." We are children
of God by the Spirit who makes the Son live in us, allowing us to
live the very life of the Son; and we are children of God in the Son
because the Son lives in us.[44] The mutual indwelling of the Divine
Persons is not exclusive but rather invites our participation and
enables it. Especially in medieval tradition, the mystical implications
of the Trinitarian dynamic of this passage come to the fore, as when
William of St. Thierry in *On Contemplating God* writes that God
loves Godself in us and that we love each other in God and learn to
love God by the diffusion of God's love in our hearts. God sends the
Spirit of God's Son into our hearts by the sweetness of love and the
ardor of God's good wishes, and the Spirit is our love, through which
we embrace God.[45]

As masculine metaphors used in reference to the First Person of
the Trinity, the words "Abba" and "Father" have been used to cement
patriarchal privileges and customs. This happens particularly whenever divine "fatherhood" becomes an anchor for the use of exclusively male metaphors for God, and males are thought to reflect
God's nature more closely than females. That is Mary Daly's point

---

43. Bruce Metzger, *A Textual Commentary on the Greek New Testament* (Stuttgart: United Bible
Societies, 1975), 595–96.
44. Cf. Silverio Zedda, *L'adozione a figli di Dio e lo Spirito Santo: Storia dell'interpretazione e
teologia mistica di Gal. 4,6* (Roma: Pontificio Istituto Biblico, 1952), 153.
45. William of St. Thierry, *On Contemplating God, Prayer, Meditations*, trans. Sister Penelope, The
Works of William of St. Thierry, vol. 1, 42–9; cf. also Zedda, *L'adozione a figli di Dio*, 163–64,
who suggests William is alluding to Galatians 4:6.

when she speaks of the necessity of going "beyond God the Father." As she puts it: "If God in 'his' heaven is a father ruling 'his' people, then it is in the 'nature' of things and according to divine plan the order of the universe that society be male-dominated."[46] It is also true, as Janet Soskice points out, that the insistence that God is *literally* a "Father" occurs within Christian heresy (not orthodoxy), as in the case of Arianism.[47] Though Christian theologians have always stressed that God is "beyond" categories such as sex and gender, many of them have nevertheless insisted on exclusively male imagery (and in English, male nouns and pronouns) to refer to God, most often on the basis of the male imagery for God used in Scripture.

Admittedly, the Bible is androcentric, but its language for God is not as uniformly male-oriented as it might seem at first glance. Not only is God described in Scripture with female-oriented metaphors often having to do with generativity and motherhood (Gen. 1:2; Deut. 32:18; Isa. 42:14; Matt. 23:37; John 3:5), but some of the classic titles for God that seem to be quite masculine in translation may have female connotations. For instance, *El Shaddai* (Exod. 6:3) and *Shaddai* (Gen. 49:25) are normally rendered "God Almighty" or "Almighty" in English. However, another viable translation of the Hebrew is "God of the breasts" or "breasted God," a variant not often chosen by translators. Clearly such a title would seem absurd to them if they were convinced a priori that they are speaking of what is basically a male deity.[48]

The actual title "Father" for God is comparatively rare in the Hebrew Bible, though the use of parental and spousal images in connection with God is extensive, and can be rooted in patriarchal social expectations in distressing ways. At the same time, parental imagery for God in the Old Testament is often an expression of "God's deepest and tenderest love for the people and of God's vulnerability in the face of this love" and is sometimes couched in

---

46. Mary Daly, *Beyond God the Father: Toward a Philosophy of Women's Liberation* (Boston: Beacon Press, 1973), 13.

47. Janet Martin Soskice, *The Kindness of God: Metaphor, Gender, and Religious Language* (Oxford: Oxford University Press, 2007), 69.

48. Johanna W. H. van Wijk-Bos, *Reimagining God: The Case for Scriptural Diversity* (Louisville, KY: Westminster John Knox Press, 1995), 26–28.

language that is both motherly and fatherly (cf. Hos. 11:1–4).[49]
Those who justify a male-centered worldview on the Bible are on
shakier ground than they might think, and yet the Bible is by no
means a straightforwardly feminist book. It is an ambiguous set
of writings that require us to make a series of interpretive decisions on the basis of what the Spirit helps us discern as faithful
to the good news of the gospel. Here is where understanding the
liberative and pneumatic potential of Paul's theology is of particular importance, since Pauline hermeneutics are so influential for
Christian understandings of just what kind of a "Father" we are
empowered to address by the Spirit of the Son.

Though historically this has not often been the case, addressing the First Person as "Father" can actually serve as a tool for dismantling patriarchal presuppositions. Jerome points out that he is
astounded that despite the explicit prohibition (attributed to Jesus
in Matt. 23:9) of giving anyone except God the honorific "Father,"
the title is so often used in the church for "men of God." He criticizes
both the custom of calling others "abba," or "father," in the monaster-
ies of his time and the habit that some of his readers had of allowing
others to address them as such.[50] His logic is sound, even though he
does not press it to its logical conclusion. Not only is it questionable
to use patriarchal titles for leaders in the church, but the meaning of
fatherhood itself is subverted by the application of the metaphor of
fatherhood to the First Person. God as "Father" is the One who ten-
derly searches for a way to give all persons the rights and privileges
that tend to be reserved only for a few in most societies and who by
so doing unravels a patriarchal logic of exclusion and hierarchy.

In thinking through what this "fatherhood" of the First Person
might mean, it is important always to keep in mind both pneumatological and christological dimensions. The "Father" addressed
in Galatians with a male title is not invested in the maintenance of
hierarchies of any sort and for that reason sends the Spirit "into our
hearts," who is not a Spirit of submission and control but a Spirit
of freedom and liberation. At the same time, the Spirit reminds us
of the way of Jesus and actualizes it for us in our present contexts,

49. Ibid., 44.
50. Jerome, *Commentary on Galatians*, 160–61.

for "within the religious dynamics of Christianity, only the Son can show us the Father. Without the Son, 'the Father' is not God, but an idol."[51] In the path shown concretely by Jesus in his struggle against the powers and principalities of "this evil age," calling God "Abba, Father," makes sense and can function in opposition to the many "fathers" of an unjust system.

A further twist to the question of the "fatherhood" of God comes from looking at the metaphor from the perspective of God's sons and daughters living in poverty and need. As Sobrino points out, it is scandalous to call people "children of God" who seem to live *etsi Deus non daretur* (as if God did not exist). This is not because they do not believe in God but because the dire conditions in which they live are so heartbreaking that they evoke the theodicy question: How can a good God allow this? The real conditions of the world are horrific for immense segments of the population, even though this truth of reality is often covered up by indifference or propaganda. As Sobrino reminds us, whether we call God our "*Abba*, Father," our "Mother," our "Everything," or some other name, God's beloved children are too often innocent victims of injustice, whose rights and dignity in practice depend more on where they were born than on their intrinsic humanity.[52]

To speak of the "children of God" in any sort of significant way, as opposed to justifying with fine but empty words the inequalities and iniquity of our world system, Sobrino holds that theology needs to make progress at least on three fronts. First of all, it needs to seek the way of honesty, speaking about the real conditions of this world rather than covering up the truth. Second, it needs to seek the way of praxis, looking for concrete ways to show what the paternity and maternity of God in this world really mean for God's children. Third, it needs to traverse the way of boldness in faith, countering the discourse of power and showing in what ways the poor of this world are beloved by God, refusing to forget them. Unless the weakest of the weak, with whom Jesus lived in utmost solidarity, are taken into account, any talk of filiation becomes empty and meaningless.[53]

---

51. Soskice, *The Kindness of God*, 83.
52. Sobrino, *La fe en Jesucristo*, 271.
53. Ibid., 268–76.

When the Spirit empowers us to say "Abba, Father" we are saying a word to the world and also to God. Marius Victorinus speculates that by coming to know the Father through Jesus, "we are made into a word of the Father" and on that account become God's children (literally "sons"). This happens in analogy to Christ who knows God and is the Word of God. By the Spirit and the Son, we too become "knowers" of God, enabled to become "a word both to Christ and to God" and "a word of the Father." The implication is that the process of filiation by God's mercy and grace is singularly empowering: "For that reason let us cry out as people who know!"[54] Once again, the metaphor is ambiguous: "word" has often been used in phallocentric ways to displace women and to silence them, not least by the very Marius Victorinus who is providing this interpretive insight. However, it need not be so, given the character of the Spirit doing the empowering.

Once the power of "being" a word and speaking a word is unleashed, possibilities for communication, dialogue, and transformation open up. In my native country of Argentina during the military dictatorship of the 1970s, a huge circular sign was placed on the large Obelisk that is a symbol of Buenos Aires, as a ring is placed on a finger. It read "Silence is health." The slogan ostensibly referred to noise pollution in the city but was an effective reminder to the population that to speak up against injustice was dangerous to one's health and could lead to disappearance or death. The Mothers of Plaza de Mayo disregarded the warning and spoke through their actions, marching every Thursday in front of the federal government buildings: they insisted that they wanted to know where their young adult children were, who had been silenced and made to disappear. It was at this time that to "disappear someone" became a transitive verb in Spanish, and the mothers insisted on finding out who had authorized and carried out such actions. They spoke justice into being by the force of their insistence, against all odds. The strength of their protest was sustained by the bond of filiation that connected them to their children, a force that simply could not be broken, even by death. It is precisely that kind of filial connection that Paul depicts

---

54. Cooper, *Marius Victorinus' Commentary on Galatians*, 310–11.

in this passage as the fierce and tender link that God forges with each of God's children, one that cannot be broken, no matter what the circumstances.

FURTHER REFLECTIONS
Human Trafficking

Discussion about slaves and slavery may seem at first glance like a reference to a problem of the past, but in truth various forms of slave labor are in full force today all over the world. One of the major forms of current human trafficking is forced labor or involuntary servitude. It may happen to a migrant abroad or in a person's home country: for example, in clandestine factories or in domestic settings that may include sexual exploitation. Sex trafficking primarily involves women forced, coerced, or deceived into prostitution. Bonded labor or debt bondage involves the unlawful exploitation of a person's work in order to pay off debt, including debts incurred by relatives and ancestors. According to UNICEF, at least 27 million people in the world are trafficked. Millions of children are forced into the sex trade, abducted, and compelled to be combatants, guards, messengers, porters, cooks, prostitutes, and domestic servants in the context of armed conflict.[55]

Worldwide human trafficking generates billions of dollars annually and continues to expand. Slavery is not limited to poor countries; the United States is a source, transit, and destination country for men, women, and children subjected to forced labor and sex trafficking. Trafficking provides slaves to work in street prostitution, massage parlors, brothels, strip clubs, and domestic service as well as in agriculture, manufacturing, hotel and janitorial services, construction, and health and elder care.[56]

When Paul affirms that we are no longer slaves but rather beloved children of God whose hearts receive God's Spirit of liberation and

55. Cf. UNICEF, "End Trafficking Toolkit," at https://www.unicefusa.org/sites/default/files/USF15_ET_Toolkit.pdf.
56. Cf. "Trafficking in Persons Report," Department of State, United States of America, July 2015, http://www.state.gov/documents/organization/245365.pdf.

freedom, his statement collides with the reality of slavery that is not just a matter of our ancestors who may have been slaves or slave-owners but of our neighbors and family members and perhaps of our own direct experiences. If we are consumers of chocolate, electronics, or many other products, then we are probably colluding directly or indirectly in the economics of slave labor practices as well. If we are to take seriously God's economy of grace and justice, as well as a filial relationship with God that breaks with our slavery "to the elemental spirits" of the world, then the church's mission— literally its sending out by God—will need to take on the economic dimensions of discipleship. If consumption of bodies, services, and products is what drives human trafficking globally, then in order to leave behind the old economy of slavery and death, the church needs to learn concrete ways to refuse to do business that colludes with the contemporary globalized logic of human trafficking within and across national borders.

C.' 4:8–5:26
Walking by Faith in Freedom
(Reprise)

4:8–11
Idolatry Then and Now

In this section Paul picks up the theme of the "rudiments" once again, the "weak and beggarly elemental spirits" (v. 9) that by nature are not gods (v. 8) and yet function in the world as such, to the detriment of those who are enslaved by them. Sobrino makes the important point that although much of modern Western discussion about God has centered on atheism or on the "death of God," what is often lacking is precisely the consideration of the continuing importance of idolatry: that is, the power of false gods among all human groups, whether they think of themselves as religious or not. He emphasizes that Christian theology should not only be a matter of ascertaining whether a person is a "believer" in the existence of God but also deal with a person's disbeliefs: namely, the idols against which a person struggles. Unless there is a dialectical formulation that complements any confession of faith in Christ with a corollary refusal to deposit one's faith in idols, faith remains abstract, empty, and perhaps dangerous, as it allows the coexistence of belief and idolatry.[1]

Christopher Morse constructs an entire dogmatics on the strength of the insight that there is a kind of disbelief central to faithfulness toward God. Said otherwise, "having faith in God means that some things are to be refused credence and trust." It is important, therefore, in doing theology to refuse to give allegiance to that which

1. Jon Sobrino, *El principio-misericordia: Bajar de la cruz a los pueblos crucificados* (Santander: Sal Terrae, 1992), 24–25.

is not of God, which Scripture describes variously as false gods, false prophets, idols, unclean spirits, "and even the Antichrist." Such disbelief is not identical to simple skepticism or to existential doubt, as important as the latter is as a theological theme, but rather hås to do with the insistent recognition that the struggle to be faithful to God (with all our doubts) entails distrust of much that claims to come from God or to be of God.[2] This insight is profoundly (though not exclusively) Pauline, and helpful as a hermeneutical tool in trying to understand Paul's concerns as he writes Galatians: he is consistently aware of the problem of idolatry as a temptation not only outside of the Christian faith, but equally important, *within* it.

> How many there are that would do better not to call themselves Christians because they have no faith! They have more faith in their money and possessions than in the God who fashioned their possessions and their money.
>
> Monseñor Oscar Arnulfo Romero, "Pentecost: Spirit and Life of the New Covenant" (homily, June 3, 1979), http://www.romerotrust.org.uk/homilies/159/159_pdf.pdf.

In societies driven by consumerism and competition, many people, regardless of whether or not they profess a religious faith, share a way of life centered on symbolic and material consumption. Even if we are agnostic or profess atheism, we can still be blind to our own small or large devotion to such "rudiments." Accordingly, to limit the understanding of the "rudiments" only to the Galatians' supposed reliance on the law for their justification, as Luther does, is not only questionable in the context of the epistle (since Paul probably is speaking of the Galatians' fascination with pagan practices, not Jewish ones) but limits its heuristic power for readers today.[3]

To a degree, we all construct our identities through complex processes of consumption of material things as well as of seemingly immaterial ideas that then often gain traction in material ways. Desire and consumption are not necessarily "bad"—we all need to

2. Christopher Morse, *Not Every Spirit: A Dogmatics of Christian Disbelief*, 2nd ed. (New York: Continuum, 2009), 4–6.
3. For Luther's understanding of the passage, cf. Martin Luther, *Luther's Works*, vol. 26, *Lectures on Galatians, 1535 Chapters 1–4*, ed. Jaroslav Pelikan (Saint Louis: Concordia Publishing House, 1963), 402–12.

consume food in order to exist, for instance. Furthermore, there is a sense in which we are consumed with a desire for a deep connection to creation, to other human beings, to beauty, and to God in ways that are profoundly transformative and meaningful. The mystical tradition in Christianity is keenly aware that we are drawn to God and that God generously draws close to us in order to quench our spiritual thirst.[4] The problem comes when our desires and our consumption become distorted and destructive of life; that is when they become "basic principles" or "rudiments" in the Pauline sense.

Some of the "basic principles" that constitute the dominant way of being in the world in a system of globalized capitalism are greed, selfishness, a short-term mentality, anthropocentrism, and trust in violence as a method of conflict resolution. In such a context, consumption becomes a primary practice in everyday life, regardless of income. Even people who cannot afford to buy prestige items can consume them at the level of desire. Religion in various forms is also "consumed," as are cultural artifacts. What is particularly problematic is the interweaving of such consumption patterns with what Hugo Assmann calls the intense "messianization" of the free market economy. By this he means that its unlimited virtues are extolled and its inexorable laws are upheld no matter what the consequences for humanity and for the planet.[5] In discerning the kind of distortions implicit in an unquestioning belief of this kind, it is important to pay attention to the sacrifices that such loyalty demands. If the cost of upholding the principles of any system is marginalization or death for human beings and distress for God's good creation, then its idolatrous character becomes clear.

As Marion Grau has shown, biblical and patristic traditions have much to say about economic desires, expressing a series of convictions about wealth, power, and consumption. Such convictions are then "written" on the bodies of Christians, not always in positive ways. Yet at the core of God's unpredictable divine economy we can discover many forms of "economic" relationships that "resist

---

4. This is one of the convictions that drives the architecture of Augustine's *Confessions* as well as of much of the writing of the medieval mystics of the Latin (Western) tradition, such as Julian of Norwich, Meister Eckhart, and Teresa of Ávila.

5. Cf. Hugo Assmann, *Las falacias religiosas del Mercado* (Barcelona: Cristianisme i Justícia, 1997), 8.

tyranny, stasis and oppression" and allow us to envision strategies of "flexible, miraculous exchanges." For that reason, at its best, theology points—for example—"toward the redemption and release of those women and slaves expropriated by the domination of the profit-driven deified economies of late, or extreme, capitalism."[6] Pauline theology can be helpful in imagining practices of resistance in the face of the kind of consumption and idolatry that drive much of what passes for "normal" in our societies.

In Galatians 4:8–11 Paul describes a situation that is contrary to the liberating potential of the gospel and yet is probably familiar to many of us: the Galatians are letting themselves be driven by "basic principles" that threaten to curtail their freedom and their capacity to resist oppressive structures. The Galatians, when they did not know God (literally, "not knowing God," *ouk eidotes theon*) were formerly bound to the alienating "rudiments" of hegemonic common sense (economic, cultural, religious, social, or a combination of all of them). They were "enthralled" to false gods, literally serving them slavishly. Paul holds that in serving those who are by nature not gods, they had become enslaved to them, a polemic with Old Testament undertones (see 2 Chr. 13:9 and Isa. 37:19). This changed when they came to know God (literally, "knowing God," *gnontes theon*). The "knowing" (v. 9) is placed in a position parallel to the previous "unknowing" of verse 8 and in contrast to it.

Immediately, however, Paul shifts his emphasis, restating the participle he had used in the active voice (knowing God) as a participle in the passive voice: "being known by God" (*gnōsthentes hypo theou*). For Paul we only know God inasmuch as we are fully known by God, a knowledge that is inextricable from love and is expressed in praxis, not in purely theoretical or noetic terms (cf. 1 Cor. 8:2–3 and 13:12). Being known by God is connected closely to the work of the Holy Spirit, so that this text is also an echo of the idea in verse 6 that the Spirit is the one in our hearts, crying "Abba!" As Marius Victorinus puts it, "Having been known by God, they receive the Spirit by which they come to know God."[7]

In what amounts to a denial of the divine economy, however,

---

6. Marion Grau, *Of Divine Economy: Refinancing Redemption* (New York: T. & T. Clark, 2004), 14.
7. Stephan Andrew Cooper, *Marius Victorinus' Commentary on Galatians: Introduction, Translation and Notes* (Oxford: Oxford University Press, 2005), 313.

though the Galatians have been liberated and adopted by God, they continue to bind themselves willingly to the reigning false gods of their society, once again enthralled by them. Such gods have real power and purchase, which increase when more and more people appease them. Though all followers of Jesus should be living according to the counter-hegemonic logic of God's economy of grace, in practice many or perhaps most of us do not, which is one of the great tragedies and sins of the Christian church through history. It ends up eroding the capacity of the church to be light and salt in society.

It is of course in practice difficult to find the right balance between being "in the world" influencing the system from within, and being "against the world," persevering in a counter-hegemonic mode. Sometimes the latter can become so sectarian as to be fully unintelligible to those outside the group. What is required is a certain pneumatic fluidity in ecclesial thought and praxis able to discern contextually what might be in accordance with the divine economy of liberation and what not. When the prevailing ethos of a given time and place crystallizes servitude to gods that are not worthy of service, then the gospel as good news should push the church to act in a counter-hegemonic way. However, wherever a given culture makes space for flourishing, then the gospel as good news should act in cooperation with it. This has to be done skillfully: Traci West speaks of a necessary "strategic resistance," meaning the capacity to recognize multiple contexts and to avoid "a tendency to simplistically assume an oppositional stance to values in the dominant culture," lest we miss opportunities to find genuine accountability and solidarity.[8]

In the case of the Galatians, Paul points out their continued, scrupulous observance of certain religious rituals revolving around the calendar: days, months, seasons, and years (v. 10). What Paul criticizes is not the existence of an early form of the liturgical calendar. Clearly, from the beginning, Christians celebrated Sunday as the Lord's Day, as well as Easter and other important dates. His comments elsewhere also show that he does not consider physical elements involved in the rituals of other religions, such as "food

---

8. Traci C. West, *Disruptive Christian Ethics: When Racism and Women's Lives Matter* (Louisville, KY: Westminster John Knox Press, 2006), 70–71.

sacrificed to the idols," as somehow contaminated or problematic in themselves, as long as they are not hurtful to the growing faith of other people (1 Cor. 8). It is not clear exactly what days, months, seasons, and years are occupying the energies of the Galatians and whether they are Jewish Christian adaptations of festivals such as the Feast of Tabernacles or the Passover or, as is more likely, Gentile non-Jewish practices. It might even be a combination of both.

Augustine thinks that most of the letter is a polemic against exclusive Jewish Christian interpretations of the gospel. However, aware as a pastor of the shortcomings of his own Gentile Christian flock, he takes this passage to be about the relapse of the Galatians "to the superstitions of the Gentiles" and perhaps to the custom of consulting astrologers to designate dates for certain activities.[9] Regardless of the exact nature of the observances, the problem comes when the ritual observance of certain dates and festivals becomes—consciously or unconsciously—an end in itself, one that encroaches on the glorious freedom of the children of God to live lovingly and compassionately in the world, as Jesus did.

Faced with the dismal tendency of human beings to return to their old ways, even if the old ways are alienating, in verse 11 Paul expresses the frustration known by many a minister: Has his work on their behalf, a labor that has taken him to the point of exhaustion, been a complete waste of time? In reflecting on this passage, as a pastor and as the leader of a movement, Luther identifies deeply with these sentiments. He is quite sure that at some point or another, perhaps after he has died, false leaders (which he identifies with the "sectarians") will "take over other churches as well and will infect and overthrow them with their poison." Although Luther's continual polemic against Anabaptists and Roman Catholics can be wearisome and misrepresent them sharply, what is insightful about his commentary on this text is his confidence that, in the end, the church belongs to Christ and is never fully corrupted by our infidelities: "Nevertheless, Christ will continue to reign to the end of the world, but in a wondrous way, as He did

---

9. Eric Plumer, *Augustine's Commentary on Galatians: Introduction, Text, Translation, and Notes,* Oxford Early Christian Studies (Oxford: Oxford University Press, 2003) 185.

under the papacy."[10] From a pastoral perspective Luther sees that though one can attempt to form and to influence the church, it is impossible in the long run fully to determine the course of a congregation's life, for good or for ill.

What surely makes the whole situation with the Galatians all the more frustrating for Paul is that it is precisely a mark of a false god to expect servitude and enslavement from followers. The God of life wants exactly the opposite, namely, to empower all those who are willing to live in freedom as beloved children. The Galatians seem to be disposed to enslave themselves "once again and anew" (Paul uses a redundancy to hammer in his point) to "weak and poor" forces (*ta asthenē kai ptōcha stoicheia*), possibly as a kind of umbrella insurance in the face of a harsh universe. This shows that the Galatians have not yet internalized the character of God. Beyond that, as one who loves them, Paul fears for the Galatians; he is literally afraid for their well-being, given the implications of a life enslaved by the "rudiments." He therefore poses the rhetorical question: "How is it possible that you would want to be enslaved once more?" It seems to him almost inconceivable, and yet it is happening.

4:12–20
Paul as Mother

Paul applies his christological notion of exchange not only to the relation between God and people but also to relationships among people as well. He consequently beseeches the Galatians to become as he is, just as he became as they are. Perhaps this means that he is willing to take on the ways of the Gentiles, that they might come to know God in a manner that previously was possible only in the context of Judaism. The phrase gives us a glimpse of how Paul envisions the practice of discipleship and of ministry: it does not so much consist in an imitation of Christ in every detail, given the cultural and religious differences between the spaces of Jesus' ministry and those of Paul's apostleship. Rather, with the help of the Spirit he tries to

10. Martin Luther, *Luther's Works*, vol. 26, *Lectures on Galatians, 1535 Chapters 1–4*, ed. Jaroslav Pelikan (Saint Louis: Concordia Publishing House, 1963), 402.

internalize the patterns of Christ's way, including that of the wonderful exchange, in a primarily Gentile context.

Paul calls to mind the fact that the Galatians have done him no wrong (v. 12). This may indicate that the Galatians have not yet abandoned the teachings of Paul, yet implies that he fears that they are on the verge of doing so. In the past, they had received him and his gospel at a time when he was afflicted by a physical limitation, perhaps an ailment relating to his vision, as verse 15 may suggest when Paul says that the Galatians would have been willing even to tear out their own eyes to give to him.

Paul's health or lack thereof is a disputed topic among interpreters. Tertullian and Jerome thought that Paul's "thorn in the flesh" (2 Cor. 12:7) was that he suffered from severe headaches, whereas Augustine and Chrysostom held that this simply meant that Paul had to put up with the painful resistance of his opponents.[11] In Galatians he speaks of a physical infirmity or sickness of the flesh (v. 13) and also of a condition in the flesh that put the Galatians to the test (v. 14). It may even be, as Troy W. Martin suggests, that his "weakness" in the Galatian context was the very fact of his circumcision, because in that culture it would have "made him a prime target for derision," as can be seen in writers such as Tacitus, Petronius, Juvenal, and Martial, as well as indirectly in Philo's apology for the practice.[12]

Despite his situation (whether an illness or his status as a circumcised male), Paul makes the point that the Galatians neither made light of him (*exouthenēsate*) nor disdained him (*exeptysate*) on that basis.[13] The former verb could mean treating someone as a nonentity, and the latter verb, which literally means to "spit out," was used at times in ancient literature to speak of warding off evil spirits. Here, much to the contrary, Paul remembers how he was welcomed warmly, as a very angel of God, embraced and received as kindly by the Galatians as Christ himself might have been. Said otherwise, his

---

11. J. B. Lightfoot, *St. Paul's Epistle to the Galatians* (London: MacMillan, 1896), 186–91.
12. Cf. Troy W. Martin, "Whose Flesh? What Temptation? (Galatians 4.13–14)," *Journal for the Study of the New Testament* 74 (1999): 65–91.
13. Cf. Alfio Marcello Buscemi, *L'uso delle preposizioni nella lettera ai Galati* (Jerusalem: Franciscan Printing Press, 1987), 57, for the material force of this construction.

words were received as a message of divine origin and his mission perceived as genuine.

Whatever the nature of his ailment, Paul had been in a place of vulnerability but was not made to suffer additionally because of it. When he had been weak, the Galatians were strong for him; in turn he allowed himself to become as they were, aliens to the ways of God revealed to Israel, so that they might become as he was: namely, a child of God according to the promises made to Abraham. However, rather than the christological pattern of exchange that he advocates and has already experienced with them in the past, at the moment when he writes the letter two variants of wrong kind of exchange seem to be emerging. The first wrongful sort of exchange has to do with the relationship between the Galatians and Paul and the second with the dynamic between the Galatians and Paul's opponents.

First of all, though in the past when he was weak and vulnerable, the Galatians received him warmly, treating him as a friend, now that he is presumably well and strong, they are treating him coldly, and even as an enemy. Though previously they did not scorn him, now they seem on the verge of doing so. He therefore addresses them with pointed rhetorical questions (vv. 15–16): "What has become of the goodwill you felt?" This question (which can more literally be rendered "where, then, is your blessing?") refers to a former frame of mind, in which they were able to bless themselves and others. It echoes the language of Psalm 31:1–2 (LXX).[14]

Paul sees them tottering on the verge of cursing rather than blessing. "Have I now become your enemy by telling you the truth?" In this question Paul sets himself up implicitly as a representative of truth, so that if the Galatians indeed move to enmity with him, they will position themselves in opposition to God's truth. Jerome speculates that Paul had exhorted the Galatians to leave behind "childish elements, syllables, and reading habits, and to aspire to more advanced things," but they reacted by rebelling and becoming angry. He suggests that church people often appreciate literal explanations of Scripture but that when "a modest attempt" is made "to nudge

14. Walter Bauer, *A Greek-English Lexicon of the New Testament and Other Early Christian Literature*, trans. and adapt. William F. Arndt and F. Wilbur Gingrich, 2nd ed. (Chicago: University of Chicago Press, 1979), 487.

them on to greater things," in order that they might mature spiritually, they turn against their teachers and go "from being panegyrists
to being our enemies."[15] If he is correct, when the first excitement of
conversion wore off and the adverse consequences of discipleship
for life in an imperial setting became more vivid, Paul's Christology
of exchange may have begun to seem unexpectedly burdensome to
the Galatians.

Second, Paul argues that his opponents seem to make much of the
Galatians, but in reality they do so in order to exclude them, so that
the Galatians might in turn make much of them as their new objects
of desire (v. 17). It is not evident precisely what kind of exclusion
Paul has in mind, whether an exclusion through insulation or exclusion by withdrawing fellowship. He may mean that the Galatians
are in danger of being cut off from him or even from Christ. What
is clear is that he vividly describes the power dynamics of a certain
kind of seduction whereby the Galatians are simultaneously courted
and pushed away. The verb he uses three times in verses 17–18 when
he speaks of "making much" of someone (*zēloō*) is related to the
English word "zeal" and can also be translated as "paying court." It
can be used both in a good sense, as in being deeply concerned with
somebody's well-being, or more negatively, as when somebody is
filled with envy. Paul is using the word in its positive sense but with
a tinge of irony. Much zeal is being manifested on all sides, but as for
the Galatians, they should always direct their energies toward what
is good, regardless of whether or not Paul is around.

Paul then shifts rhetorical gears and addresses the Galatians as
his children, in a more tender tone. Contrasting himself implicitly
with those who want to seduce the Galatians, he places himself in
the peculiar standpoint of a mother, a person who can speak with
authority because she has put her body on the line for her children.
Not only did he suffer the pangs of birthing them in the past but is
now reliving that pain "until Christ is formed" in them (v. 19). He
says that he wishes he could be with his spiritual children and speak
to them in person in order to find the right way to communicate

---

15. Jerome, *Commentary on Galatians*, in *The Fathers of the Church: A New Translation*, vol. 121,
trans. Andrew Cain (Washington, DC: The Catholic University of America Press, 2010),
173–74.

with them and to be able to change the tone of their conversation. As it is, he is sorely perplexed.

The idea of becoming ever more Christlike appears often elsewhere in Paul's epistles: for instance, in Romans 8:29, 2 Corinthians 3:18, and Philippians 3:10. In this passage, Paul links the notion of likeness to Christ to the metaphor of pregnancy and childbirth. After the Exodus from Egypt, during the time of wandering in the desert, Numbers 11 depicts Moses as overwhelmed with trying to deal with all the needs of the children of Israel. He angrily demands of God whether his duties as the leader of Israel are to include mothering the people: "Did I conceive all this people? Did I give birth to them, that you should say to me 'Carry them in your bosom' . . . ?" (Num. 11:12).[16] The implication is that God is Israel's Mother, not Moses, and therefore that God should provide the needed mothering. Here, by contrast, Paul willingly presents himself as a mother to the Galatians (v. 19), engaged in "messianic labors," trying to rebirth them and to "metamorphose them back into the conformity with Christ" that they are tempted to give up in order to conform again to the dominant order.[17]

What are we to make of Paul's assumption of motherhood? Is it a case of creative gender-bending or does he assume a maternal role in a way that pushes actual women aside? Some caution is warranted here, as it is not unusual in Christian tradition and elsewhere for some men to claim that they are better at carrying out what they have identified as a female role than women themselves. This can serve both to naturalize culturally determined gender roles and then to displace women even from the advantages that might be linked to aspects of those roles. Feminist philosopher Celia Amorós rightly points out that it is a quite common discursive strategy for a male writer to become a "woman" (*devenir femme*) in order supposedly to inhabit a place of otherness, only to then depoliticize it.[18] Another common strategy is briefly to acknowledge the female metaphor, but then immediately either to ignore it or to masculinize it. That

16. Jerome mentions this parallel of Moses with Paul; cf. *Commentary on Galatians*, 179.
17. Brigitte Kahl, *Galatians Re-Imagined: Reading with the Eyes of the Vanquished* (Minneapolis: Fortress, 2010), 284.
18. Cf. Celia Amorós, *Tiempo de feminismo: Sobre feminismo, proyecto ilustrado y postmodernidad* (Valencia: Ediciones Cátedra, 2000), 334–49.

is Luther's move when he says that Paul's words when he calls the Galatians his little children are "gentle and soothing" but then immediately shifts in his commentary to a focus on apostolic fatherhood and—interestingly—on the "fatherhood" of Christ.[19]

Despite these possible pitfalls, it is worthwhile to try to take "Paul's reconfigured self-image seriously," as Davina Lopez recommends: "Paul as a mother crying out in labor with her Christ-shaped children is a provocative (trans)gendered image that should be just 'sat with' in its complexity."[20] It is suggestive that Paul's emphasis on masculinity (the "seed") should shift, after Galatians 3:28, in the second half of the chiasm, to female-oriented metaphors, such as that of his own motherhood of the Galatians and the paradigmatic roles of Hagar and Sarah. This hints at the fact that Galatians 3:28 may be more of a piece with the logic of the whole epistle than some feminist critics have feared when they have suggested that the equality presented in that text mirrors neither the lived social experience of early Christians nor is a deep reflection of Pauline theology.[21] Taking into account the intersectionalities of sex, gender, race, economics, and politics, Lopez suggests that Paul's birth pangs signify the formation of new relationships in a new creation within the "present evil age" of Roman imperial domination and in opposition to it. Thus, "Paul's fertility with the Galatians is born of the physical pain and struggle of care and support among the conquered."[22]

Though a cult of motherhood can certainly be one of the faces of patriarchal logic, when motherhood is linked to Christ and to the Godhead it can actually undermine the monopoly of masculine metaphors for God and God's work, opening doors for more expansive metaphors for the Divine than have been customary in most of Christian tradition. If one reads Paul's claim with a christological dynamic of exchange in mind, whereby what he means to do is to take on the patterns and attitudes of Christ with respect to the

19. Luther, *Luther's Works*, vol. 26, *Lectures on Galatians, 1535 Chapters 1–4*, 430–31.
20. Davina C. Lopez, *Apostle to the Conquered: Reimagining Paul's Mission* (Minneapolis: Fortress, 2008), 142.
21. Sheila Briggs, "Galatians," in *Searching the Scriptures*, vol. 2, *A Feminist Commentary*, ed. Elisabeth Schüssler Fiorenza (New York: Crossroad, 1994), 218–21, is representative of many feminist suspicions in this regard, which are understandable but perhaps not the whole story.
22. Lopez, *Apostle to the Conquered*, 144–45.

Galatians, the passage can be seen to point indirectly to the maternal love of Jesus for the children of God.

In this sense, Julian of Norwich's development of the idea of Jesus as Mother has a certain Pauline flavor: in being as a mother to the Galatians, Paul is being Christlike, and if they become like Paul, then they in turn will become maternally generative and Christomorphic. For Julian, "all the lovely works and all the sweet loving offices of beloved motherhood are appropriated to the second person."[23] In contrast, Augustine links Paul's maternal office in Galatians not to Christ or to God but to "the person of Mother Church."[24] Julian's insight seems to get more profoundly at the heart of what is at stake in Paul's christological logic of exchange. If, as Julian states, "as truly as God is our Father, so truly is God our Mother," what the "faith of the Holy Church" should do is lead us to find "our beloved Mother" in God.[25] Paul's "motherhood" likewise only makes sense at a more profound theological level if it links the Galatians to the motherhood of Christ and ultimately to the maternal generativity of the Triune God.

Paul ends the section almost poignantly, stating that he wishes he could be present with the Galatians in order to be able to change his tone (literally, his "voice") and presumably experience and thus express a different kind of mood, one less stern and more akin to the positive moments of the past. He knows that he has influence on the Galatians and that his actual presence would make a difference, yet as things stand and he receives news of them from afar, he is almost at his wits' end.

FURTHER REFLECTIONS
Paul's Logic of Exchange

A christological logic of interchange is consistently present in Paul's theology. Christ became as we are that we might become

---

23. Julian of Norwich, *Showings*, trans. Edmund Colledge and James Walsh, The Classics of Western Spirituality (Mahwah, NJ: The Paulist Press, 1978), 296.
24. Plumer, *Augustine's Commentary on Galatians*, 191.
25. Julian, *Showings*, 296–302.

as Christ is. Christ becomes a curse that we might attain God's blessing (Gal. 3:13–14). Christ, who was rich, becomes poor that we might be enriched (2 Cor. 8:9). Likewise, Paul becomes as the Gentiles are, so that they (we) might be in Christ, as he is (Gal. 4:12; cf. 1 Cor. 9:19).

The Pauline logic of exchange is also at the heart of early Greek theology. For instance, in the *Epistle to Diognetus* from the late second century we read: "O the sweet exchange! O work of God beyond all searching out, O blessings past our expectation, that the wickedness of many should be hidden in one righteous Man and the righteousness of the One should justify many wicked!"[26] Around the same time, Irenaeus of Lyon writes that the Word becomes human and the Son of God becomes the Son of the human being, so that the human being might be adopted as a child of God.[27] Perhaps the best known version of the interchange is that of Athanasius of Alexandria, in the fourth century, who states quite simply that Christ assumed humanity that we might become God.[28] In the Latin tradition Augustine of Hippo also picks up a similar theme in the *Confessions*. Speaking of Christ, he writes: "He who for us is life itself descended here and endured our death and slew it, by the abundance of his life."[29]

The Reformers continue in this vein. Martin Luther speaks of the "joyous" or "fortunate exchange" (*fröhlicher Wechsel*), though he connects it less to the doctrine of the incarnation than he does to the cross. He conceives of a kind of interchange of attributes between Christ and human beings.[30] For his part John Calvin writes of the marvelous exchange (*mirifica commutatio*) made possible by God's great kindness towards us. In the context of a discussion of the Lord's Supper, he waxes poetic:

26. *The Epistle to Diognetus* (IX.5), trans. Henry G. Meecham (Manchester: Manchester University Press, 1949), 87.
27. Irenaeus, *Against Heresies* (III.19.1), in *The Writings of the Fathers down to A.D. 325. The Ante-Nicene Fathers*, vol. 1, ed. Alexander Roberts and James Donaldson (repr., Grand Rapids: Eerdmans, 1993), 448.
28. Athanasius, *On the Incarnation* (LIV), trans. and ed. A Religious of C.S.M.V. (Crestwood, NY: St. Vladimir's Orthodox Theological Seminary, 1953), 92–93.
29. Augustine, *Confessions* (IV.12.19), trans. Henry Chadwick (Oxford: Oxford University Press, 2008), 64.
30. Luther, *Luther's Works*, vol. 26, *Lectures on Galatians, 1535 Chapters 1–4*, 284.

This is the wonderful exchange, which, out of his measure-less benevolence, he has made with us; that, becoming Son of man with us, he has made us sons of God with him; that, by his descent to earth, he has prepared an ascent to heaven for us; that, taking on our mortality, he has conferred his immortal-ity on us; that, accepting our weakness, he has strengthened us by his power; that, receiving our poverty unto himself, he has transferred his wealth to us; that taking the weight of our iniquity upon himself (which oppressed us), he has clothed us with his righteousness.[31]

The pattern of exchange combines asymmetry (the situation of human beings and of God) with symmetry (God becomes one of us that we might become as God is) in a poetic, satisfying way. It cannot function as a theory: it is not primarily an explanation but rather a description of the Christian experience of transformation and identification with God. It has the merit of bringing to the fore a profoundly mystical vein of Christian experience, but it loses force if it is cut off from the concrete human history of Jesus of Nazareth. That God in Christ becomes poor, that the poor might become rich, is not only metaphorical: it has specific social, economic, and politi-cal implications.

4:21–5:1
Covenant Relation with God: Hagar and Sarah

This passage is uncomfortable on many levels. It seems that Paul manages to use language that today could easily alienate both Jews and Muslims by seeming to disengage historical Judaism from the "heavenly Jerusalem" while at the same time setting up the Abraha-mic lineage through Hagar, now claimed by Islam, as inferior. At the same time, given the history of chattel slavery in the United States and its relation to white racism, the references to Hagar are doubly troubling.

Regardless of Paul's intentions, given the history of white racism,

31. John Calvin, *Institutes of the Christian Religion* 2.17.2; ed. John T. McNeill, trans. Ford Lewis Battles, Library of Christian Classics (Philadelphia: Westminster Press, 1960), 1362.

it becomes problematic to accept Paul's tenet that it is better to be the descendant of the free woman rather than of the slave woman. In today's context it might seem to imply that descendants of enslaved Africans in the Americas are somehow lesser human beings than those who do not descend from slaves, something that white supremacists in fact believe. Because people who quote Scripture fluently have often also been the ones buttressing white racism, an awareness of the possibly inflammatory nature of Paul's discourse in the context of countries where white racism has been a deep historical problem is essential. It is ironic that the words of the apostle of liberation, who above all else wants the Galatians to experience the glorious freedom of the children of God, could be used to shore up injustice and inequality, but it can happen all too easily.

Paul's justification for his handling of the text is that he is attempting an allegorical interpretation of the covenant relationship with God based on the stories of two mothers, Hagar and Sarah, along with their respective sons by Abraham, Ishmael and Isaac. Allegories can be problematic because they harden the plurivalent meaning of a narrative, editing it down to focus on details that fit into the allegorical structure while leaving out important pieces of the story. Scholars argue about what Paul even meant by the expression "spoken in allegory" or "the things being allegorized" (*allēgoroumena*) in verse 24, in part because the verb "to allegorize" does not appear elsewhere in the New Testament or in the Septuagint. It seems that he is interpreting Sarah and Hagar as representatives of two different covenants so that he utilizes what was later called typology: that is, the study of Old Testament "types" as precursors to New Testament persons or events. Typology is a specific variant of what is usually called allegory: namely, describing one thing under the guise of another and therefore assigning a new "spiritual" meaning to elements or images in a story.

The early church, following Paul's lead in this passage, often employed *allēgoresis* in the sense of typological interpretations of the Old Testament, for example taking the sacrifice of Isaac to prefigure the death of Jesus or Jonah's three days in the great fish's belly to foreshadow the days between the cross and the resurrection. This allowed for a christological interpretation of the Old

Testament, as practiced most famously by Origen, who went as far as to argue that *all* of Scripture consists of mysteries to be uncovered spiritually.[32]

The tendency to universalize allegorical interpretation earned distrust already in Origen's own day (for instance on the part of some of the Antiochene theologians) because of its intrinsic arbitrariness. That is one reason why the Reformation eventually reacted against "allegorical" readings and tried to return to a historical and literal understanding of Scripture, confident that the literal meaning of a passage has its own spiritual significance. Given the ambiguities of some passages of the Bible, however, a "plain sense" reading is not always possible, so that subtle forms of allegorizing tend to appear even among the most historically or literally minded interpreters.[33]

In this passage, Paul—who himself could be accused of arbitrariness in his choice of images and interpretation—uses typology in order to continue to hammer away at his argument that if as Gentile Christians the Galatians think they are obliged to become Jewish Christians, then they will be giving up a central tenet of the good news of the gospel: freedom. His so-called allegory is therefore meant to challenge the Galatians to act according to the freedom that he believes is inherent to the gospel, not according to the logic of the "elemental spirits" or of certain religious rites or customs, whatever their origins. His argument is set out on the basis of two premises he has already tried to develop in the previous sections. First, subjection to the law results in a lack of freedom whenever the law is treated as something of ultimate rather than penultimate value. Second, through Christ, the Galatians have become heirs to the promises of God to Abraham. Their inheritance is not based on their subjection to the law but on their status as adopted children of God with full rights.

By developing the allegory on the basis of the story of two mothers, perhaps Paul is building further on the theme of his own role as a "mother" to the Galatians. He may even be giving a nod to a

---

32. Origen, *On First Principles* (IV.3.5), trans. G. W. Butterworth (Gloucester, MA: Peter Smith, 1973), 296–97.
33. Cf. Jean Grondin, *Introduction to Philosophical Hermeneutics*, trans. Joel Weinsheimer (New Haven: Yale University Press, 1994), 28–41.

cultural context in which mother goddesses were commonly worshiped.[34] He wants them to identify with Sarah, whom he presents as a free woman, a type of the free, heavenly Jerusalem, and mother of a child born by the work of the Spirit. He does not want them to choose the lot of Hagar, whom he depicts as a slave, a type of the enslaved, earthly Jerusalem, and mother of a child born from the work of the flesh. By setting up this opposition, Paul identifies Jewish Christianity, and perhaps also Judaism proper, with what is "earthly," as contrasted to Gentile Christianity, which is identified with what is "spiritual" or "heavenly." He further accuses Jewish Christianity (and presumably also Judaism in the iteration to which he had previously belonged) of persecuting Gentile Christianity, as Ishmael supposedly persecuted Isaac, according to the Septuagint version of Genesis 21:9–10.

Paul says nothing of the power differential between Sarah and Hagar or between Isaac and Ishmael. Neither does he mention the Genesis narrative's emphasis on the care of God for Hagar and Ishmael, including God's promise that they would become the ancestors of a great people. As Jerome points out, Ishmael was also begotten according to God's promise, even if the covenant promise was given to Isaac.[35] As he did with his reflections on the promise to Abraham, Paul edits out of the narrative whatever does not serve his argument. For example, he omits the fact that the son of a free man with a slave woman would have at that time been considered free, so that Ishmael and Isaac would have actually been equals on that count, whatever the legal status of their mothers.[36] He also flattens out the story in order to make his allegorical argument, leaving out the character nuances and ironies present in the Genesis narrative.

As Delores S. Williams points out in her influential interpretation of Hagar from the perspective of womanist theology, Hagar is the first female in Scripture to liberate herself from oppressive power

---

34. Cf. Susan M. Elliott, "Choose Your Mother, Choose Your Master: Galatians 4:21–5:1 in the Shadow of the Anatolian Mother of the Gods," *Journal of Biblical Literature* 118 (1999): 661–83, who argues for a central Anatolian context where many mountain mother goddesses, local expressions of the great Mother goddess, were worshiped and served by self-castrated functionaries, or *galli*.

35. Jerome, *Commentary on Galatians*, 183–86.

36. Elsa Tamez, "Hagar and Sarah in Galatians: A Case Study in Freedom," *Word and World* 22 (2000): 265–71.

structures, including brutal treatment on the part of Sarah. She is depicted in Genesis as a woman with great autonomy who performs tasks (such as choosing a wife for her son Ishmael in Gen. 21:21) that in that culture were often reserved for men. With faith, hope, and resilience this African slave woman struggles and works through "issues of survival, surrogacy, motherhood, rape, homelessness and economic and sexual oppression;" she has inspired "generation after generation of black women because her story has been validated as true by suffering black people."[37]

In Islam, Hagar is remembered as "Our Lady Hajar." Parts of her story are reenacted by pilgrims on the hajj as they move swiftly between Safa and Marwa and recall God's saving intervention on Hagar's behalf at the well of Zamzam. Hagar is revered by many Muslims and Christians all over the world, especially by "women without land, humiliated, excluded, with lost identities and frustrated dreams," because she embodies the hope that God sees them, goes out to meet them, and takes their needs into account, no matter what their social, economic, cultural, ethnic, or geographic provenance.[38]

In the Old Testament account, Hagar calls God *El-roi*, "God of seeing" or "God who sees" (Gen. 16:13), and God tells her to name her son *Ishmael*, "God hears," for God hearkens to her and shines God's face on her. She encounters God and lives to tell the tale (Gen. 16:13). By contrast, the clarity of Hagar as a paragon of liberation and comfort is diluted in Paul's allegory, because he is not interested in her as a historical figure, only as a negative type. That is what allows him to present her paradigmatically as the outsider and the "other" to Sarah, with whom we are to identify as heirs of the promise.

Some classic rabbinical interpretations also take Sarah to represent Jerusalem, while Hagar stands for otherness or even for paganism. Later, in the ninth and tenth centuries, the nature of Hagar's servitude takes on significance not only in the context of debates between Muslims and non-Muslims but also within Islam, specifically between Arab and non-Arab Muslims (such as the Persians),

37. Delores S. Williams, *Sisters in the Wilderness: The Challenge of Womanist God-Talk* (Maryknoll, NY: Orbis, 1993), 33.
38. Rita M. Ceballos, "Agar, una experiencia de Dios liberadora," in *Actas del Primer Congreso de Teólogas Latinoamericanas y Alemanas: Biografías, Instituciones y Ciudadanías,* CD format, ed. Carolina Bacher Martínez et al. (Buenos Aires: Teologanda, 2008), 13.

with the latter identifying as descendants of Isaac and looking down on the Arab descendants of Hagar as the *lakhnā*, the slave. Those Arab Muslims who, in turn, defended the honor of Hagar as their ancestral mother, often depreciated Sarah. Today the two sons and their respective mothers sometimes are made to stand in paradigmatically for tensions between Israeli Jews and their Arab Muslim neighbors.[39] None of these polemical binaries are very satisfying theologically, based as they are on an ethnic or religious othering that masks the profound commonalities between the groups in question and focuses only on delineating a difference based on exclusion or caricature.

The inherent difficulties of following Paul's argument too straightforwardly when he identifies Israel with Hagar and the Christian church with Sarah led some interpreters early on to identify "Sarah" with the capacity for mystical interpretation and "Hagar" with literal readings that engendered a "spirit of fear."[40] This solution allows for a bit of interpretive leeway. Augustine, for example, expands the allegory to fit his context. He adds the sons of Abraham with his later wife Keturah (Gen. 25:1–2), the "sons of a free woman," yet born "according to the flesh" in order to symbolize the "heresies and schisms" of the Manichees and Donatists against whom he was struggling in his North African church.[41] Augustine's free hand with the text, if not necessarily convincing with regard to his argument, is at least an example of the need for a contextual interpretation, even if it does not resolve the internal tensions within Paul's allegory or do justice to the patterns of injustice and grace within the Hagar and Sarah dynamic as it is depicted in Genesis.

No matter how it is read, Paul's allegory does not constitute his finest theological hour. Luther, who warns that to use allegories is often a dangerous thing, excuses Paul's use of it because he sees him as a "very fine craftsman" in handling allegories. Luther allows for a limited use of allegories because they are sometimes helpful for moving and persuading the common people, especially the simple

39. Zakaria Rhani, "Les récits abrahamiques dans les traditions judaïque et islamique," *Archives de Sciences Sociales des Religions* 53 (2008): 27–46.
40. See Jerome, *Commentary on Galatians*, 88.
41. Plumer, *Augustine's Commentary on Galatians* Augustine, 195.

and uneducated.[42] However, even in the best of cases, for Luther they "do not provide solid proofs in theology" but serve as icing on the cake, or as he puts it, "as an ornament for a house that has already been constructed."[43]

In the case of this passage it may well be that Paul's allegory does more to harm than to decorate the house he wants to build. In particular, the tendency toward dualism that appears in the dyad of flesh and spirit in his allegory pushes against the strong commitment to materiality present in the doctrine of the incarnation, elsewhere a strong undercurrent of the epistle. That commitment is what grounds Paul's Christology of the marvelous exchange and bolsters his defense of a contextual path of faith for Gentile Christianity, so that in one sense the implications of his allegory tend to weaken his own position, rather than strengthening it. Given its intrinsic theological debility, it comes as no great surprise that Paul's allegory has not served him or Gentile Christianity very well through the centuries.

The motherhood theme reappears, once again as a positive dimension of his argument, when Paul relates Sarah to the "Jerusalem above" as one who is free herself and mother of the free (v. 26). Sarah was once barren but by God's grace bore a child of the promise, something that Paul seems to link to a quotation from Isaiah 54:1 (LXX), which in its Old Testament context hearkens back to the exilic Jews who joyfully returned to Jerusalem from Babylon. It would seem that for Paul the way to be a child both of mother Jerusalem and of mother Sarah is through the work of the Holy Spirit (v. 29). Freedom in Christ drives out any sort of bondage to the "rudiments," who are not to share in the inheritance of the "free woman." The Galatians, as children of their "mother" Paul, are called to renounce any practices that are contrary to the freedom of the gospel and to rejoice.

The section ends with a conclusion more vigorous than the weakness of the allegory perhaps warrants but which is nevertheless bracing, reaching the level of Paul's better moments: "For freedom Christ has set us free." As Elsa Tamez reminds us, Paul's allegory

---

42. Luther, *Luther's Works*, vol. 26, *Lectures on Galatians, 1535 Chapters 1–4*, 433.
43. Ibid., 435–36.

about Hagar and Sarah is ultimately incomprehensible if we pluck it out of the larger context of the epistle and its urgent call to live firmly in freedom.[44] Luther immediately moves to interpret this freedom not politically, as he says that the sectarians do, but as a freedom that takes place in the conscience and provides liberty from God's wrath.[45] However, especially for oppressed groups throughout history, the prospect of the glorious freedom of the children of God continues to hold a political and material promise, imbued with a spirituality that is never divorced from the flesh. This is perhaps the best perspective from which to read Paul's circuitous argument, if it is to not become in itself an excuse to diminish the freedom of others. When we consider freedom in Christ from this perspective we will always ask how it translates into "specific freedoms for free human beings with specific bodies."[46]

5:2-6
Faith Working through Love

Paul ratchets up the intensity of his argument here even further, with the interjection "Look!" or as the NRSV has it, "Listen!" The imperative followed by "I, Paul" is emphatic indeed. He seems to continue to speak as a "mother" to the Galatians in a tone that mixes reproach, admonishment, and a certain confidence born of mutual love and affection. It is not just anyone speaking, but Paul, whom they know so well. Given their shared history, he believes that he has the right to speak out forcefully and command their attention. He wants their full concentration, because he will now speak of circumcision.

Paul had mentioned the topic peripherally in 2:3 when he recalled that the Jerusalem leaders did not ask him to circumcise his coworker Titus, a Greek. In 2:7 he had mentioned the gospel for the circumcised (Peter's ministry) and the gospel for the uncircumcised (his own mission). Nevertheless, to this point in the letter, the practice of circumcision has not been at the forefront of his critique,

---

44. Tamez, "Hagar and Sarah in Galatians," 265.
45. Cf. Luther, *Luther's Works*, vol. 26, *Lectures on Galatians, 1535 Chapters 1–4*, 439–61.
46. Tamez, "Hagar and Sarah in Galatians," 271.

though he does identify his opponents as "those of the circumcision" or the "circumcision faction" (*tous ek peritomēs*) in 2:12. After having circled around the problem of making Jewish Christian practices indispensable or even salvific for Gentile Christians, he suddenly moves to discuss circumcision, quite bluntly and straightforwardly.

He paints himself as a kind of witness for the prosecution (v. 3) who testifies in no uncertain terms, and not for the first time, that for Gentile Christians to enter into the logic of the circumcision and to allow themselves to be circumcised means for them to become debtors to the law in its entirety, in a way that obligates them morally to fulfill it. Gentile Christians such as the Galatians are in danger of letting themselves be talked into circumcision because they mistakenly understand certain aspects of the law to guarantee their connection to God as God's children and heirs to Abraham's promise. In reality what they are doing is to misunderstand the law, making it into something ultimate rather than penultimate and building an unnecessary fence around the gospel.

Calvin, who is unwilling to discard the value of circumcision either for Abraham in the Old Testament or for Timothy in the New Testament, observes that Paul's reasoning is directed not so much "against the outward rite or ceremony, as against the wicked doctrine of the false apostles." For the Reformer, that false doctrine consisted in making circumcision in the Gentile context a "necessary part of the worship of God" or a "ground of confidence as meritorious work."[47]

Paul allows himself a pun in verse 4, pointing to an idea that he will pick up in much more vigorous language in verse 12. Here he plays on the notion of something being "dissevered" or "cut off" (*katērgēthēte*), as indeed happens in circumcision; he then tells the Galatians that what they are really

> Are you a lover of the Law? Keep the basics of the Law: have love for your neighbor, the whole Law being fulfilled in this. Faith has removed the difference between circumcision and uncircumcision.
>
> "The Letter to the Galatians," in Theodoret of Cyrus, *Commentary on the Letters of St. Paul*, vol. 2, trans. Robert Charles Hill (Brookline, MA: Holy Cross Orthodox Press, 2001) 19.

47. Calvin, *Calvin's Bible Commentaries: Galatians and Ephesians*, 128.

about to cut off is their reliance on the grace of Christ to provide sufficient access to God's promises for them as Gentile Christians. Christ will be "profitless" or of "no benefit" to them if they persist in adding on burdens and obligations to what is meant to be a gift from God. To embroider on grace or to reject it means to be graceless. Said otherwise, justification is a gift given in and through Christ; to add the obligation of circumcision to the Gentile practice of Christianity is tantamount to "falling from grace" (v. 4).

The verb chosen here by Paul, *ekpiptō*, can be used of a withered flower that falls to the ground, of a boat that drifts off its course or runs aground, or it can be applied figuratively, as it is here, to losing something—in this case God's grace or favor.[48] The expression should probably be understood in the context of Paul's rather grim humor about what is being "cut off" and what is "falling" given the Galatians' flirtation with the need to add requirements from Judaism to shore up their grasp on the gospel of Jesus Christ. If they focus on circumcision, what they will lose is their own grip on grace rather than gaining a deeper connection to the God they desire to know.

Rather than this "falling" into a life not buoyed by grace, Paul wants to promote life in the Spirit. He believes that the faith that characterizes the existence of those who follow Jesus in the Spirit promotes their capacity to experience the hope of justice intensely (v. 5). Furthermore, faith is energized by love through the work of the Spirit (v. 6) so that it becomes not only faith seeking understanding but also faith seeking effectiveness (*fides quaerens efficacitatem*), as José Míguez Bonino has put it.

Míguez Bonino remembers the life of Camilo Torres, a Colombian university professor and Roman Catholic priest from a rich and aristocratic family who, to the amazement and horror of many in his context of origin, became a left wing guerrilla fighter and was killed in 1966. Míguez Bonino describes Torres's understanding of the Christian life: It means taking into account the particular and concrete needs of human beings and developing the practice of love not as a mere sentiment but rather as "a conscious and intelligent effort"

---

48. Cf. Bauer, *A Greek-English Lexicon of the New Testament*, 245.

under given historical conditions "to change the basic economic and social structures that produced the misery of the majority of his people." In this way, faith becomes efficacious or effective through love, a love that in turn must be effective.[49] Whether or not Torres's application of just war theory to his context was efficacious in the way he would have desired, the principle that Christian faith is a pneumatic force that demands concrete expression in love is a central tenet of liberation theology, and without it no theology can claim to be liberating. It is also profoundly Pauline: circumcision or uncircumcision are penultimate; what really is serviceable, worthwhile, or counts (*ischuei*) in Jesus Christ is faith that makes itself active or works effectually through love (*pistis di' agapēs energoumenē*), as Paul states in verse 6.

Only a lived-out, concrete faith expressed in love is truly able to connect us to what is ultimate. Faith without love is meaningless, or as Balthasar Hubmaier put it, "[m]ere faith alone is not sufficient for salvation." He adds, "mere faith does not deserve to be called faith, for a true faith can never exist without deeds of love."[50] Here is where one sees the limits of "justification by faith alone" when it is separated out from the praxis of the Holy Spirit, which always entails love. "Faith alone" is too abstract a concept to function well as a description of the active, concrete, material way of Jesus Christ, which requires action in the midst of a messy, ambiguous world.

> "Neither circumcision nor uncircumcision is of any *empowerment* but faith working through love."
>
> Aliou Cissé Niang, *Faith and Freedom in Galatia and Senegal: The Apostle Paul, Colonists and Sending Gods* (Leiden: Brill, 2009), 131.

The effectiveness sought by faith does not function according to the logic of pragmatism. It has nothing to do with instrumental reason and everything to do with taking incarnation and its implications seriously. It is all too easy to spiritualize the justice for which

---

49. José Míguez Bonino, *La fe en busca de eficacia: Una interpretación de la reflexión teológica latinoamericana de liberación* (Salamanca: Sígueme, 1977), 69–71.
50. See Balthasar Hubmaier, *Theologian of Anabaptism*, ed. and trans. H. Wayne Pipkin and John H. Yoder (Scottsdale, PA: Herald Press, 1989), 526–27.

we hope, as Jerome seems to do by circumscribing our hoped-for justice to the event of the second coming of Christ.[51] Paul was not talking only in terms of futuristic eschatology but always also of a realized or present eschatology: the realized aspects of hope do not cancel out hope's future dimensions; one actually drives the other. Those who follow Jesus by the Spirit are called to be involved in the peace and justice of God's reign as it takes shape concretely on earth in large or small ways, in anticipation of Christ's desired and imminent return.

There is a gender subtext in Paul's polemic against circumcision as envisioned by his Jewish Christian opponents and presumably also increasingly by the Galatians. Though he speaks in generic terms (v. 3) of those who allow themselves to be circumcised, by definition his admonition can only fully apply to males. If in Christ there is no "male and female" as well as no "Jew or Greek" and "slave or free" as he has tried to establish in 3:28, then it makes sense for the central rites and symbols of God's gift of grace in Christ to be less gender-specific than the male circumcision being contemplated by the Galatians.

As Maurus Victorinus realizes, for Paul, "when it comes to faith, all else ceases to count." That includes "social status, gender, or anything done that concerns the body, whether about, on, or for the sake of the body."[52] It is not that the bodily dimension can ever be unimportant, given the doctrine of the incarnation, but rather that certain bodily markers (for instance gonads and what is done to them in ritual fashion) are not at the center of what symbolizes grace in Christ. From a gender perspective, this can be good news. Circumcision is phallocentric, both literally and figuratively. To allow it to remain secondary in our consideration of grace could help disarticulate male-centered understandings of how God works in the world. In turn, that could open up spaces for reimagining circumcision as a practice in new contexts, such as that of the reality of combating HIV/AIDS.

51. Jerome, Commentary on Galatians, 199.
52. Cooper, Marius Victorinus' Commentary on Galatians, 330.

FURTHER REFLECTIONS
Male Circumcision and HIV/AIDS

The significance of male circumcision changes according to context and circumstances, which is why Christian theology cannot take the logic undergirding Paul's strictures about circumcision seriously without taking into account the cultural fluidity of its meaning. HIV/AIDS brings this sharply into focus. In the world today there are millions of people infected with the virus, and it has become the primary killer of young adults globally. Though expensive treatments do now exist that can prolong life, there is still no cure for the disease. Many people do not have access to such medical care. Indeed, HIV/AIDS has become primarily a disease of the poor, both of poor people in wealthy nations and of poor nations.[53] It is also in many ways a gendered disease: married women, for instance, are one of the most vulnerable groups to infection, and women and girls are primarily tasked with taking care of the sick.[54] The area most affected at present by the pandemic is sub-Saharan Africa, which at the same time is one of the areas of the world where Christianity continues to grow and find contextual expressions of great dynamism.

   In the conversation about how to prevent the spread of HIV/AIDS, male circumcision has become an important topic. Scientific research has shown that uncircumcised men who are sexually active are much more vulnerable to the virus than those who are circumcised. This is because the virus binds itself to cells called Langerhans cells, contained in the foreskin and the area under the foreskin, allowing it more easily to penetrate the skin. Circumcised men are therefore not as likely as uncircumcised men to contract the virus or to pass it on to others. Even though circumcision cannot in itself stop the spread of the virus, the World Health Organization and UNAIDS have suggested that it would be helpful to implement

---

53. Alan Whiteside, *HIV/AIDS: A Very Short Introduction*, Very Short Introductions, vol. 174 (Oxford: Oxford University Press, 2008), xi–xii.
54. Mandy Marshall and Nigel Taylor, "Tackling HIV and AIDS with Faith-Based Communities: Learning from Attitudes on Gender Relations and Sexual Rights within Local Evangelical Churches in Burkina Faso, Zimbabwe, and South Africa," *Gender and Development* 14, no. 3 (2006): 363–74.

circumcision of male infants as a prevention strategy.[55] In Southern Africa circumcision has begun to emerge as a rite of passage in puberty for many boys, but ironically the practice itself, if carried out with an infected knife, can actually serve to spread the disease.

Notably, in the past what primarily determined whether a boy was circumcised in Africa was religion: as a rule, Christians did not practice it, while Muslims did. In that sense, it could be said that Paul's influence reached deep into the continent, where Gentile Christian churches have generally discarded circumcision. Could it be time to change this practice, given shifting circumstances? It would seem that anything that churches might do to alleviate the transmission of the virus would be consonant with the good news for the Gentiles that Paul tried to preach. It might be possible simply to shift circumcision to the realm of health care, largely uncoupling it from religious meaning. However, when communities of faith are able to work alongside health experts, the results are encouraging. This has happened in Zimbabwe, for example, where Muslims have worked with the national Ministry of Health and Child Welfare and health oriented nongovernmental organizations to promote male circumcision, as have some traditionally circumcising communities such as the Tshangani.[56]

A brave and significant step theologically for Christians worldwide would be for churches not only to find ways to rethink and perhaps even to promote infant male circumcision in the context of frank discussions of Christian sexual ethics and gender justice but also to rethink baptism as a symbol of gender equality. In other words, in the face of HIV/AIDS, it would be good to revisit not only Paul's arguments about circumcision but also the gendered implications of his understanding of "putting on Christ." Otherwise, it may well be that distorted Christian beliefs about the one-sided submission of women to men and of wives to husbands will continue, feeding into a gendered sexual double standard in Christian communities of faith. When this is the case, "married women within

55. Cf. Whiteside, *HIV/AIDS*, 37–38.
56. Julia Samuelson and Kim Dickson, *Progress in Scale-Up of Male Circumcision for HIV Prevention in Eastern and Southern Africa: Focus on Service Delivery*, revised (Geneva: World Health Organization Document Production Services, 2011), 19. Available at http://whqlibdoc.who.int/publications/2011/9789241502511_eng.pdf.

the church are unable to challenge the unfaithfulness of their husbands, or negotiate the use of a condom for safer sex. Both these situations may increase the risk of infection with HIV."[57]

Paul's argument against circumcision in the Galatian Gentile context is about allowing an emerging indigenous expression of Christianity to find its way without adding rituals or practices that are not negative per se but are also not intrinsic to the flourishing of life in Christ in a non-Jewish context. Could it be that in the era of HIV/AIDS, those very principles of contextual expression of the materiality of the gospel could lead Gentile Christian communities to readopt male circumcision as part of a wider commitment to the sexual health of the churches?

The obstacle to circumcision as Paul believes it is practiced among his Jewish Christian opponents is not that circumcision is a bad thing in itself. As Augustine correctly points out, if circumcision were to cut a person off from Christ by definition, then Paul never would have circumcised Timothy (Acts 16:3). The problem is that his opponents "had placed their hope for salvation in circumcision of the flesh."[58] As Jerome puts it, "circumcision is of no value when it is thought to confer intrinsic benefit."[59] In the end for Paul the central question is not circumcision in itself: its presence or its absence is simply not the operative point. He makes almost exactly the same observation in 1 Corinthians 7:19, where he remarks that both circumcision and uncircumcision are "nothing," but what matters is "obeying the commandments of God in everything."

What is most important for Paul in this passage is the way in which faith and hope are worked out. By the work of the Spirit of God in our world, faith becomes active and is made effective through love (v. 6). Citing Galatians 5:5, 2 Corinthians 1:22, and Ephesians 1:13–14, José Comblin argues that the Holy Spirit is the presence of God's kingdom in the present time and the beginning of God's reign or commonweal on this earth. The problem historically has been the

57. Marshall and Taylor, "Tackling HIV and AIDS," 370.
58. Plumer, *Augustine's Commentary on Galatians*, 199.
59. Jerome, *Commentary on Galatians*, 196.

loss of the link between the kingdom of God as proclaimed by Jesus in the gospels and the emphasis on the Holy Spirit in Paul.

At times Christianity has tended to understand the Spirit as the "sign of a purely internal transformation within the human being," forgetting the social and historical dimensions of pneumatology and projecting onto Scripture the Church's increasingly narrow understanding of God's reign, especially within Christendom.[60] Here as always in Galatians, being conscious of the pneumatological dimension of Paul's writing in view of the concrete life of Jesus of Nazareth and his followers in a given time and place is not only an important key to interpretation but a safeguard against losing the counter-hegemonic, subversive edge always latent in the epistle.

Ultimately, despite his polemical tone, Paul does not pit circumcision against uncircumcision, or the Christian circumcised against the Christian uncircumcised, but rather places all such matters squarely in the realm of the penultimate. What is central to those "in Christ Jesus" is faith expressed materially and concretely through the active love of God and neighbor, which after all is arguably the same thing that is aimed at in the Torah (Paul will quote Lev. 19:18 to this effect in 5:14). Under closer scrutiny, by this logic, in light of the life and teachings of Jesus as recorded in the gospels, any deep division between "faith" and "works" makes no sense, for the outcome of a loving faith is expressed in tangible, concrete ways. Paul and James (2:18) are not really opposed to each other after all.

It would be easy to overlook the glue that holds the exercise of a faithful love and of a loving faith together in hope, but it can be seen through the lens of a pneumatic Christology and conversely of a Christological pneumatology. Christians are in the Spirit and they are in Christ, so that the hope of justice emerges in the

> **Faith must be confessed *on earth*. For this reason, love is its sign, which means that it may not be flight from the world or navel-gazing.**
>
> Ernst Käsemann, *On Being a Disciple of the Crucified Nazarene: Unpublished Lectures and Sermons,* trans. Roy A. Harrisville (Grand Rapids: Eerdmans, 2010), 163.

60. José Comblin, "Espíritu Santo," in *Mysterium Liberationis: Conceptos Fundamentales de la Teología de la Liberación* vol. 1, ed. Ignacio Ellacuría and Jon Sobrino (Madrid: Trotta, 1990), 631.

Spirit (v. 5), just as in Christ faith is made active through love (v. 6). Pneumatologically based hope stays firm in the face of injustice, or as Theodoret puts it, "having received the pledge of the Spirit and believing in the promises, we look forward to the life awaiting us, which is adorned with immortality and not subject to the assault of sin."[61]

Hope for the future is not—Theodoret's emphasis notwithstanding—just a matter of a future after death, for it is embedded "in Christ." It is anchored in the life of faith manifested concretely in love in the present, so that just as the Spirit is never without the Son nor the Son without the Spirit, our present hope is never without our future hope, even as the future of God is already coming toward us in Jesus Christ. Theodoret's adornment of immortality or (as Paul had expressed in 3:27) being clothed with Christ begins here and now. As Jürgen Moltmann reminds us, because the God of hope is the "coming God" (Isa. 35:4; 40:5), entering into God's future makes possible a new "human becoming" in the present.[62]

5:7–15
Freedom for Service

Paul, who is fond of athletic metaphors, comes back in verse 7 to the image he had used in 2:2, comparing the way of discipleship to the discipline of running. In 2:2 he describes how he met with the leaders of the Jerusalem church in order to make sure—or more accurately to garner their agreement to the effect—that he was himself not running "in vain." He now wonders whether the Galatians may themselves be running in vain, for though they had previously been running well, they are now letting themselves be confused by the obstacles being put on their course. Whereas the NRSV translates his question as "who prevented you from obeying the truth?", one might also render the phrase as "Who put obstacles in the way of you being persuaded by the truth?"

---

61. "The Letter to the Galatians," in Theodoret of Cyrus, *Commentary on the Letters of St. Paul*, vol. 2, trans. Robert Charles Hill (Brookline, MA: Holy Cross Orthodox Press, 2001), 19.
62. Jürgen Moltmann, *The Coming of God: Christian Eschatology*, trans. Margaret Kohl (Minneapolis: Fortress, 2004), 24.

Something or someone is impeding their way and hindering them from hitting their stride, and Paul thinks he knows what is happening. In his view, they are being persuaded by an argument that does not come from God (v. 8). God is the One whose very character it is to call what is good into being and who continues to call them to run in the direction of grace, and God does not put needless obstacles in the path of those who are committed to running well in the footsteps of Jesus.

A proverb then illustrates the problem at hand: "A little yeast leavens the whole batch of dough" (v. 9). Paul uses the same saying in 1 Corinthians 5:6 to indicate how a negative influence can grow. The gospels also sometimes use the figure of yeast as something that spreads and is negative, for instance a lack of trust in God or religiously inspired hypocrisy (Mark 8:15; Luke 12:1). However, yeast can also be used as a metaphor for the expansion of a good influence, as happens in Jesus' parable where the kingdom of God is like a yeast that leavens three measures of flour (Matt. 13:33 and Luke 13:21). For Paul the connotation is always negative (see also 1 Cor. 5:7–8). The implication here is that if the Galatians allow certain attitudes to ferment, such as placing circumcision or other religious obligations (whether of Jewish or pagan origin) as requirements for receiving the gift of grace in Christ, their whole experience of God will be distorted.

Having uttered the proverb, Paul continues speak as a mother who expresses confidence that her children will not allow themselves to be detoured from their course by those to whom they now seem to be giving too much of their attention. He begins his sentence in verse 10 once more with the emphatic "I" that he used in verse 2, as if to say, "I, at least, no matter what others might think, continue to trust in you." He plays up his own powers of persuasion, against the persuasive powers of his opponents, playing on variations of the same root word in verses 7, 8, and 10 to describe the Galatians (in the process of being persuaded), his opponents (the persuaders), and himself (persuaded in the Lord). His own expression of confidence, equated with being "in the Lord," is in itself meant to be persuasive: "if you are indeed in Christ, then I know you won't be fooled." As an added measure, he also warns of the consequences for those who mislead the Galatians: regardless of who they might be, and no matter what their status, they will bear the burden of judgment. Augustine does not think that the "persuaders" had yet succeeded in gaining control over the Galatians, and if he is right, then Paul's desire to persuade the Galatians himself becomes all the more urgent.[63]

For a third time Paul has recourse to the emphatic first person singular (v. 11) in order to ask a rhetorical question: Why would I still be persecuted by my Jewish Christian opponents, if I continued to uphold the centrality of circumcision for Gentile Christians? The phrasing seems to imply that perhaps the Galatians thought he did not care one way or the other about the matter or that he even supported circumcision for the Gentile church. As a matter of fact, he is so much opposed to the introduction of additional ritual requirements to the gospel of Christ for a Gentile context that he holds that to defend such requirements, or even to be indifferent to them, would be tantamount to abolishing the "scandal of the cross." The persecution to which he refers may be included in the catalog of troubles that he mentions in 2 Corinthians 11:26, which includes dangers that he faces due to his "false siblings" in Christ.

What does Paul mean by the offense or scandal of the cross (*skandalon tou staurou*) in verse 11? It may well refer to the scandal or offense caused by the crucifixion of Jesus. The expression could also mean the scandal or offense constituted by the cross itself as an instrument of torture and execution. The cross is scandalous and is a cause for stumbling because it was a punishment reserved for persons who somehow undermined the law and order of the Roman Empire and were therefore seen as "terrorists" or "subversives." The death of Jesus on the cross was so ignominious that the very idea of a "crucified Messiah" seemed laughable if not destructive to the hope of messianic transformation of a corrupt order. Yet this person, executed as a criminal, was the one confessed as "Christ" or "Messiah" by the early church.

There are at least two senses in which the cross should always be a "scandal" to theology. First, we should never forget that it is shocking

---

63. Plumer, *Augustine's Commentary on Galatians*, 201.

and scandalous to torture and execute human beings under any circumstances, even when they seem culpable according to prevailing logic. The reasoning of empire always tends to justify the execution of those branded as enemies and to accommodate the death of innocent people who cannot be accused of enmity, such as infants and children, as inevitable "collateral damage" in the pursuit of enemies. This has been the reasoning of the United States government in using bomb-laden drones to target areas in Pakistan inhabited by people suspected of leadership in terrorist organizations such as al-Qaeda or in executing men such as Osama bin Laden without the benefit of a trial. The death of Jesus on the cross likewise means that for the Roman Empire he was considered either "collateral damage" or—more likely—potentially a threat to Roman hegemony. On the cross Jesus takes on not just any human death, but the kind of death that is considered "justified" by imperial power and is a signal of the success of its policies of governance and control.

Second, the cross should be a "scandal" to theology whenever the history of God's solidarity with the human condition, as symbolized by Jesus' death on the cross, is used to excuse and even to glorify torture and execution, rather than to put an end to it. This is at the heart of the feminist critique of certain approaches to substitutionary atonement that seem to celebrate suffering as good in itself and to use the cross to encourage women or others to endure mistreatment willingly, as if enduring abuse had in itself salvific value.

The notion of the cross as a salvific message only makes sense if it represents God's absolute solidarity with humanity in even the toughest of situations (that is, if God really was present and acting in Jesus). The "cross" should also serve as shorthand for the subversion of death in the resurrection. The "scandal of the cross" can only represent hope if it is a symbol of the wonderful exchange whereby God enters into the plight of creation, in order that creation might enter fully into the life and glory of God. Yet even for those who find in the cross such a symbol of hope, it is scandalous, impossible to explain fully, and difficult to digest. In the face of dominant common sense, as a model for God's commitment to the world and God's involvement with creation, it is a continual provocation.

As Paul is learning through his experiences in ministry, it is all too easy for people of faith to disarm the power symbolized by the cross, sometimes inadvertently. He has no patience at all with any sort of Christian leadership that only weakens the scandal of the cross. That is why, in vexation, he throws out one of his most memorable phrases (v. 12). If the people (in this case, clearly men) who are disturbing the Galatians indeed think circumcision is so indispensable to Gentile Christianity as to make it central to discipleship, then Paul can only wish, quite heartily, that they would go all the way and emasculate themselves! Augustine calls this Paul's "elegant ambiguity," by which he inserts a blessing in the guise of a curse, for he provides a way at least for them to become "eunuchs for the kingdom."[64] Marius Victorinus puts it more bluntly: "Let them not only be snipped around, but let them also get it cut off."[65] The interjection *ophelon*, which can be translated "I wish," or more poetically "oh that" or "would that," presupposes an impossible wish rather than a concrete hope yet clearly exposes Paul's exasperation. He uses the interjection in a similar ironic vein in his polemic against the Corinthians, whom he perceives as "puffing themselves up," when he tells them "I wish you had become kings, so that we might be kings with you!" (1 Cor. 4:8).

Jerome quite cleverly uses Paul's hyperbole to illustrate the errors of Marcion, Valentinus, or anyone else wishing to undermine the Old Testament on the pretext of its supposed depiction of "the Creator as a savage, bloodthirsty war-monger and unrelenting judge." He points out that as a matter of fact nowhere in Old Testament law is there ever pronounced "a sentence nearly so harsh and cruel" as Paul the apostle of the good God enunciates here against his opponents, when he wishes they would be "forcibly castrated." He concludes: "Whatever excuse they give for Paul, we shall return in kind with a defense of the old Law."[66]

Paul's hyperbolic statement in verse 12 is problematic at many levels, and we should probably not try to "harmonize" it into a smooth interpretation or try to justify it. Joseph Marchal, who finds Paul's words "flippantly violent," reminds us that surgical castration still occurs regularly in the case of intersex infants (whose external

---

64. Plumer, *Augustine's Commentary on Galatians*, 203.
65. Cooper, *Marius Victorinus' Commentary on Galatians*, 334.
66. Jerome, *Commentary on Galatians*, 216.

organs don't "match up" to their internal ones according to medical protocol) in the interest of fitting them up with socially prescribed "male" or "female" bodies, before they reach the age of consent. Such surgeries lead to mental and physical pain and suffering, to "marks" on the body that cannot be undone, and should be taken into account as we read this text today and ponder how bodies continue to be conceptualized and marginalized and how religious argumentation about bodies can be used to justify cruelty and exclusion.[67] Perhaps this is a case of *Paulus contra Paulum*: Paul's own words may need to be "anathemized" for the sake of the good news of the gospel.

Paul now makes an abrupt rhetorical shift. He addresses the Galatians directly, no longer as a mother speaking to her children, but now as a brother speaking to his siblings in Christ (v. 13). He reminds them that they were called to freedom, yet he qualifies that freedom in a very particular way: it does not mean freedom for narcissism and self-indulgence but rather the freedom to love, to serve and to do good to others. The phrase literally means "do not use liberty to give opportunity to the flesh" (*eis aphormēn tē sarki*). It needs to be interpreted carefully, without falling into the habitual trap of making the "flesh" out to be simply synonymous with human embodiment or human sexuality. A fragment of Origen's *Miscellanies*, preserved by Jerome, is helpful here. Origen understands Paul to say that those who have pursued the Spirit and truth and thus have attained a deep understanding of spiritual realities should not look down on those "who cannot grasp spiritual profundities." On the contrary, such a person should minister to the weaker siblings, to make sure that a person "for whom Christ died may not perish in deficiency of knowledge."[68]

Paul clinches his argument by quoting Leviticus 19:18, by which the continuity of his thought with the Old Testament is made once again very clear. Indeed, as the prophets had stated before him, mercy, compassion, and love manifested in concrete and practical ways, not in any particular religious rite, are the point of the law. That

67. Joseph Marchal, "Bodies Bound for Circumcision and Baptism: An Intersex Critique and the Interpretation of Galatians," *Theology and Sexuality* 16 (2010): 163–82. In part because of Paul's shift toward "motherly" language in the next section, I do not think Paul's discourse in the letter is as androcentric as Marchal does.
68. Origen, *Miscellanies*, quoted in Jerome, *Commentary on Galatians*, 217.

is why Jeremiah 4:4 speaks of the circumcision of the "foreskin of the heart," which unlike physical circumcision is gender-inclusive. Paul's polemical style waxes and wanes and can all too easily be coaxed by people of bad faith in directions that seem anti-Jewish or to crush whatever other opponent du jour may be at hand, but one sees consistently in Paul that he is not against circumcision or the law per se, simply against their distortion.

> What business in the Christian's heart has the wildness of wolves and the savagery of dogs, and the deadly poison of snakes, and the bloody cruelty of wild beasts?
>
> Cyprian of Carthage, *The Unity of the Catholic Church*, IX, in: *On the Church: Select Treatises*, ed. and trans. Allen Brent (Crestwood, NY: St. Vladimir's Seminary Press, 2006), 161.

The imperative to fulfill the spirit of the law by loving and serving one another is not just a lofty goal but a profoundly practical one for the life of the community. Augustine asks himself why Paul chooses to summarize the whole meaning of the law, both here and in Romans 13:8–10, in terms of the manifestation of love for neighbors, without mentioning love for God. He concludes that it is quite easy to lie and dissimulate about one's love of God but that a clear test of whether or not love for God is genuine can be seen in whether or not a person loves others, as 1 John 4:20 also points out.[69] Those who do not practice love and compassion, and in fact treat each other aggressively, "biting and devouring each other," easily end up destroying or consuming each other (v. 15). The verbs that Paul chooses here, namely, to bite, to devour, and to consume, had been used in Greek since classical times to describe wild animals struggling to the death.[70] It is not clear whether there was such extreme strife in the Galatian communities, but Paul has painted in a few words the type of dynamic that can ultimately destroy a congregation.

Cyprian of Carthage, in the face of ecclesial strife in his third-century North African context, points out that the dove, the symbol of the indwelling of the Holy Spirit in the church, "is a purely simple and joyful living creature." He adds, pointedly, that "it is not

---

69. Plumer, *Augustine's Commentary on Galatians*, 207.
70. Kenneth S. Wuest, *Galatians in the Greek New Testament* (Grand Rapids: Eerdmans, 1944), 152.

venomously bitter, it does not bite savagely, its claws do not clash
with violence." Doves, he says, "recognize the concord of peace in
the kiss of a beak," and that is the kind of divine affection that should
prevail in a church setting.[71] Whether in Galatia, North Africa, or
elsewhere, when church members begin to attack each other, they end
up destroying the community.

> The powers of God that
> counter evil and the forces
> of sin, freeing creation from
> self-jeopardy and self-
> destruction, often come in
> most astounding modesty.
>
> Michael Welker, *The Work of the Spirit:
> Pneumatology and Pentecostalism* (Grand
> Rapids: Eerdmans, 2009), 229.

Perhaps, given the enormity
of our challenges not only within
church communities but also the
church's responsibilities to society
and creation, the image of the mild
dove evoked by Cyprian should
be supplemented with the Spirit
as the "Wild Bird who heals," the
Spirit as the green face of God, evoking "wildness, chaotic creativity
and embodiment" as well as healing, pushing us to love not just our
human neighbor as ourselves but also to love all of God's beautiful creation, of which we are a part.[72] Self-destructive behavior in
the church cannot be understood in isolation from the wider self-
destructive habits of humanity in society and in nature.

FURTHER REFLECTIONS
Loving Oneself

The ethical structure evident both in Paul and in the Leviticus tradition that he quotes is based on the presupposition that a person
has a measure of self-regard. In this vein, Juan Luis Segundo writes
movingly about faith as a basic human experience, since everyone
needs to have confidence in something or somebody, as well as
a basic modicum of self-confidence, in order to be able to negotiate even the simplest tasks of life. He calls this "anthropological

---

71. Cyprian of Carthage, *The Unity of the Catholic Church* (IX), in *On the Church: Select Treatises,*
ed. and trans. Allen Brent (Crestwood, NY: St. Vladimir's Seminary Press, 2006), 160.
72. Mary C. Grey, *Sacred Longings: The Ecological Spirit and Global Culture* (Minneapolis:
Fortress Press, 2004), 116–17.

faith"— the necessary human trust that has to exist before trust and faith in God can emerge.[73] Love for oneself along with the capacity to love and trust others is taken for granted in all of these formulations, yet the matter of self-hatred along with the consequent hatred of the neighbor is worth pondering. What happens when people despise their neighbors because they despise themselves and despise themselves because nothing in their life experience has taught them they are lovable and worthwhile?

If a whole societal structure (such as the logic of the U.S. incarceration system or of its immigration laws) continually tells certain people in actions, if not in words, that they are despicable and worthless, how are such people to find their way to loving themselves? How are they to be loved as neighbors if they are not considered lovable or even fully human? Judith Butler makes the point that in our society certain lives are not considered worth taking into account, and certain deaths have become literally unthinkable and therefore ungrievable.[74] She is thinking primarily of the "collateral damage" of U.S. military strikes abroad, but the same goes for undocumented immigrants dying in the desert as they try to cross the Mexican-U.S. border or for the young people of color dying daily of gunfire wounds on the south and the west sides of Chicago. In the face of a system that renders the vulnerable faceless and insignificant, love of neighbor requires making space for that neighbor to love himself or herself—and to live. Here the profound wisdom of Alice Walker's description of a womanist falls sharply into relief: "Loves music. Loves dance. Loves the moon. *Loves* the Spirit. Loves love and food and roundness. Loves struggle. *Loves* the Folk. Loves herself. *Regardless.*"[75] From the perspective of Galatians, that *regardless* reflects the power of the Holy Spirit opening up spaces for love and for life.

73. Juan Luis Segundo, *La historia perdida y recuperada de Jesús de Nazaret: De los Sinópticos a Pablo* (Santander: Sal Terrae, 1991), 20–25 and 40–46.
74. Judith Butler, *Precarious Life: The Powers of Mourning and Violence* (New York: Verso, 2004), 19–49.
75. Alice Walker, *In Search of Our Mothers' Gardens: Womanist Prose* (New York: Harcourt Brace Jovanovich, 1983), xi–xii.

5:16-21
Living in Opposition to the Spirit

In this section Paul illustrates in a detailed way, through the use of a catalog of attitudes and actions, what a life of freedom should look like for followers of Jesus. It is a life infused by the Holy Spirit, able to avoid the traps of self-indulgence and narcissism, and is guided by the Spirit to follow creatively in the path of Jesus. Especially in Paul's extensive portrayals of the work of the Spirit in this passage and in Romans 8:1-17, the "sheer range of the Spirit's scope and activity" becomes apparent. The Spirit enables "everything from justification to the final manifestation of the children of God, from faith to prayer," from ethical behavior to a filial relationship to God.[76] The wideness and variety of the range of the Spirit's activity in Paul's depiction means that the Spirit is not only at work sporadically in occasional miraculous manifestations, or exclusively in human interiority, but is present and at work in all of the cosmos, without neglecting the human dimension of God's liberating and transforming work.

Kathryn Tanner has pointed out that in modern times a bifurcation has emerged between two understandings of the Spirit's role. The first is that of the Spirit at work in exceptional events (rather than in everyday life), bypassing human fallibility and appearing only when ordinary human operation comes to an end. She argues that this understanding easily lends itself to justifying an "infallible certainty of moral insight" because what is attributed to the Spirit seemingly has no human mediation and therefore admits no ambiguity. The second is a conception of the Spirit at work "gradually, and without final resolution, in and through the usual fully human and fully fallible" processes of ordinary life. The second understanding is important because it shows "the ability of the Spirit to make do with the fallibility, corruptions and confusions of human life" for the Spirit's own purposes. Working in, through, and with human limitations, the Spirit opens up surprising possibilities. The second conception also holds great potential, Tanner thinks, for the dialogue between science and religion, allowing for the investigation of the complexities of natural

---

76. Alasdair I. C. Heron, *The Holy Spirit: The Holy Spirit in the Bible, the History of Christian Thought, and Recent Theology* (Philadelphia: Westminster Press, 1983), 46.

processes.[77] Paul's reflections in Galatians on living in the Spirit are akin to the second understanding. They reflect the complexity of living in the way of Jesus in an embodied manner in the midst of the ambiguities of our relationships in and with the world.

In order to drive his point home, Paul first contrasts a life guided by the Spirit with a life dedicated to the "works of the flesh." Living "in the Spirit" requires that a person should not carry out "the desire of the flesh" (v. 16). The desire of the "flesh" is antagonistic to the Spirit, and the Spirit is "against the flesh," for they are in opposition to each other and have their hearts set upon different objectives (v. 17). Paul's language can be very tricky to interpret, for in the wrong hands, the hostility he posits between "Spirit" and "flesh" becomes an excuse for polemic against bodies in general and female or other subaltern bodies in particular.

Jerome, for instance, construes verse 17 in the light of ascetic practices aimed at conquering bodily desires through fasting and prayer: the flesh, he writes (referring primarily to the body) "fears the cold, despises hunger" and is "attenuated by vigils."[78] Even though he also interprets verse 17 figuratively as the antagonism between a literal, superficial understanding of Scripture and an allegorical, spiritual sense, distrust and dislike of the body persists as a subtext of his discussion of the "carnal" sense of Scripture.[79] From the subjugation of the "flesh" to the castigation of the body as a regular spiritual practice is a very short step, one already taken to extremes quite early in Christian history.

One sees in the Desert Fathers and Mothers, for instance, a struggle to keep a balance between the bodily practices of asceticism and the centrality of charity and mercy. They sometimes exhibit a very negative attitude toward their own bodies and equate sexuality with "lust" and (if they are men) habitually see women as agents of temptation or of the devil.[80] At the same time, one finds in their sayings

---

77. Kathryn Tanner, "Workings of the Spirit: Simplicity or Complexity?," *The Work of the Spirit: Pneumatology and Pentecostalism*, ed. Michael Welker (Grand Rapids: Eerdmans, 2009), 87–88.
78. Jerome, *Commentary on Galatians*, 226.
79. Ibid., 226–27.
80. Cf. *The Desert Fathers: Sayings of the Early Christian Monks*, trans. Benedicta Ward (London: Penguin Books, 2003), 33–52.

subtler perspectives: for instance the notion that the human body is like a coat that will last a long time if it is treated carefully but will fall apart if it is neglected[81] or that it is better to eat meat and drink wine than to "eat the flesh of the brothers by disparaging them."[82]

Sadly, from the severe ascetic discipline and punishment of one's own body "for the good of the soul," which was impressive to many in the Greco-Roman world, we can trace a fairly direct trajectory to a justification of the use of such practices against the bodies of others. We see this throughout history in majority-Christian societies both inside and outside of the church: not only in the Inquisition or the Middle Ages but also much more recently by military and paramilitary interrogators in Latin America in the 1970s and 1980s, by contemporary U.S. forces through the use of waterboarding and other extreme interrogation practices, or in the U.S. system of incarceration with its "solitary confinement." All of these practices are justified by their users in that they invoke "a greater good" to be had from this harsh treatment of bodies, either for the individual being tortured or for the wider ecclesial or national community.

Kelly Brown Douglas describes the demonization of the flesh/body and the tendency to promote antagonistic dualisms such as body/spirit as a "Platonized Christianity," which she links to the Christian justification of torture and lynching of black bodies by white people. She rightly describes such dualism as a heretical tradition. She also points out that there are some significant elements of Christian theology that resist this dualism, in particular the incarnation and the event of the crucifixion/resurrection, when they are taken seriously and their implications worked out.[83] On the other hand, she identifies Paul as "perhaps the earliest and certainly most influential representative of this Platonized tradition," especially given his preference for celibacy and his rigoristic sexual ethic.[84]

However, given the centrality of the incarnation and the cross/resurrection event for his theology, an argument can be made that Paul does not subscribe to the Platonized dualism she rightly

81. Ibid., 49.
82. Ibid., 28.
83. Kelly Brown Douglas, *What's Faith Got to Do With It? Black Bodies/Christian Souls* (Maryknoll, NY: Orbis, 2005), xv–xix et passim.
84. Ibid., 30.

critiques but rather subverts it in accordance with the "divine opposition to dualistic relationality" that she finds in the path of Jesus
of Nazareth and in Black church traditions that are not antagonistic to the body or to sexuality.[85] As she confesses, "to me, as long as
there continues to be a Christian story that has protected, empowered and advanced the sacred dignity of human bodies—especially
those of black women—then I can continue to be a Christian."[86] The
question remains, then, whether Paul's theology promotes a hurtful
dualism or whether it can play out differently and function as good
news for all bodies, especially for those who have suffered the consequences of the dualism Brown Douglas describes.

Any consideration of the "flesh" in Galatians should keep in mind
the centrality of the incarnation for Paul's theology and the fact that
the backbone of the epistle is a Christology of the exchange by which
Christ becomes what we are in order that that we might become as
Christ is: namely, children of the promise, free to live and flourish
in love. To interpret "flesh" simply as "body" or "embodiment" does
not make sense if the cornerstone of God's work of redemption in the
world is the incarnation of the Second Person, "born of a woman" in
the fullness of time (4:4). Despite the centrality of incarnation and
resurrection to Paul's Christology, all too often the "desires of the
flesh," as he describes them, have been interpreted in ways that focus
one-sidedly on human sexuality. The remedy against "illicit" sexuality has been understood as the pursuit of a disembodied spirituality
that tries to repress or ignore bodily needs and desires.

What Paul actually says to the Galatians about the "flesh" (*sarx*)
is that it is a way of life characterized by desires that go against the
Spirit of life and of freedom. Such desires end up driving people
to live in ways they really do not want to live (v. 17), somewhat as
addictions tend to do. The force of such desires is that they have the
ability to co-opt the deep human longing to live in peace and harmony by satisfying various lesser cravings or ambitions in ways that
are ultimately hurtful to human freedom.

Among the distorted desires of the "flesh" Paul does mention a
trio of attitudes that seem to refer primarily to expressions of human

85. Ibid., 86.
86. Ibid., 221.

sexuality: *porneia* (lewdness or fornication, a word sometimes used elsewhere in the Bible figuratively for idolatry, as in Rev. 17:2), *akatharsia* (which again can be translated as lewdness or impurity and is also used sometimes in a metaphorical sense as impurity of motives, as in 1 Thess. 2:3) and *aselgeia* (licentiousness, lasciviousness, intemperance, or even insolence, as perhaps in Mark 7:22). None of these imply that sexuality is in itself bad but rather that an obsession with sex as one's primary focus in life is detrimental. Each of these attitudes, when considered in their sexual dimension, have in common that they ultimately require treating another human being as an object to be used in obtaining gratification.

The main gist of Paul's catalogue of vices is focused on attitudes that have little to do with sexuality, save inasmuch as a person's attitude as a human being generally also affects his or her approach to sexuality or to any other dimension of existence. All of them affect human relationships. The twelve other attitudes that he mentions are nonsexual, and only two of those, *methai* (drunkenness) and *kōmoi* (carousing) have much to do directly with the body, though of course all of the attitudes mentioned are necessarily embodied in one way or another. They include attitudes having to do with the transcendent dimension, such as idolatry (treating entities that are not divine as if they were) and sorcery (or more literally, the abuse of drugs or *pharmakeia*). They particularly address negative human interactions, such as enmities, strife or altercations, and jealousy (*zēlos*), a word that can be positive when it means a noble aspiration or zeal but that can turn negative, as here, where it is manifested as envy and malice. He furthermore lists anger (literally, outbursts or "swellings" of ire), quarrels (specifically, rivalries that lead to feuds), dissensions or divisions, factions driven by discord and contention, and envy, followed by murder in some manuscript traditions.

What Paul is contrasting in this passage is not the "body" versus the "spirit." As Theodoret reminds us, idolatry and its ilk are works that proceed not from the flesh in the sense of our bodies but from our understanding.[87] Paul is opposing two different kinds of spirituality: a spirituality of conflict and hate versus a spirituality of

---

87. "The Letter to the Galatians," in Theodoret of Cyrus, *Commentary on the Letters of St. Paul*, 21.

peacemaking and love in the Spirit of Jesus. Augustine and other church fathers tend to think of the spirit in verse 17 as the human spirit or mind (*mens*), in the sense of Romans 7:23. However, most likely what Paul is doing is to contrast the Holy Spirit with the tenor of a "fleshly" spirituality that looks away from God. That unprepossessing spirituality is not to be confused with the incarnate spirituality in the footsteps of Jesus that Paul proposes and tries to exemplify as best he can.

When we look at Paul's list of the "works of the flesh" it is vital to remember how many of them have been linked to women directly or blamed indirectly on women in the social and cultural imaginary, and to avoid repeating that mistake. The projections have often included accusations that women by their very nature incite fornication, that they have a propensity for practicing witchcraft or sorcery (including erotic spells) or that they tend to be very jealous and vindictive. Poor women and women of color have suffered disproportionately from such accusations. Other subaltern subjects, such as men of color or those not identifying as heterosexual, have also been linked to the "works of the flesh" by the dominant cultural and religious imaginary. One consequence of linking certain people to these "vices" is the conviction that they need to be constrained, contained, and controlled by many customs and laws in order to keep them in line. Some theologians have often been all too ready to assist in such maneuvers.[88]

For Paul's catalog to have value as a tool for analysis and discernment, as he probably meant it to be used, it cannot be a pretext for projecting negative attitudes onto particular groups of "others." It is also not meant as an exercise in self-condemnation. As Jerome comments in an aside, "I have no idea who can inherit the kingdom of God, seeing that anyone who gets riled is kept out of it."[89] It would seem that nobody, Christian or not, can wholly avoid the pitfalls in Paul's list, but if the list is primarily of value as a catalog for self-analysis, a person who wants to exult in the freedom of the gospel

---

88. A classic example of this is the fifteenth-century *Malleus Maleficarum*, or *Hexenhammer* ("Witches' Hammer"), attributed to Heinrich Kramer, which though it was condemned by the Roman Catholic Church soon after its publication, became a handbook for persecution of those suspected of witchcraft.

89. Jerome, *Commentary on Galatians*, 232.

can consult with it to make sure that he or she is not using that freedom as a pretext to turn other people into commodities for consumption or otherwise disrupting human relationships.

For the Christian faith, the conviction that all human beings are
created in God's image should mean that mistreating other human
beings is always also a sin against the God in whose image they move
and live and have their being. That is why Paul says that those who
practice such ways of treating others will not inherit God's reign (v.
21): it would be a fundamental contradiction for those who mistreat
others to claim simultaneously to be heirs of the God who so dearly
loves all human beings and cherishes all of creation. Paul's catalog
is not a record of God's moralistic horror at human mistakes, given
that for the apostle, God's characteristic work is to claim and reclaim
humans for life in and with God, no matter what our past mistakes,
as seen in his comments in 1 Corinthians 1:26–29 and elsewhere.
Paul's point is rather that for supposed followers of Jesus to treat
others with disdain and simultaneously to claim with impunity the
inheritance of God's kingdom would put God in a position of com-
plicity with oppression and injustice. Religious faith should never be
used as a cover for a spirituality of conflict and hate.

5:22–26
Living by the Spirit

Paul now turns from the "works" of a way of life antagonistic to the
Spirit of life to the "fruit" of God's Spirit in the lives of those who
truly follow Jesus. The metaphor of fruit (*karpos*) is used in the New
Testament variously to refer to pregnancy and childbirth (fruit of
the womb) as in Luke 1:42, to praising God (fruit of the lips) as in
Hebrews 13:15, and even to indicate a spiritual reward or profit, as
in Philippians 4:17. Here, a singular fruit is brought to maturity by
the Spirit. Similar metaphors are found in Ephesians 5:9 (the fruit
of the light) and Philippians 1:11 (the fruit of justice). The fruit of
the Spirit as described by Paul in Galatians has multiple dimensions
and manifestations, all of them positive and conducive to a life that
respects and values other people. The results of the fruit of the Spirit

are sometimes called the nine Christian graces, though in verse 23 some manuscript traditions add patience (*hypomonē*) or chastity (*agneia*) to the list to bring the number up to ten, perhaps as a counterpart to the Ten Commandments.[90]

It would be a mistake to interpret the fruit of the Spirit in an individualistic or spiritualistic manner. God's Spirit of life, who renews the face of the earth (Ps. 104:30) works to bring forth fruit able to transform both individual lives and communities or societies in a wider sense. Paul's list begins with the triad of love (*agapē*), joy (*chara*), and peace (*eirēne*). Each of these has a personal and individual application but also a social or systemic dimension, as becomes immediately evident when they are understood in light of the Old Testament and of the life of Jesus. God's love is manifested concretely in God's profound engagement with human reality, as seen in the sending of the Son (1 John 4:9). Human reception of that love consists not only in loving the unseen God but also in the capacity to love others (1 John 4:20). Joy or delight is a marker of the reception of the good news of the gospel, that is, of God's tender mercies for creation as shown in the solidarity of God with human particularity in the birth of Jesus and the unfolding of his life (Luke 2:10). Peace as understood in the New Testament reflects the prophetic understanding of shalom as peace with wholeness and justice, which always includes a socio-political component. In Revelation 6:4, for instance, the red horse of the apocalypse and its rider symbolically take peace from the earth with a great sword, with the result that people slaughter each other in wars. God's children, by contrast, are called to become doers or makers of peace (Matt. 5:9).

The second triad generated by God's Spirit is patience or forbearance (*makrothymia*), kindness or benevolence (*chrēstotēs*), and generosity or kindness (*agathōsynē*). Patience in this sense, though it is sometimes translated as "longsuffering," is not a passive or indifferent endurance. It literally means having a long (*makros*) temper (*thymia*), and like peacemaking requires both fortitude and a persistent expectation infused with hope. Abraham, for instance, is described in this sense in Hebrews 6:15 as having "patiently

90. Bruce Metzger, *A Textual Commentary on the Greek New Testament* (Stuttgart: United Bible Societies, 1975), 598.

endured" (*makrothymēsas*) and thereby "obtained the promise." This attitude is often cultivated by those who have to endure conditions of injustice but have hopes and plans about changing their situation, and take small or large steps in that direction whenever they are able.

Kindness (*chrēstotēs*) means "goodness of heart." Jerome describes it as "a virtue which is gentle, charming, peaceful, adept at getting along with all good people."[91] It appears throughout the Pauline and Deutero-Pauline letters to describe the qualities of those who serve God (2 Cor. 6:6). The word is also used in reference to the gracious kindness and benignity of God as richly manifested in Christ (Eph. 2:7; Titus 3:4). To be kind is not to be weak, but rather to be able, thanks to the transformative work of the Spirit, to express good-heartedness in a way reminiscent of God's own heart.

The next quality, *agathōsynē*, translated "generosity" by the NRSV, is similar and also refers to goodness. Jerome comments that the two do not differ much, because the goal of both is "to do good voluntarily," but he sees the second as a more somber or stern understanding of goodness.[92] If he is correct, then the implication once again is that goodness can include a certain severity of purpose and is not synonymous with mere affability; J. B. Lightfoot calls it active goodness or beneficence as an energetic principle.[93]

For Paul this kind of goodness is, again, characteristic not only of those led by the Spirit, but even more profoundly of God, as can be seen in Romans 2:4, where he ascribes directly to God several dimensions that here appear as the fruit of the Spirit. From a Trinitarian point of view this makes sense on two levels: first, for Paul the work of the Spirit is the work of God, for the Spirit is God, so that whatever fruit the Spirit brings forth will by definition be congruent with God's character. Second, the wonderful exchange made possible by the work of Christ in the world leads those who are in Christ to share in the very life of God and therefore to begin taking on godly qualities. Each of the qualities that appear in Paul's list are parsed out concretely in specific situations by Jesus, who in his life shows how the fruit of the Spirit looks in the midst of conflict,

91. Jerome, *Commentary on Galatians*, 238.
92. Ibid., 238.
93. J. B. Lightfoot, *Saint Paul's Epistle to the Galatians* (London: MacMillan, 1905), 213.

injustice, social and gender inequity, empire, religious strife, family tensions, and economic distress.

The final triad describing the fruit of the Spirit is composed of faith or faithfulness (*pistis*), gentleness or mildness (*prautēs*), and self-control or temperance (*egkrateia*). *Pistis* is usually rendered in this context in the sense of good faith, fidelity, integrity, and honesty, or as the NRSV has it, as "faithfulness," in a vein similar to that of Matthew 23:23, where it appears in the triad "justice and mercy and faith" as what Jesus says should characterize a true follower of the torah. In his 1519 commentary on Galatians, Luther understands "faith" doubly, both as directed toward God (where faithfulness means believing in God's promises) and as expressed in the fidelity and humanity of one person toward another.[94] In the 1535 commentary he concludes that in this passage it probably means the latter, for when the dimension of interpersonal trust is lacking, people become suspicious and dogged, unable ever to trust anyone, and therefore unable ever to find friendship and concord with others.[95] This quality can once more be easily attributed to God as well as to those in whom the Spirit brings forth fruit, whereas *pistis* in its other common meaning, faith or belief, is for Paul a penultimate quality necessary now, but to be left behind along with hope when we see God face to face (1 Cor. 13:8–13). God is faithful, but God does not "believe" or "have faith" in God.

Gentleness or forbearance is sometimes also translated as mildness or meekness and therefore can seem in some cultural contexts to convey a quality of weakness, rather than of strength. Paul uses the same word in 2 Corinthians 10:1 to describe Jesus, when he speaks of the "meekness and gentleness of Christ." This is an important clue, because the mildness in question here is not that of a person who has no force of character, but a gentleness chosen by someone who is strong and able to relate to others in a way that does not coerce and compel them to assent to anything by brute force. That is why it makes sense for the word to be paired with "self-control." The latter is a quality that requires strength in order for someone

---

94. Martin Luther, *Luther's Works*, vol. 27, *Lectures on Galatians, 1535 Chapters 5–6, 1519 Chapters 1–6*, ed. Jaroslav Pelikan (Saint Louis: Concordia Publishing House, 1964), 377.
95. Ibid., 95.

to exercise restraint and temperance rather than to be carried away
immediately by whatever is desired at the moment. Neither of these
qualities is prized highly in our climate of globalized capitalism and
consumer-driven economies since both attitudes chip away at the
ruthlessness, individualism, and exercise of immediate gratification
that often help drive competition and sales.

The two qualities, gentleness and self-control, have often carried
with them a gendered subtext, linked to so-called feminine and masculine qualities respectively. After the industrial revolution in the
West and the rise of capitalism, in some social contexts to be "gentle" began to be portrayed as "feminine" and therefore weak, pliable,
childlike, and perhaps asexual, linked to the relegation of women to
the private and domestic sphere.[96] For women who have been forced
to perform meekness against the grain and to flee any expression of
sensuality lest they be labeled "loose," as well as for working-class,
rural, or non-white women who have not had the opportunity of
inhabiting a serene domesticity, extolling meekness can seem like
one more nail in a moralistic Christian coffin. The need for "self-
control," on the other hand, can sometimes contain a veiled admiration for male vitality and virility, so often portrayed in literature and
art as difficult to curb in the case of particularly "manly" men.

Paul's use of the word here and elsewhere does not seem particularly skewed in either of those directions. In 1 Corinthians 7:9
egkrateia does refer to "practicing self-control" with regard to sexual
desire, but his recommendation is explicitly oriented equally toward
men and women: he counsels marriage as a realistic option if the
continence he practices in his own life does not seem achievable to
them. In 1 Corinthians 9:25 he uses "self-control" to describe the
discipline of athletes. These qualities should not be coded by gender.
Human beings as a whole are sexual beings, and their sexual vitality
and expression is part of their humanity. Gentleness and self-control
refer to an attitude of respect for the other that should traverse all
aspects of life, including human sexuality, in all spheres, whether
domestic or public. They are simply qualities that Paul considers

96. Cristiana Molina Petit, *Dialéctica feminista de la ilustración* (Madrid: Anthropos, 1994),
    115–35.

Christlike, in that they require both spiritual strength and an attitude of respectful love for others in order to be exercised.

Paul concludes his list with a rhetorical flourish, stating (v. 23) that there is "no law against such things." Such qualities are prized by the torah and by civil law, as opposed to the attitudes in his previous list. Just as those who carry out the "works of the flesh" habitually, disregarding the welfare of others, disqualify themselves from inheriting God's kingdom, those who allow the Spirit to bring forth the fruit of a Christlike life show that they are citizens of God's commonweal. However, since God's kingdom is "coming" but not in full effect yet, and the laws of the empire do have force, being led by the Spirit (v. 18) can lead a person into trouble in the hands of the law, as indeed was the case of Jesus himself, crucified by the Romans as a potential terrorist. Christ's Spirit of resistance particularly questions and contests empire as "that which seeks to control all aspects of life and all of reality."[97]

As Joerg Rieger points out, nobody can entirely escape the "force fields" of empire, and yet at the same time, no empire has been able to co-opt Christianity completely. He adds: "If empire is that which seeks to control, the Holy Spirit is by contrast that which cannot be controlled," just as Christ cannot be controlled. There is a "pneumatological surplus" that materially resists the encroachment of empire at all levels: geographic, political, economic, intellectual, emotional, spiritual, psychological, cultural, and religious.[98] The fruit of the Spirit described by Paul is not meant to lead Christians to submission to the empire or to any other penultimate reality masquerading as an absolute but rather is a way of pneumatic resistance in the footsteps of Jesus.

The material consequences of living out the fruit of the Spirit in an unjust society can indeed be death, even for those who initially have privilege on their side, as a few white persons, acting in solidarity with slaves escaping from bondage in the United States, found out. William Still tells the story of a white man, Seth Concklin, who

---

97. Joerg Rieger, "Resistance Spirit: The Holy Spirit and Empire," in *The Lord and Giver of Life: Perspectives on Constructive Pneumatology*, ed. David H. Jensen (Louisville, KY: Westminster John Knox Press, 2008), 130.
98. Ibid., 130–31.

as an active part of the Underground Railroad perished in 1851 trying to help Vina Still and her three children escape from what Concklin called the "Christian wolves" that pursued them from Alabama to Indiana. Concklin was found drowned, his skull fractured, and his hands and feet in chains. The escapees were reclaimed for slave labor.[99]

Sobrino points out that persecution by the "Anti-Kingdom" in its many manifestations is a common consequence of following Jesus wholeheartedly in an unjust system. Martyrdom, such as the one experienced in El Salvador in 1980 by Monseñor Romero, and in 1989 by the six Jesuits and the two women killed by paramilitary forces (along with so many thousands of others whose names are largely unknown to us) is an extreme manifestation of such persecution.[100] That context challenges any dualistic and moralistic reading of Paul's next comment to the effect that that those who "belong to Jesus Christ have crucified the flesh with its passions and desires" (v. 24). If we have already crucified with Christ a way of life that is primarily about self-gratification and objectifying others, we are liberated to live in a way that questions common sense about how a given society functions, for example incarcerating so many bodies of color or putting tax money toward sustaining military infrastructure all over the world. And yet that commitment is not easy; as Jerome wryly suggests, "it takes no small effort to live in the present age in such a way that the life of Jesus is revealed in our flesh right now."[101]

The wonderful exchange, by which Christ dies that we might live, and lives that all that separates us from true life might die, has many implications for the way we relate and contribute to our societies. Paul's exhortation to be guided by the Spirit or to advance together by the Spirit if indeed we live by the Spirit (v. 25) means much more than being "nice" or "moral" or conforming to a set of societal rules and expectations. It is a call for honesty, commitment to the community of faith as an agent of transformation, and consistency with

99. Cf. William Still, *The Underground Railroad: A Record of Facts, Authentic Narratives, Letters, Etc., Narrating the Hardships, Hair-breadth Escapes and Death Struggles of the Slaves in Their Efforts of Freedom* (Philadelphia: Porter & Coates, 1872).

100. Jon Sobrino, *Jesucristo Liberador: Lectura histórico-teológica de Jesús de Nazaret* (Madrid: Trotta, 1991), 167–68.

101. Jerome, *Commentary on Galatians*, 241.

the ramifications of the path of Jesus in our particular space and place: "if we live (by the Spirit), then let us also walk (by the Spirit)." The type of walking evoked as a metaphor is disciplined and constant, the gait of people determined to move forward even if the path is stony. Paul uses the same verb in Romans 4:12 to describe all those who follow the example (literally, walk in the footsteps) of Abraham's faith, whether or not they are circumcised. In Philippians 3:16 he uses the image in the context of pressing doggedly ahead toward the goal, looking forward in eschatological hope to our transformation in Christ. Here also he frames a shared exhortation, directed toward the Philippians and toward himself as part of a community of faith: "let us hold fast to what we have attained," or more literally, "given what we have achieved, let us continue to advance together" (*stoichein*). Paul will come back to the same metaphor of walking forward together in Galatians 6:16, as he concludes his epistle with a blessing.

As Eldin Villafañe points out, to live in the Spirit (theological self-understanding) is to walk in the Spirit (ethical self-understanding). The Spirit's historical project is to participate in the reign of God, challenging structures of evil and sin and empowering disenfranchised congregations to find the spiritual and material resources to carry out necessary social struggles.[102] Walking together by the Spirit entails an attitude of humility and love in our relationships with those who walk with us along the same path: conceit, competition, and envy should be left behind (v. 26).

Once again, Paul puts his finger in the wound of what so often derails social movements for change or communities of faith caught up in the possibilities of transformation. Conceit refers to empty glorying, to a boastful attitude that has little substance and is therefore hollow. Jerome makes the point about the futility of "empty glory" that even martyrdom, if it is undergone with the intention of evoking admiration, means shedding blood in vain. The same goes for seeking any of the Christian virtues if it is done out of a desire for glory, in order to evoke praise.[103] Likewise for Luther, vainglory

102. Eldin Villafañe, *The Liberating Spirit: Toward an Hispanic American Pentecostal Social Ethic* (Grand Rapids: Eerdmans, 1993), 195.
103. Jerome, *Commentary on Galatians*, 245.

is a "detestable vice" that is the most dangerous of all for the church, especially when it arises among church leadership.[104]

To provoke one another, to incite each other to combat or to have a competitive attitude toward one another, also undermines a community, though such tactics are often used in our society for short term gains, such as winning a game. That is not the kind of "sportsmanship" that Paul strives for, as much as he likes athletic metaphors. Irritating others and provoking rivalries does little if the goal is to walk together as a community in a path of justice and transformation. It serves only to make others stumble.

The final attitude to avoid in verse 26, envy, is the verbal form of the noun Paul had mentioned in the catalog of vices of verse 21. All three attitudes enable each other: a person who is competitive and boastful about real or inflated achievements may act out of envy or provoke envy in others. Such practices are destructive of friendship and community, and when they are mirrored and take on their own dynamic, easily unsettle or disrupt a group's direction.

---

104. Luther, *Luther's Works*, vol. 27, *Lectures on Galatians, 1535 Chapters 5-6, 1519 Chapters 1-6*, 98-99.

B'. 6:1–17

The Gospel Is Truly Good News (Reprise)

6:1–6

Burdens and Baggage

Restoration in the Spirit means the capacity to lead persons who have lost their way gently back toward the path of justice. Given that the Holy Spirit is the Spirit of gentleness, any correction of others should be in the Spirit, lest it become neither humble nor gentle. Correction is sometimes needed, but when we find ourselves in the position of having to correct one another, we should do so in the awareness of our own fragility and of our tendencies to fall exactly into the sort of situations we critique. As Augustine points out, nothing proves that a person is truly "spiritual" like the way that person handles another's sin: whether with insults or the desire to liberate that person, whether with verbal abuse or with help.[1]

Ironically, Paul himself does not always seem to follow his own advice. He certainly is not particularly gentle with the Galatians in this letter, though he says he aims to love them like a mother. He has no patience with his Jewish Christian opponents, who after all are also part of the church. However, he does show keen insight into the human psyche and into the dynamic of relationships in the community of faith. As Dietrich Bonhoeffer points out, it is only by carrying each other's burdens—by suffering and enduring each other—that we truly can become siblings in Christ to each other: "Only as a burden is the other really a brother or sister and not just an object to be

---

1. Eric Plumer, *Augustine's Commentary on Galatians: Introduction, Text, Translation, and Notes,* Oxford Early Christian Studies (Oxford: Oxford University Press, 2003), 221.

> We should never undertake
> the task of rebuking another's
> sin without first examining
> our own conscience by
> inner questioning and then
> responding—unequivocally
> before God—that we are
> acting out of love.
>
> Plumer, *Augustine's Commentary on Galatians*, 225.

controlled."[2] Paul seems to realize that one crucial way in which people in the community truly become human beings to each other rather than simply things to be manipulated is through this involvement in each other's difficulties.

Paul starts out the section with a hypothetical example: let us imagine that someone is detected (literally taken by surprise or overtaken) in some sort of transgression (v. 1). The word translated "transgression" by the NRSV (*paraptōma*) metaphorically implies a false step or blunder and therefore by extension is used in the New Testament to convey the idea of a trespass or fault. It is the same word used by Jesus in Matthew's account of the Sermon on the Mount to explain part of the Lord's Prayer: "If you forgive others their trespasses, your heavenly Father will also forgive you; but if you do not forgive others, neither will your Father forgive your trespasses" (Matt. 6:14–15). The sense that one gets in reading this and other New Testament passages that use the expression (see Mark 11:25) is that such "stumbling" is part of our imperfect human condition and therefore is a given, but that God provides ways for us to forgive each other and to be forgiven for our mistakes.

The "if" of verse 1 should be understood also as a "when" or a "whenever:" Paul knows that we all occasionally fall into the kind of attitudes "according to the flesh" that he depicted in 5:19–21 and 26 and begin to walk in a way that is not guided by the Spirit, yet God's grace can catch us when we stumble. As Paul points out in 2 Corinthians 5:19, in Christ God does not count our trespasses (*paraptōmata*) against us but rather is able to turn us into ambassadors of reconciliation. Paul seems to like to use the expression in the context of variations on the marvelous exchange. For instance, our human actions ("our trespasses") led to the execution of Jesus, but that did not

---

2. Dietrich Bonhoeffer, *Life Together: Prayerbook of the Bible*, Dietrich Bonhoeffer Works, vol. 5, ed. Geffrey B. Kelly, trans. Daniel W. Bloesch and James H. Burtness (Minneapolis: Fortress, 1996), 100.

ultimately put an end to his work, for he was raised "for our justification" (Rom. 4:25). Likewise, the "stumbling" (*paraptōmati*) of Israel
did not lead to the "fall" of Israel but rather has allowed salvation to
come also for the Gentiles (Rom. 11:11–12).

Paul suggests that when a person stumbles, then other members of the community ("you, who are spiritual"), with the help of
the Spirit, should work gently to restore that person. Sadly, in such
circumstances a gentle spirit is often lacking. Calvin, who himself
can seem severe in his judgments, is aware that injury "is frequently
done by unseasonable and excessive severity," which disguises itself
as zeal but actually "springs in many instances from pride, and from
dislike and contempt of the brethren." He further suggests that if a
reproof does not "breathe the spirit of meekness" then it should not
be considered to partake in a "religious and Christian character."[3]
In other words, the test of a genuine, helpful response to another's
sin is whether or not it is made in a spirit of gentleness and love. It
is not surprising that Augustine first gave expression to a version of
his famous axiom "Love and do as you please" (*Dilige, et quod vis
fac*) in response to this passage, when in his commentary on verse 1
he wrote "Love, and say what you like" (*Dilige et dic, quod voles*).[4]

A built-in problem in trying to restore each other when we do
stumble is that we can easily become blind to our own propensities
to blunder (v. 1), as is so clearly illustrated in the Sermon on the
Mount, in the saying about our capacity to notice a speck in someone else's eye yet be blind to the log in our own (Matt. 7:1–5). Paul's
advice for fulfilling the "law of Christ" in the face of this human
tendency is for us consciously to practice "bearing one another's
burdens" (v. 2). Because just three verses later, he will make a statement that seems to contradict this one, namely that "all must carry
their own loads" (v. 5), the section has led to a good bit of confusion. What Paul seems to want to underline in this counterpoint is
the "both-and" of solidarity with others and personal responsibility.

The expression "the law of Christ" in verse 2 can be a challenging one. What exactly does Paul mean with the expression, used

3. John Calvin, *Calvin's Bible Commentaries: Galatians and Ephesians*, trans. John King
(Forgotten Books: 2007), 148.
4. Cf. Plumer, *Augustine's Commentary on Galatians*, 224–25.

nowhere else in the Pauline corpus? There have been three main lines of interpretation of the expression: the idea that it refers to Old Testament law as it is reinterpreted by Jesus; the notion that it is a reference to terminology used by Paul's opponents; and an understanding based on the idea that the law of Christ is identical to the commandment to love God and our neighbors: *lex Christi, lex amoris*.[5] The latter does not necessarily exclude elements of the other two and it seems the most convincing approach, as long as it is understood pneumatologically, in conjunction with the mention of the Spirit in verse 1. The "law" is not a bad word for Paul or something to be rejected, but a way of walking in the world in accordance with God's mercy, as Jesus showed concretely in his life and as the Spirit makes real and illuminates in ever new situations to those who follow Jesus in their lives. Such a "law" is never implemented in abstractions but is worked out in the specific solidarity of living alongside others, taking their burdens seriously.

Bonhoeffer connects the "law of Christ" with forbearance. Through the incarnation and in the cross "God truly suffered and endured human beings," bearing them "as a mother carries her child, as a shepherd the lost lamb." As a result of God's forbearance with human beings, Christians now are empowered to bear with each other and to suffer one another. This entails bearing with "the freedom of the other," including all those "weaknesses and peculiarities that sorely try our patience." For Bonhoeffer, bearing the burden of the other means affirming the reality of the other's creation by God. Because our abuse of freedom can lead to sin against the other, our practice of forbearance is bound up with forgiveness, intercessory prayer, listening, and active helpfulness: "We may suffer the sins of one another; we do not need to judge. That is grace for Christians."[6]

The word used for "burdens" in verse 2 (*baros*) tends to refer literally or figuratively in the New Testament to anything difficult to carry which may be imposed on a person by a third party, such as a long and heavy workday (Matt. 20:12), the obligation to observe

---

5. Cf. Claude Pigeon, "La loi du Christ en Galates 6,2," *Studies in Religion/Sciences Religieuses* 29 (2000): 425–38.
6. Bonhoeffer, *Life Together*, 102.

detailed religious precepts or rituals (Acts 15), or even the burden of ethical responsibilities (Rev. 2:24) and demands (1 Thess. 2:7). Paul can also use it in a positive sense, as in the "weight of glory" of 2 Corinthians 4:17. His point here is that church life should not lead us into a situation in which the demands and challenges that come our way, whether positive or negative, are met in solitude and isolation. Paul knows that the practice of mutual support is vital for our spiritual health. If we in the community of faith do not help each other carry the weight of existence, we will begin to lose touch with our true identities and fall into self-deception (v. 3). At this point in his exhortation he therefore shifts toward the need for self-awareness.

We fool ourselves if we think we are "something" (*ti*) when in reality we are "nothing" (*mēden*). Though this saying seems harsh at first sight, it can be helpful in understanding how self-deception shifts needless burdens onto other people. The problem of "white obliviousness" in a racist society is a case in point. When people believe that they are "something" special simply because their skin lacks pigmentation, they begin to lose touch with God's perspective on reality and God's promise of justice. They are fooled not only because they fail to recognize that they are "nothing" more or better than others whose skin's melanin is more apparent. They are blind to the inequities built into life in a society where those with darker skin are detained and incarcerated more often than those with lighter skin, regardless of how they live. The self-deception involved in living blindly in the face of injustice is toxic to others but also harmful to those who fool themselves. It is therefore necessary for all members of a given community to exercise discernment about who they are and equally about what they do, putting their work to the test (v. 4).

To test one's own work requires self-examination of the kind also recommended by Paul in 2 Corinthians 13:5: "Examine yourselves to see whether you are living in the faith. Test yourselves." The need for this sort of self-scrutiny appears in all strands of the New Testament and is a characteristic of walking in the Spirit. It is the same word that is used to test a metal to see whether it is pure (see 1 Pet. 1:7). For Paul and the other writers of the New Testament, the standard of what it means to live without self-deception is always Jesus

Christ. Only if we put our deeds and our labor to the test with help of the Spirit and with Jesus in mind as our paradigm can we truly measure the value of what we are doing. In this sense we are not to ride on our neighbor's coattails, much less take credit for the work of others; we need to take responsibility for the way we live. Marius Victorinus therefore renders the phrase "let each one appraise his own work."[7]

Paul holds that only when we have truly exercised discernment about ourselves and our accomplishments is it acceptable for us to take pride in what we have achieved (v. 4). That "pride" (*kauchēma*) is an expression that Paul uses often when he speaks of grounds for "glorying" or "boasting," as he will in verse 14. He seems to see it as an ambiguous trait, which can all too easily become negative (Rom. 4:2; 1 Cor. 5:6). It is only truly warranted when it is done "in Christ Jesus," living out the gospel in concrete ways (1 Cor. 9:15; 2 Cor. 12:5; Phil. 1:26).

We are each tasked with the examination of our own lives. We can neither take credit for the lives of others nor push aside our responsibility to put our own work to the test. It is in this sense that we must each carry our own loads (v. 5). Paul uses a different word here for "load" or "cargo" (*photion*) than he did in verse 2 when he spoke of our shared burdens (*bare*). He frames it in the future tense: "each one will carry" his or her own backpack. We are thus commissioned to take responsibility for our own freight or baggage. Perhaps we too easily miss the positive dimension of this commission, which is that empowered by the Spirit we are each charged with working on our specific "baggage" in ways that lead us to greater freedom, joy, and (perhaps) even to "boasting" in Pauline fashion of the great things that God has done for us. Only when we deal with our own baggage responsibly can we meaningfully share in carrying the burdens of others in a way that is truly helpful. Aquinas distinguishes the "burdens" from the "baggage" by explaining that in the former case it is a matter of "supporting weakness, a burden that we ought to carry for

7. Stephen Andrew Cooper, *Marius Victorinus' Commentary on Galatians: Introduction, Translation and Notes* (Oxford: Oxford University Press, 2005), 338.

one another," but in the latter case Paul is speaking of "the burden of rendering an account."[8]

For example, if a person, regardless of origin, passes for "white" in a society such as the contemporary United States and enjoys "white privilege," that person can only truly cooperate in bearing the burdens of those who are not granted the benefits of white privilege by working on such things as his or her internalized racism and personal complicities with unjust societal structures. It is not up to the persons of color in a congregation or group to deal with a white member's "baggage" in this sense, given that such baggage is usually based on self-deception and willful blindness.

Into his recommendations about how to maintain the difficult balance between solidarity in carrying the burdens of others and responsibility for one's own baggage, Paul then inserts an exhortation about the treatment of teachers in the community of faith. Those who receive instruction in the word should share "in all good things" with those who teach them (v. 6), or as Marius Victorinus puts it, "Let the one who is catechized in the word grant a share in all good things to the one who catechizes."[9] Jerome thinks that the good things in question refer to bodily necessities such as "food, clothing, and other commodities which people classify as good things."[10] In Romans 15:25–27 Paul uses a similar expression in speaking of how the Gentile Christians in Macedonia and Achaia were pleased to share "material things" with the poor among the Jewish Christian community in Jerusalem, which was especially appropriate because they as Gentile believers had received spiritual blessings from their Jewish Christian counterparts. His statement in Galatians seems to be along the line of laborers being worthy of their hire (Matt. 10:10) or of Paul's own statements elsewhere to the effect that those who proclaim the gospel should be able to make their living by the gospel (see 1 Cor. 9:14). Perhaps Paul wanted to make sure that in the process of dealing with their own baggage the Galatians did not forget the responsibility of the community to support the very teachers

---

8. Thomas Aquinas, *Commentary on Saint Paul's Epistle to the Galatians*, trans. Fabian R. Larcher, Aquinas Scripture Series Vol. 1 (Albany, NY: Magi Books, 1966), 192.

9. Cooper, *Marius Victorinus' Commentary on Galatians*, 338.

10. Jerome, *Commentary on Galatians*, in *The Fathers of the Church: A New Translation*, vol. 121, trans. Andrew Cain (Washington, DC: The Catholic University of America Press, 2010), 254.

> It is, and always has been, the disposition of the world, freely to bestow on the ministers of Satan every luxury, and hardly to supply godly pastors with necessary food.
>
> John Calvin, *Calvin's Bible Commentaries: Galatians and Ephesians*, trans. John King (Forgotten Books: 2007), 154.

who helped them make sense of God's word.

James Dunn points out that the fact that Paul supports the ministry of teaching suggests that "there was already a substantial amount of Christian tradition to learn and to teach," and that the persons who were well-informed about the traditions around Jesus and the interpretation of Scripture would have been "expected to serve the church by instructing new members in what the new faith was all about." As a time-consuming endeavor in a growing movement it would have been difficult for teachers in the church community to find the time to make a living by other means. Indeed, on the basis of this text, it would seem that "the first 'professional' ministry mentioned in the New Testament was teaching."[11]

6:7–10
Reaping and Sowing in the Spirit

Although self-deception could serve as an excuse for the Galatians not to deal with their own "baggage" or not to provide for their teachers, Paul reminds them that

> Whoever sows something evil is a harvester of evil. One sows something good? One will enjoy the harvest of the good. As is the seed, so too is the harvest.
>
> Marius Victorinus, *Galatians*, 340

they should not deceive themselves about a central truth: God cannot be fooled (v. 7). As Jerome remarks, a plausible excuse can satisfy just about anyone, but it cannot trick God.[12] The expression graphically indicates that one cannot turn up one's nose in contempt

---

11. James D. G. Dunn, *The Theology of Paul's Letter to the Galatians* (Cambridge: Cambridge University Press, 1993), 128–29.
12. Jerome, *Commentary on Galatians*, 255.

and derision in God's face, for one will indeed harvest what one has planted. The image of sowing and reaping is used throughout Scripture, and there are several variations on this particular aphorism as well. Eliphaz the Temanite quotes the saying ("Those who plow iniquity and sow trouble reap the same") when he accuses Job of sinning and therefore indirectly of deserving the calamities he is experiencing (Job 4:8). A more poetic rendering of the idea appears in Hosea 8:7, "They sow the wind, and they shall reap the whirlwind." A parallel, positively rendered suggestion appears later in the book: "Sow for yourselves righteousness; reap steadfast love" (Hos. 10:12). In Proverbs 22:8 we find the adage "Whoever sows injustice will reap calamity." Paul first approvingly quotes a concise version of this saying, "you reap whatever you sow" or rendered more literally, "whatever a human being (*anthrōpos*) sows, that is also what [that person] will reap" (v. 7). He then adapts the maxim to his theme about walking in a manner contrary to the Spirit ("according to the flesh") or guided by the Spirit, to speak of "sowing to one's own flesh" or "sowing to the Spirit" (v. 8).

The idea Paul is positing is that a person who puts all effort or "sows" only for the benefit of his or her "flesh" will inevitably reap "corruption" (*phthora*) out of the "flesh." Flesh is not meant here in the sense of the body but in the ethical sense already explained in the previous chapter, yet the verse has been used to try to argue for the sinfulness of the body and specifically of human sexuality. Jerome mentions Julius Cassianus, "the most astute heresiarch among the Encratites," who quoted this passage to shore up his belief that "every sexual union between man and woman is foul." The Encratites or "abstainers" were second-century gnostic Christians who held that sex was evil. Jerome rebuts that argument by pointing out that in verse 8 Paul does not say that a person "sows in the flesh" but "sows in his own flesh" (*eis ten sarka eautou*) and that it cannot apply to intercourse because people do not have sex with themselves.[13]

Jerome and Cassianus think the matter through from a

13. Jerome, *Commentary on Galatians*, 256; cf. Irenaeus, *Against Heresies*, in *The Writings of the Fathers down to A.D. 325, The Ante-Nicene Fathers*, vol. 1, ed. Alexander Roberts and James Donaldson (repr., Grand Rapids: Eerdmans, 1993), 353 (I. 28).

male-oriented perspective that connects "sowing the seed" to male ejaculation, but Jerome ends up discarding that point of view and forcefully counters the tendency to demonize sexuality and human reproduction.[14] Even for Jerome, who is steeped in asceticism and abstains from sex himself, it is not permissible to fall into a dualistic perspective by which "flesh" is understood as "the body" or as a "bodily function."

Augustine suggests that those who "sow in the flesh" are persons who "do everything, even what appears to be good," for the sake of their own short-term prosperity.[15] The root of the word translated corruption (*phthora*) implies the idea of perishability and therefore metaphorically of spiritual ruin. The same kind of expression appears in Col. 2:22 with regard to human regulations and prohibitions that inexorably perish with use. On the other hand, a person who sows to the Spirit or for the Spirit (*eis to pneuma*) will reap eternal life out of the Spirit. The implication is that only the Holy Spirit, the maker and giver of life, can endow us with life everlasting. Such life is not simply the continuation of existence as we know it but an invitation to share in the very life of God. Once again Paul underlines the agency of the Spirit to transform and enliven us.

If the Galatians have confidence in the work of the Spirit both now and in the future, Paul says that they should not grow weary in doing what is good, that is, in walking in the path of the Spirit, who as God alone is truly good. In due time, by the power of the Spirit, they will indeed harvest what has been planted in the Spirit, so they should not "give up" (*ekloumenoi*) in exhaustion. The verb used is the same one that appears in the context of the feeding of the four thousand to describe what would happen if the people, famished and drained after three days, were sent home without food (Matt. 15:32; Mark 8:3). Elsewhere in the gospels the crowds are also depicted as exhausted, something that evokes compassion in Jesus (Matt. 9:36). In Hebrews 12:3–5, the expression is used in exhorting those who are running the race of faith not to lose heart, echoing also Proverbs 3:11.

Clearly, exhaustion and fatigue are real challenges for those who

---

14. Jerome, *Commentary on Galatians*, 257.
15. Plumer, *Augustine's Commentary on Galatians*, 229.

try to follow Jesus, and it is sometimes hard to continue on the right track when the season of harvest seems never to arrive. Given the resistance and perseverance needed in the face of adversity, Paul's exhortation has been an inspiration to people involved in the struggle for justice and peace through the centuries. For example the hymn "I'll Overcome Some Day" (which by most accounts later served as the basis for the well-known civil rights anthem "We Shall Overcome"), written by Charles Tindley in 1900, was based on Galatians 6:9.[16]

In the face of the genuine challenge posed by the seeming intractability of this "evil age," Paul suggests that the frustrating "in-between" time until our eschatological hope is fulfilled is a *kairos*, a fitting season and an opportunity for action (v. 10). After all, as Calvin points out, "every season is not adapted to tillage and plowing."[17] During this time, we are to work for the good of all. Such activity is anything but busy work, since it implies sharing in the creative labor of God, and it requires perseverance. Paul also instructs the Galatians to focus such labors primarily, though not exclusively, on the "household" or the "family" of faith. With his habitual pastoral sense, Paul seems to be indicating that given our limitations, we should marshal our energies wisely: not neglecting the needs of those closest to us, though at the same time aware of the need to work for the good of all.

Augustine interprets Paul to the effect that "eternal life ought to be desired with equal love for everyone, but the same duties of love cannot be fulfilled for everyone."[18] The sentiment can be read in a way self-serving for the community, as if one were to share only what little is left of one's energies and resources with those outside the immediate Christian community once all the community's needs are met. Bruno the Carthusian seems to read the verse precisely in that way: "For first we should provide the necessities of life to the faithful, and thereupon, if there is more than enough, also to the infidel."[19] However, if such labors are undertaken in the Spirit by followers of

16. Charles Albert Tindley, "I'll Overcome Some Day," http://www.hymnary.org/text/this_world_is_one_great_battlefield

17. Calvin, *Calvin's Bible Commentaries: Galatians and Ephesians,* 157.

18. Plumer, *Augustine's Commentary on Galatians,* 231.

19. Bruno the Carthusian, "Complete Galatians," in Ian Christopher Levy, trans. and ed., *The Letter to the Galatians: The Bible in Medieval Tradition* (Grand Rapids: Eerdmans, 2011), 181.

Jesus as coworkers in God's economy of salvation and liberation, such a reading would be a distortion. It seems more appropriate to posit here an embedded practical theology of "think globally, act locally:" do not neglect your siblings in the faith all around you, but do not forget the needs of "all" either. As Aquinas puts it, Paul suggests that the Galatians should in the first place serve readily, in the second place serve perseveringly, and in the third place serve all.[20]

FURTHER REFLECTIONS
Hope

In reading Galatians it is perhaps easy to get distracted by the many topics and ideas that emerge in the letter, but it is important to remember that one key thread that ties everything together for Paul is hope. It is not limited to the actual word "hope" (*elpis*), as in the "hope of righteousness" or "hope of justice" of 5:5. It is also a theme latent whenever he makes explicit or implicit reference to the work of the Holy Spirit. For Paul, the Spirit is a Spirit of hope, and true hope emerges as a result of the creative work of the Spirit, who is the agent of a new creation in Christ (6:15).

The possibilities opened up by a pneumatic "new creation" are one reason Paul's theology can be read fruitfully from a feminist perspective. As Sandra Hack Polaski points out, the notion of a new creation, continually being birthed by the Spirit, "articulates the conviction that God has done something radically new in the Christ event," and it opens up many possibilities of transformation for the present and the future. This includes the transformation of elements of the Christian tradition that have been hurtful to women as well as the rediscovery of liberative themes in Scripture and tradition that had been neglected or forgotten.[21] The hope that the Spirit brings is not a facile optimism or a naïve negation of the real power and consequences of evil. On the contrary, it empowers people to imagine and begin to live into God's justice in the face of empire, human

---

20. Aquinas, *Commentary on Saint Paul's Epistle to the Galatians*, 193.
21. Cf. Sandra Hack Polaski, *A Feminist Introduction to Paul* (St. Louis, MO: Chalice, 2005), 119.

destructiveness, the idols of the present age, and the distortions of religion.

6:11–17
The Christological Verifiability of the Gospel

Paul is moving toward the end of his epistle and is almost ready to sign off. He therefore pens a few words himself, in his own hand and in visibly large letters (v. 11), in preparation for his final admonitions and benediction. The expression has led to speculation about the deeper meaning of the "large letters." Are they metaphorically large, in accordance to the weighty matters he has brought before the Galatians and the profundity of his thought, or are they the actual overlarge and thus recognizable scrawl of a man whose eyesight might be failing? In the Greek the phrase clearly refers to handwriting, but the Latin translation *qualibis litteris* is ambiguous, so that some commentators in the Latin tradition understand the phrase to refer to the *kind* of letter Paul is writing.[22] The "large letters" in Paul's own handwriting would have also been a guarantee that the epistle had not been forged, since false letters written in Paul's name were known to be circulated to the confusion of the churches (see 2 Thess. 2:1–3).[23] At any rate it is a cue for listeners or readers to settle down because the concluding section is forthcoming.

In a quick summary of the themes of the epistle, he returns a final time to the topic of the "flesh" and circumcision, and to his Jewish Christian opponents, with what may be a pun. Those who wish to make a good showing, or speciously to be "seen well" in the flesh, are the ones wanting to force the Galatians—the male Galatians, at least—to be circumcised. He adds an intriguing reason why the opponents might suggest circumcision: "that they may not be persecuted for the cross of Christ" (v. 12). Jerome, who is probably quoting Josephus, mentions that Julius Caesar, Octavian Augustus, and Tiberius had afforded Jews living in the Roman Empire some protection by allowing them to practice their own rites and carry

---

22. Cf. Plumer, *Augustine's Commentary on Galatians*, 231; see also Eric Plumer's footnote 277 on p. 230.
23. Cf. Jerome, *Commentary on Galatians*, 260–62.

out their ancestral ceremonies. Therefore it would have been in the interest of the community to be circumcised in order to "pass" for Jews and avoid Roman sanctions.[24] Paul was disdainful of such maneuvers and skeptical about the integrity of those who proposed them, since he perceived them as ambitious.

He therefore returns to the inconsistencies of his opponents (v. 13) and sets out a series of four contrasts between their approach and his own as the apostle to the Gentiles. His opponents boast in circumcision (vv. 12–13), while he boasts only in the cross of Christ (v. 14). His opponents avoid persecution (v. 12), while he accepts persecution in the form of the marks of Jesus (v. 17). His opponents compel the Galatians to be circumcised (vv. 12–13), while he claims that circumcision and uncircumcision ultimately do not matter (v. 15). Finally, his opponents live "in the world" and under its powers (v. 14), while he lives "in the new creation" under the aegis of Christ (v. 15). The watershed in all these contrasts is the cross of Christ, which ushers in the new creation and stands in tension with the "present evil age" (1:4) with its imperial pretensions.[25]

Just as Peter had not been consistent in his upholding of the law, the opponents are also inconsistent. They want the (male) Galatians to be circumcised only in order to be able to boast about the Galatians' flesh. Here again, Paul is playing with a double meaning: the "flesh" in the ethical sense of acting selfishly for short-term benefit and the "flesh" that is cut in circumcision. He is also contrasting the kind of boasting he believes is carried out by his opponents with the only kind of "boasting" that he can find acceptable, namely, boasting in the cross (v. 14).

The cross "of our Lord Jesus Christ" is at the heart of everything that is worthwhile according to Paul. Through it, he affirms, "the world is crucified to me, and I to the world." The "world" or cosmos refers here not to material creation but to the same unjust organization of reality that was meant in his comment about this "present evil age" at the beginning of the epistle (1:4). Once again, Paul puts forward a variation on the marvelous exchange. On the basis of the

24. Ibid., 262.
25. Cf. Jeffrey A. D. Weima, "Gal. 6:11–18: A Hermeneutical Key to the Galatian Letter," *Calvin Theological Journal* 28 (1993): 90–107.

work of the Triune God, symbolized by the cross of Christ, the present world system is flipped on its head and loses its power to enslave Paul and by extension anyone who takes seriously the good news of the gospel he has preached. The cross, furthermore, as Luther argues, does not only represent "the wood that Christ carried on his shoulders and to which he was then nailed" but also incorporates "all the many afflictions of the faithful, whose sufferings are Christ's sufferings."[26] All such sufferings are to be subverted and turned around, left behind in the new creation. If the cross is understood in this way, it should never become an excuse for imposing suffering or for naturalizing it in the name of Jesus.

Rather than the "world" with its various systems of religious prestige (which in the Galatian context include circumcision or uncircumcision, Jewish Christianity or Gentile Christianity), what now counts is a new creation (*kainē ktisis*). For one last time, the clear implication is that for Paul, as Augustine correctly points out, circumcision in itself is not harmful, but that the problem comes when hope for salvation depends on the observance.[27] All Christians look forward to a body "that neither Jew can circumcise nor Gentile keep uncircumcised."[28] The "new creation" of verse 15 is also mentioned by Paul in 2 Corinthians 5:17, where he states similarly that anyone who is in Christ is a new creation, not merely a new "creature."

Those being recreated by the God who makes all things new are part of a wider story that goes beyond each individual experience, though their singularity is valued and made part of God's new creation. Within the logic of God's new creation can be found a unity in which people can walk forward in concord yet without uniformity. The NRSV renders the expression (v. 16) as "those who will follow this rule." The "following" (from the verb *stoicheō*) conveys the idea of moving forward along with others, framing one's conduct according to a certain rule of life. It is the same verb Paul had used in 5:25 when he spoke of being guided by the Spirit to move forward together according to the logic of God's peace, love, and justice. The

---

26. Luther, *Luther's Works*, vol. 27, *Lectures on Galatians, 1535 Chapters 5–6, 1519 Chapters 1–6*, 134.

27. Plumer, *Augustine's Commentary on Galatians*, 233.

28. Jerome, *Commentary on Galatians*, 265.

"rule" (*kanōn*) evokes a measuring stick and by extension a rule of conduct. This is not a stiff and stifling sort of rule but rather the kind of flexible pneumatic way of life that allows for contextual constructions of the meaning of the gospel for a given time and space (including variously circumcision and uncircumcision) without sacrificing a deeper union in Christ.

One senses almost a palpable emotion in Paul, who upon speaking of that kind of unity breaks into a blessing, granting those who follow in the way of Jesus and the Israel of God both peace and mercy or compassion. It is not wholly clear whether he means that those who follow God in the way of love manifested in the cross are synonymous with the "Israel of God," but it would seem that the conjunction "and" implies a blessing on the Gentile people of God in Christ *and* on the Israel of God (v. 16). The latter may mean Jewish Christianity or (in view of Paul's writings in Rom. 9–11) simply Judaism.

There is not much more to be said. For the rest (v. 17), or given the remaining time we have, says Paul, "let no one make trouble for me," for I have cast my lot with Jesus and am branded with his marks. As Augustine remarks, Paul has no "desire to be worn down by turbulent conflicts over a matter sufficiently explained" in this epistle and elsewhere.[29]

In Paul's time, slaves were marked with brand marks to indicate to whom they belonged, and people also had the custom of marking their bodies with signs similar to present-day tattoos in order to indicate their religious loyalties. Paul's dedication to following in the way of Jesus had resulted in a fully embodied identification with Jesus, which included bodily wounds and scars suffered as a result of persecution (see 2 Cor. 11:23–27). As Mayra Rivera reminds us, all kinds of past and present relationships leave their marks in our bodies. Likewise, when we encounter others we encounter the marks of their lives: "When we see, hear, or touch the Other, we touch upon the Other's scars." From a Trinitarian perspective, this holds for God as well, since for human beings the "glory of God is always encountered as flesh."[30]

29. Plumer, *Augustine's Commentary on Galatians*, 235.
30. Mayra Rivera, *The Touch of Transcendence: A Postcolonial Theology of God* (Louisville, KY: Westminster John Knox Press, 2007), 138–39.

It would be a mistake to think of immanence and transcendence in too binary a fashion, as if presence and immanence eradicated transcendence or as if transcendence dissolved materiality and relationship. Whenever we interact as human beings, in our very relationality, as concrete and material as it may be, we encounter transcendence, because we cannot "grasp" the human or non-human Other. In the incarnation, God enters into materiality and relationship in a very specific and historical way, namely in the life of Jesus of Nazareth, yet God continues to be transcendent even in that concreteness and closeness. One dimension does not cancel out the other. Paul bears the "marks" of Jesus Christ in a specific and material way that bears witness to the closeness and immanence of God, and yet those marks and scars simultaneously make reference to something beyond themselves that we might call God's transcendence.

The mystical tradition of the stigmata, quite popular in the Middle Ages and perhaps most famously manifested in Francis of Assisi, not surprisingly builds on this passage. Those who follow Jesus with their life are "marked" in various ways by that path, and such "marks" are more important to Paul than the mark of circumcision, which he had also received. This is true although such marks are not prestigious according to the common sense that prevails in the world as we know it, but quite to the contrary are seen as disgraceful, the marks of the lowest of the low within society.[31] As Ernst Käsemann puts it, "the disciples of Jesus are stigmatized."[32] Such "marks" should never be the result of self-flagellation but rather a visible sign of sharing God's option for the weakest and the most marginalized and therefore have a subversive sociopolitical potency that hearkens back to the political nature of the crucifixion of Jesus as an enemy of the Roman Empire.

Anthropologist Clifford Geertz, speaking of religions generally, makes the important point that as "a religious problem, the problem of suffering is, paradoxically, not how to avoid suffering but how to suffer," how to deal with inevitable physical pain, personal losses,

---

31. See Calvin, *Calvin's Bible Commentaries: Galatians and Ephesians*, 164.
32. Ernst Käsemann, *On Being a Disciple of the Crucified Nazarene: Unpublished Lectures and Sermons*, trans. Roy A. Harrisville (Grand Rapids: Eerdmans, 2010), 215.

and encounter with the agony of others that life entails.[33] In this case, the mention of the marks of Jesus branded in pain on his body may also be a final nod to pregnancy in Paul's role as "mother" to the Galatians. The language he uses for "bearing" is reminiscent of bearing or carrying a child in the womb (cf. Luke 11:27).

The marks of pregnancy are borne not as an end in themselves but as a sign of what is to come. Though it might be pleasurable at times to bear with such marks because of what they symbolize, it is by no means always agreeable to do so. Paul knows that it is not a matter of rushing out to put on such "marks" or of making suffering an end in itself. He "puts up" or endures with the consequences of following in the way of Jesus, looking forward from within the beginning of the new creation toward its culmination. And with that, save for a short blessing, Paul rather abruptly closes off the letter. Perhaps he ran out of steam or out of room on the scroll, or maybe there is nothing left to say: the new creation is to speak for itself.

33. Clifford Geertz, "Religion as a Cultural System," in *The Interpretation of Cultures* (New York: Basic Books, 1973), 104.

A'. 6:18
Final Blessing/Conclusion

The letter ends as it began, with the grace that is ours through Jesus Christ (see 1:3). Paul's prayer, as Calvin points out, is not only that God might bestow grace on the Galatians "in great measure" but also that "they might have a proper feeling of it in their hearts."[1] The concluding formula is very similar to the closing blessing used by Paul in Philippians 4:23 and Philemon 25. In 2 Timothy 4:22 a similar expression is also used. Notably, in our epistle Paul adds *adelphoi* to the formula, literally "brothers," but in this case best understood inclusively as "siblings" or "brothers and sisters," as if to mark in his final words the close ties that bind him to the Galatians in Christ. He has acted as a mother to them, in their spiritual life and in the letter, but he ends on a note of equality, as an older sibling who shares with the Galatians in the grace of their common Lord and Brother, Jesus Christ.

In several manuscript traditions, including those attested by Marius Victorinus and Ambrosiaster, the concluding "amen" is lacking, and though the omission may be accidental, in those versions the very last word in the epistle is *adelphoi*.[2] This underlines a certain narrative arc between the harsh beginnings of the gospel, where Paul writes to the Galatians along with the *adelphoi* who are with him and reprimands his addressees severely for five verses (1:6–10) before finally addressing them as *adelphoi* in 1:11. At the conclusion, in

---

1. John Calvin, *Calvin's Bible Commentaries: Galatians and Ephesians*, trans. John King (Forgotten Books: 2007), 164.
2. Bruce Metzger, *A Textual Commentary on the Greek New Testament* (Stuttgart: United Bible Societies, 1975), 599.

6:18, with or without the concluding *amēn* (literally, "let it be so"), one has the sense that Paul finally addresses the Galatians whole-heartedly as those who truly share in a common hope, love, and grace, as if, having exhausted his arguments and reproaches, he were ready to trust in their discernment in the face of his opponents.

Final Thoughts

Once his Galatians commentary of 1519 was in print, Luther wrote to Johann Staupitz that he was sending him a copy of his "foolish Galatians" and added: "I am not as pleased with it as I was at first, and I see that it could have been expounded more completely and clearly. But who can do everything at once? In fact, who can manage to do very much continually?"[1] Still, he was confident that he had made some aspects of Paul clearer than others had before him, even though later he wrote a good deal more on the same epistle, including his important work of 1535. It seems to me that any commentator probably comes to similar conclusions: it is impossible to do all the things that one would like in dealing with a text such as Galatians. At most, one can hope for a modest contribution to theological dialogue in the form of some insights emerging from a given time and place.

As a theologian I am interested not only in speaking *about* the importance of Scripture for systematic and constructive theology but also in *using* it for theological formulation. In other words, central to my theology (and to my Christian faith) is the sense that there is a reservoir of meaning in Scripture and that our critical capacities don't hinder the access to that meaning—quite the contrary. One of the things that I learned (or perhaps remembered) in writing this commentary is the distinct pleasure of spending serious time "in the text," exploring the web of intertextual connections that connect Galatians

---

1. Quoted in Jaroslav Pelikan's introduction to Martin Luther, *Luther's Works*, vol. 27, *Lectures on Galatians, 1535 Chapters 5–6, 1519 Chapters 1–6*, ed. Jaroslav Pelikan (Saint Louis: Concordia Publishing House, 1964), x.

to other passages and themes of Scripture, both Pauline and non-Pauline. When I preach I try to dive down as deeply as possible into a given passage, but normally that is an experience of several days at the most, limited primarily to a small space carved out by the lectionary. Here I had time and opportunity to get a sense of the anatomy of the whole epistle, to make some guesses about how its ancient bones fit together, and to have a sense of how Paul's rhetorical training molded his thought processes and his dictation, even as modern patterns of English speech shaped my own writing of this book.

The contours of the Greek fonts are in themselves esthetically pleasing to me, and the critical apparatus is a source of sometimes pleasurable surprises as well: the extant manuscripts bustle up and push against each other and reveal the text to be more permeable and fluid that it tends to appear in tidy translations that have already made their interpretive decisions. The patristic tradition occasionally finds its way into the critical apparatus as well, and that opens the window into another discovery I made in the process of writing the book: the genuine pleasure to be found in spending time in the company of the ancient commentators, especially Augustine and Jerome. Though I found much to argue with and disagree about in their commentaries, I also uncovered flashes of deep understanding and canny contextual interpretation of Scripture. I looked forward to "spending time with the guys," as I put it to myself, discovering much more in their company than the wholesale irritation I had expected as a feminist. I found that I really wanted to hear what they had to say and that the fact that we are not contemporaries did not mean I could not enter into conversation with them.

I tried to take into account the historical specificity of ancient commentators without that becoming an excuse for them to "get away" with attitudes that seem contrary to the good news of the gospel. It seems to me that what kept them relevant was ultimately that their commitments to the doctrine of the incarnation and to some extent their pastoral preoccupations limited their dualistic tendencies and some of their other blind spots. Systematic theologians are sometimes (rightly) criticized for ignoring the historical context of their sources; I tried not to do that while also not losing sight of threads of theological continuity across the centuries.

Some ancient commentators, such as Chrysostom, who continually tooted an anti-Jewish horn, I found very disturbing. They did
serve to remind me of the toxic vein of Pauline interpretation that
is one of the deadly legacies of Christian history, never to be taken
lightly. We cannot as Christians afford to ignore the iniquities of our
past, whenever we have scapegoated groups (such as Jews or "infi-
dels"), justified dehumanization (such as slavery), ignored the gendered implications of freedom in Christ (by demeaning women), or
sought to use force to convert others. If Paul has been quoted to justify all of these things, from the Fathers onwards, then our reading
of Galatians is honor bound to remember and counter that legacy, or
we will be justifying the worst of the tradition rather than rescuing
the best of it.

In writing the book, I have enjoyed consulting the writings of
present day Jewish New Testament scholars who have done work
on Paul or on Galatians, such as Daniel Boyarin, Pamela Eisenbaum,
Amy-Jill Levine, and Mark D. Nanos. I find their insights helpful in
trying to take Paul's perspective as a Jewish man of his time seriously as well as in learning better to detect the anti-Jewish potholes
that dot the road even of the best-intentioned Christian theologians
and exegetes. The sense of justice and of humor that I find so often
among Jewish friends (whether or not they are interested in Galatians) is always with me as I try to traverse the treacherous waters of
Christian tradition and theology.

In reviewing the pervasive vitality of many contemporary variants of liberation theology all over the world, in particular in Latin
America and among Latinos and Latinas in the United States, Luis
Rivera-Pagán points to four elements that he perceives as central
to their continuing vigor. First, he mentions the continuing global
reality of the increasing social and economic inequity powered by a
globalized capitalist system "that validates profit as the hallmark of
success." This is a situation that cries out for God's justice and *shalom*
and challenges theology to deal seriously with the conditions of our
"present evil age." Second, in the face of such inequity and injustice, the "wretched of the earth" everywhere demand alternatives
and "forge innovative models of protest and resistance." Third, many
Christians continue to retrieve the "subversive memories hidden in

the biblical texts and Christian traditions." And fourth, "God still matters" and continues to be "reimagined as the ultimate source of hope for the oppressed and downtrodden." All of these factors contribute to theological approaches that "counter and resist the ruling imperial project of controlling and policing the frontiers of human imagination."[2]

The theology of Paul in Galatians can contribute significantly to a theology that wants to respond to realities such as those that Rivera-Pagán describes. Paul writes in the context of empire and in opposition to any reign other than that of the God manifested concretely in the apparent weakness of Jesus Christ. He holds onto the centrality of the needs of the poor as one of the nonnegotiable legacies of his Jewish tradition even as he reformulates the faith in the God of Abraham, Sarah, and Hagar for a Gentile context in light of the gospel of Jesus Christ. He provides a theology that can be retrieved and retooled in liberating ways by the power of the Spirit precisely because he believes that God matters, that the "elemental spirits" are at work to enslave us, and that God wants nothing less than life abundant for all of God's good creation. Paul also helps us to see the ambiguity of the theological task and the dangers that religion poses, even for the well-intentioned, whenever it begins to forget that it is a penultimate reality not to be confused with God.

Though he is forceful and even rhetorically violent at times in Galatians, I do not think that Paul means to shut down dialogue. The notion of *Paulus contra Paulum* (Paul against Paul) helps us remember that we can read "with" Paul and "against" Paul at the same time: indeed, to do so is consonant with the theology Paul himself proposes in the epistle. Paul Tillich reminds us that systematic theology "needs a biblical theology which is historical-critical without any restrictions and, at the same time, devotional interpretative, taking account of the fact that it deals with matters of ultimate concern." He adds that such a task helps liberate the theologian from all "sacred dishonesty."[3] My sense is that engaging the Epistle to the Galatians

---

2. Luis N. Rivera-Pagán, "God the Liberator: Theology, History and Politics," in *In Our Own Voices: Latino/a Renditions of Theology*, ed. Benjamín Valentín (Maryknoll, NY: Orbis, 2010), 14–15.

3. Paul Tillich, *Systematic Theology*, vol. 1 (Chicago: University of Chicago Press, 1951), 36.

and struggling with Paul against Paul is one worthwhile way to combat the sacred dishonesty that may tarnish our best theological efforts, allowing us to fool ourselves about injustice in the world and our part in it. For all his faults, the apostle Paul has a way of keeping us honest, engaged, and focused on faith active in love (Gal. 5:6). I am grateful to him for that.

For Further Reading

The classic commentaries by Augustine and Jerome, as well as the work of Calvin and Luther, are indispensable both for their exegetical and their theological depth. A suggestive supplement for the period between these giants of the tradition is offered by Ian Christopher Levy (trans. and ed.), *The Bible in Medieval Tradition: The Letter to the Galatians* (2011), who has made available in English six lesser known medieval commentaries on the epistle. An excellent secondary source is John Riches, *Galatians through the Centuries* (2008). Taking the epistle chapter by chapter, it goes through the main insights of the major commentators on Galatians from Marcion and Chrysostom to the writers of the Reformation and beyond, through the modern classics such as Ferdinand Christian Baur and Joseph Barber Lightfoot, and on to contemporary writers, including such authors as Daniel Boyarin and J. Louis Martyn. The book is useful for seeing the sweep of the letter's influence and for a sense of the discussion across time, though it cannot replace engagement with the individual authors. Finally, I'd be remiss not to mention James Dunn's book *The Theology of Paul's Letter to the Galatians* (1993), which is one of the few twentieth century attempts to read Galatians as "theology."

Of the many critical commentaries available in English, I'd like to mention three, since they represent different, very influential, interpretive approaches. Hans Dieter Betz's volume on Galatians in the Hermeneia series (1979) provides a painstaking exegesis in the tradition of the historical critical method. J. Louis Martyn, well-known for his emphasis on the centrality of Paul's apocalyptic

thinking, wrote the influential Anchor Bible commentary on Galatians (1997). Brigitte Kahl's *Galatians Re-Imagined: Reading with the
Eyes of the Vanquished* (2010) is a breathtaking feminist "remapping"
of Galatian exegesis and theology in the context of Roman hegemony. Last of all, *The Colonized Apostle: Paul through Postcolonial
Eyes* (2011), edited by Christopher D. Stanley, includes a thought-
provoking range of essays on Paul—though for the most part not
specifically on Galatians—informed by postcolonial criticism and
by many different social and cultural locations.

Index of Ancient Sources

Index of Subjects

abandonment, 23–24, 136
Abba, 120–22, 124–26, 132
Abram/Abraham, 6, 71–89, 116, 119,
 137, 143–48, 151, 175, 206
 covenant with, 71–79
 faith of, 72, 110, 181
 "seed" of, 41, 73, 80–82, 87, 112
 three Abrahamic religions, 44, 85
abundant life, 19, 25, 69, 84, 112, 142,
 206. *See also* flourishing
accountability, 133
Achaia, 189
action, human, 184, 193
Acts, book of, 35
Adam, new, 81
adelphoi, 20, 201
Adgistis, "Mother of the Gods," 2
adoption, 109–18, 121
adoptionism, 106
Africa, 9, 72, 155–56, 166
 enslavement of Africans, 99, 101, 144
African Americans
 mass incarceration of, 76–77
 men, 76–78
 and segregation, 96
 and voting rights, 95–96
 women, 171, 173
 See also black race; *specific topics*, e.g.,
  slavery
Against Helvidius (Jerome), 36
agency, 17, 21, 31
 of Christ/the Son, 21, 60
 of God, 17

of the Spirit, 192
of women, 108
aggression, 3, 165
agnosticism, 44, 78, 130
Ahab, King, 45
AIDS/HIV, 155–57
Akan language of Ghana, 72
alienation, 15, 56, 59, 67, 77, 87, 95, 102
allegory, 113, 144–49, 169
al-Qaeda, 162
Althaus-Reid, Marcella, 25
ambition, 15, 171, 196
Ambrose, 45
Ambrosiaster, 201
amen, 201–2
American Indians, 8–9, 99
Amorós, Celia, 139
Anabaptists, 11, 91, 134
anarchy, 105
anathema, 27, 164
Anatolia, 1–2, 146n34
ancestors, 9, 31, 41, 71–73, 127–28, 146
Anchor Bible commentary on Galatians,
 210
Ancyra, 1
angels, 26, 28, 86–87, 114–15, 121, 136
anger, 172
Anselm, 63
anthropocentrism, 131
"anti-kingdom," 120, 180
antinomianism, 74–76, 95
Antioch, 35, 41, 46–48, 51, 53, 55
Antiochene theologians, 145

as ethical guide, 94
faith and, 6–7, 10, 74, 150–54,
    157–65, 181, 196–99
of God, 96
grace and, 96
legalism, 53–61
of love, 55, 164–67
natural moral, 95
secular, 66, 75–76
threefold function of (Calvin), 94–95
unjust legal systems, 66, 75–76, 95
uses of, 93–96
the whole meaning of, 165
See also Torah; works of the law
Law of Moses, 79–87, 110. See also law,
    above
laws, dietary. See dietary laws
leadership, church, 181–82
"pillars," three, 37–44
"reputed," 39
legalism, 53–61
Levine, Amy-Jill, 56n56, 82, 205
Levy, Ian Christopher, 209
liberation, 112, 124, 194
    Holy Spirit, liberating work of, 11, 69
    Jesus, liberating work of, 18
    liberative themes, 194
    See also freedom
liberation theologies, 25, 92, 106–7, 153,
    205–6
life, 60, 116, 168. See also Christian life;
    eternal life
Lightfoot, Joseph Barber, 176, 209
liturgical calendar, 133
logic of exchange. See exchange, logic of
Longenecker, Bruce W., 41n35
Lopez, Davina, 3, 33, 98, 105–6, 140
Lord's Prayer, 184
Lord's Supper, 29, 47, 142
    not sharing with other Christians,
    52–53
love, 59, 122, 171, 173, 197–98, 202, 207
    Christ's, 60, 131
    "clothed in," 92
    for creation, 166
    faith working through, 62, 150–54, 207

freedom to, 11, 164
as fruit of the Spirit, 175
for God, 122, 158, 165, 175, 186
God's, 18, 43, 54, 74, 80, 85, 90, 102,
    122–25, 127, 174–75
human, 54, 122
for Jesus, 27
knowing/knowledge and, 132
language of, 63
law of, 55, 164–67
"Love and do as you please," 185
maternal, of Jesus, 131
for neighbor/others, 17, 122, 134,
    151, 158, 165–67, 175, 179, 181,
    184–86, 193
Paul's for the Galatians, 135, 138–41
Paul's triad of love, joy, and peace,
    175
practice of, 152–53, 164
in the present, 159
righteousness and, 191
for self, 166–67
for the weakest, 43, 125
See also charity
Luke, 5, 35, 43, 65, 119
Luther, Martin, 1–2, 12, 16, 23n1, 27–
    28, 40, 42–43, 47, 51, 53–54, 57,
    61, 66, 69–71, 74, 93–94, 104–5,
    130, 134–35, 140, 142, 148–50,
    177, 181–82, 197, 203, 209
Lutheran Church, 52, 96
Lydia, Sardis in, 2
lynching, 78n22
Lystra, 1

Macedonia, 189
Magnificat, 119
"male and female," 97–98, 101–2, 107,
    112, 154
male metaphors. See masculine
    metaphors
Manichees, 148
Marcella, 12
Marchal, Joseph, 163–64
Marcion/ Marcionism, 17, 77, 83, 163,
    209

www.ingramcontent.com/pod-product-compliance
Lightning Source LLC
Chambersburg PA
CBHW021957090426

42811CB00001B/65